G.R.E.A.T.
BURGER ESSAY
WORKSHOP:

A Helpful Advice for Students in Writing Essays!

INTRODUCTION

PARAGRAPHS

CONCLUSION

Training Average, Struggling, ESL, & Beginning Writers to Draft Prolific Essays In Merely Sixteen Weeks!

DR. STEPHEN C. SIMMS

ISBN
978-1-959314-43-1 (Paperback)
978-1-959314-44-8 (eBook)
978-1-959314-42-4 (Hardcover)

Table of Contents

Acknowledgements vii

Why this Book, Why Now? ix

Introduction.. xi

My Educational Credentials & Community Involvement....................... xiv

References xvii

Chapter 1:   The Early Years...1

Chapter 2:   Vocabulary Enrichment..7

Chapter 3:   Grammar Bellringers 13

Chapter 4:   GREAT Burger Essay Manual 116

Chapter 5:   Persuasive Essay Example 150

Chapter 6:   GREAT Burger Workshop Results 161

Chapter 7:   Comparison/Contrast Essays..171

Chapter 8:   Cause and Effect Essay 183

Chapter 9:   Cause and Effect Anchor Essays 198

Chapter 10:   2008-2009 Student Testimonials 211

Chapter 11:   2009-2010 Student Testimonials 219

Acknowledgements

I would certainly relish the opportunity to express my sincerest gratitude to some colleagues who remain in the trenches. A special thanks to Michelle and the kids who were there to support me during the tedious times. Mrs. Chico-Roman, Dr. Jenkins, Ed. Specialist Brown, Professor Annie Ruth Brown, Mrs. Andrews, and Mr. Joseph B. were all dedicated educators. These folks were 'shoulders to lean on' and greatly influential in my life. Several former students pushed me to continue my work on this writing manual as well. Their gentle nudging and sometimes coarse prodding finally spurred me into action! I am proud to be an alumnus of Miami Dade Community College, Florida Memorial University, Ashworth College, & Northcentral University.

Why this Book, Why Now?

If you googled the title, "Why Americans Can't Write", you'd certainly be shocked by nearly 73 million results that pop up! Mainstream sources would corroborate what I believe has become one of America's unspoken epidemics. Students lack the Reading-Writing connection that is absolutely essential in success during secondary grade levels and beyond. More specifically, they do not know how to confidently and expressively communicate in formal essays. This crucial skill has tragically become a roadblock to desired careers and college readiness nationwide!

The Washington Post (2015, Sept), offered "surely one reason so many Americans lack writing skills is that, for decades, most U. S. schools haven't taught them" (p. 1). In 2011, a national exam found that only 24 percent of eighth and twelfth grade writers were proficient in essay writing. Tyre (2012) "traces the problems at one troubled New York high school to a simple fact: the students couldn't write coherent sentences" (p. 2). It was in this Atlantic article called "Why Americans Can't Write" that principal DeAngelis--at a school on the verge of closure--held a schoolwide investigation! By 2008, she and her faculty found that substandard (essay) writing was their major issue. "Students' inability to translate thoughts into coherent, well-argued sentences, paragraphs and essays was severely impeding intellectual growth in many subjects" (Tyre, 2012, p. 2)

More disappointing news emphasizes just how frightened our parents, students, and elected officials have become of standardized writing tests in several states. In 2015, the state of Ohio rashly opted out of the PARCC test which was supposed to provide a more authentic picture of students' abilities. (PARCC stands for Partnership for Assessment of Readiness for College and Careers). Yet, 200,000 New York students opted out of taking this test in 2015—this was four times as many as the prior year. Ostensibly they were afraid of what the writing test might reveal about their learners.

In Illinois, some dismal results were reported from 2015's tough academic exam called PARCC. "In English language arts/literacy, 38 percent of eighth-graders passed, the high mark in that subject" (Editorial Board, 2015, p. 1). This Chicago Tribune article maintained that the numbers were even worse for high school students. Merely 31 percent passed the English exam this year which points to a tremendous downslide. Yet, the bravery of Superintendent of Illinois State Schools was quite refreshing! He touted having a realistic baseline of results from which the schools could truly grow. "Not long ago, Illinois officials were finagling ISAT scoring to inflate the results, fooling many parents into thinking their children were doing just fine" (Wexler, 2015, p. 1).

I shared these figures not to show that the sky was falling per se. Instead, I wanted to highlight the severity of the problem so that it could be adequately addressed. Understand that poor essay writing doesn't just happen in large metropolitan cities like Chicago or New York. This epidemic is happening in rural, suburban areas as well although to a lesser extent. The great news is that all is not lost. There is a better way to deal with this problem that I do disclose in this book.

Introduction

Admittedly, this workbook had been tightly locked away in the recesses of my mind for at least six years. Oftentimes, my smothered conscious would thrust forth the first-rate assertion; 'the GREAT Burger Method should be shared'. It would be my own contribution to society, and I could positively impact the Writing skills of seventh, ninth, or even eleventh graders. Thousands of White, Blacks, Hispanic, Oriental, Arab, and Native American students could become more academically influential. In addition, amplified Writing skills would make them more socially adept and confident in formal circles. Then, the frantic pace of Life and its endless chore list nearly devoured my resolve, until TODAY!

My mental ears became much more receptive to that inner voice which typically governed my actions. One menial chore of lugging the white refuse bag outside to our larger container was a fleeting distraction. Suddenly, an inaudible message gave me pause! *'Just do what you can today, nobody expects you to complete this in a single sitting anyway'*. It ironically reminded me of the 'chunking' or segmenting that teachers frequently do with their scholars. Normally, reflective educators seek to ensure that their learners are not overwhelmed with digestible mini-lessons. The notion that my grading tired fingers must hammer out the entire workbook right away disintegrated. I would have to make time.

My secondary concern became whether or not I would actually be willing to return to this preface or not. You see, supper was loudly announced at 6:14 PM! "Thump, thump" was the presumed hubbub I humorously imagined my wife heard from beneath our stairwell! Piping hot pizza, a fresh tossed salad, and a 42-inch plasma blasting CNN were quite the diversion. Yet these were some of my favorite daily trappings; another reason for me to hesitate.

This subsequent experience refocused my attention to the fact that writing educators can become creatures of habit! So, we often become trapped in a 'writing routine' or a banal revolving door! This endless maze of 'quantity versus quality' is hardly ever productive. The outcome, 'one-hour specials', are sub-standard essays just for the sake of getting them done! Usually, these repetitive drafts contain limited details and sound like very simplistic conversations, instead of quality presentations. We must break out of that futile mold! Thankfully, a larger residue of resolve remained within; no more comfort zone of complacency. By 7:03 PM, my literary urge triumphed over enjoying some well-earned creature comforts.

Treacherous thoughts of my babbling six-month old battling a bout of Bronchiolitis soon surfaced. How could I just trounce upstairs without amiably conversing with my wife about this effort? Cop out. Apparently, I had sufficiently persuaded my better half earlier. That happened when I chauffeured her home in our tiny Ford Focus. Throughout this entire story, or should I say ordeal, she must have yawned a half a dozen times. I know this because I half-drove my sedan while intermittently peering into her blood-shot eyes. During at least one instance she glared back into the rear-view mirror. It was as if she shouted through a megaphone **"enough with the infomercial; do it already"**.

Assured of her unconditional love, she was perhaps suggesting that I finally 'count up the cost'. *This, too, is a subtle cue for you that intense Writing instruction might not be immediately recognized or openly applauded. It may take an entire Semester or even an entire school year to notice appreciable growth. Fellow peers, faculty, parents, and administrators simply may be too bogged down with their own workloads. So, if a Writing coach of any type is looking for a pat on the back, they will frequently be disappointed. 'Essentially, you might find yourself completing the job that some instructor should have a year or two before'. Please implement this program because of your innate passion for student growth, not for external applause.*

Throughout this Great Burger Essay Writing Workshop, there may be moments of apprehension, or uncertainty of success. But decide 'not to go back' to the status quo or 'business as usual'. Too many teachers are internally frustrated, and their students are just doling out unskillful essays. It makes no sense sitting around and pitifully hoping for the best; do something about it! See this thing through and your pupils will have gratitude for your efforts for the rest of their lives. This is priceless. To those instructors who might even be tempted to seek quicker avenues; speed is less important than accuracy! Effectively chunking the Writing process is all-important. Honestly, retooling a person's writing Style is no quick and easy feat. But gradually connecting its GREAT components, over 15-16 weeks, will yield a much more powerful outcome. So stick with this holistic program and give it a bona fide chance to work.

In summary, re-teaching grammar, sentence types, and other language enrichment techniques are necessary building blocks. Then, your English students can confidently approach Style and Content from an empowered standpoint. Since grammar is no longer an integral focus of many middle and high schools' English programs, you must fill-in the gap. You must become a grade school teacher again reviewing the basics dropped at the end of those grades. This is how educators can meet their students where they are.

Acknowledging that, my task is to share the 'tricks of the trade' that have worked well during a seven-year Language Arts teaching period. Some will be ideas I borrowed and others original lessons that dawned on me in the field. I know there are a million proposed

Language Arts books our there. Nonetheless, I truly hope that mine will bestow very student centered, easy-to-understand, and visually compelling lessons. The interactive CD-Rom should be a big hit with those who love technology too.

Good luck and great writing!

Stephen C. Simms Sr.

P.S. *Results of GREAT Burger Workshop have been phenomenal in my classroom for the past three years!*

School year 2007-2008, my seventh grade students scored <u>an amazing 97% passing rate</u> on the Florida Writes.
(I was <u>the only 7th grade English teacher</u> at my school during school year 2007-2008).
Passing score: 3 or above.

School year 2008-2009, my 8th grade learners improved to a <u>98 % passing rate</u> on the Florida Writes.
(I was <u>the only 8th grade teacher</u> at my school during the school year 2008-2009).
Passing Score: 3 or above.

During 2009-2010, my 8th grade pupils scored <u>a brilliant 100% passing rate</u> on the Florida Writes.
(I was <u>the only 8th grade teacher</u> at my school during school year 2009-2010).
Passing Score: 3 or above. The school changed the passing rate months after the fact. So, 83 percent was final with a '4' or better that year.)

> *This is emphatic and undeniable proof of my program's success. It has been vigorously tested in my classroom for three consecutive years.*
>
> <u>**Note:**</u> My students did not only pass this state Standardized Essay Writing Test, many impressively raised their scores on the Florida Writing Rubric. I will show you these impressive scores later. They rose from a 3 to a score of 4, or jumped from a 4 to a 5 score. Others jumped by two scores as well; one young ladies failing '2' score, was replaced by an 'excellent' 5 score. *(This previous statement reflects how Writing scores altered from a practice Florida Write test to the formal Writing exam 6-7 months later).*

My Educational Credentials & Community Involvement

1. I've always been an A-student when it came to English: Associate of Arts—**3.63 GPA**, Bachelor of Science in Secondary English Education **3.71 GPA**, Master's of Business Administration—**3.58 GPA**. All four of my degrees are 'A averages' mainly because of my writing skills. I earned my Doctoral degree in Business Administration with a specialization Organizational Leadership at Northcentral University with a **3.7 GPA**!

2. I have also furthered my teacher education taking about 15-17 extra courses on Middle and High School English workshops/seminars. Some special training included ESOL (English for Speakers of Other Language) techniques, CRISS strategies, Middle and High School Reading techniques, Advanced Placement Writing, Advanced Placement Reading techniques, etc.

3. Several years back, my High school department chairperson allowed me to present my innovative method to 25 South Florida teachers. In this Vertical teaming meeting, I went through the process on the Smart board. All of these teachers eagerly accepted printed copies for their Middle and High school dates. Many still use it today.

4. I have also been trained in the International Baccalaureate Curriculum and Programme in a week-long training in Texas.

5. I was hired at one of America's best magnet schools, and worked there for three years. Magnet Schools of America judged this particular K-8 Center as 'the #3 Magnet school in the country' in 2010.

6. I directly assisted the Middle Years Programme Coordinator in creating a workable International Baccalaureate curriculum for the entire school. The principal of this institution personally recognized how valuable my assistance was in this endeavor. I created the 7th and 8th grade curriculum for Language Arts at my school Miami Frank C. Martin K-8 IB Center while it was still a K-6 school.

7. In 2015, I built the year-long curriculum for the Grand Traverse Band of Ottawa and Chippewa Indians from February to July 25, 2015. It included 30, two-hour lesson sessions, four formal exams, answer keys, Vocabulary Map exercises, and other interactive activities to teach native American adults their own language called Anishinaabemowin. I was paid handsomely as an Educational Consultant and my title was Anish. Curriculum Developer.

8. I served as the Chapter adviser, leader of the entire organization, of my school's National Junior Honor Society. My 35-student group managed to raise nearly $3,000 for Miami Children's Hospital over a two-year period. Our check hand-overs appeared in the 'Community and Giving' section of the Miami Children's Hospital Gazette.

9. Our National Junior Honor Society produced high quality Talent Shows three years in a row. In a schoolwide campaign, our members managed to collect 5,000 empty Capri Sun pouches for recycling. The money was collected to fight Cancer and other childhood, incurable illnesses.

10. In 2009-2010, we participated in the 'Autism Speaks' walk in Miami. We provided food, drinks, helped other vendors, played games, and even provided face painting for autistic children and their parents. My NJHS students and I actually participated in the one-mile walk along with over 17,000 other walkers to fight Autism.

11. *I have been actively involved in education for 14 years*. I spent five years as a substitute teacher in Miami-Dade County Public Schools. Then, I spent three years at Miami Southridge Senior High School as a full-time English teacher for grades 9, Pre-AP 9th, and 11th AP. Also, I enjoyed three years at Miami Frank C Martin K-8 Center as an English teacher for grades 6th, 7th, & 8th. and three years as a college math tutor at Miami-Dade Community College-teaching Algebra to Calculus I.

12. From 2015-2017, I was a dedicated substitute teacher four days per week while completing my doctoral degree of Business Administration (25 hours per week). I seek to demonstrate the G.R.E.A.T. Essay Workshop method as an Educational Consultant state or even nationwide.

13. My Publications include the following over the past 16 years of educating learners:

    - **Treachery by Chris Stephens (2002)** (amazon.com, barnesandnoble.com)
    - **Geo-Shifting: Social Cause Games by Stephen C. Simms (2012)**-(amazon.com, barnesandnoble.com, parkroadbooks.com
    - **Beat the Gionni's: An Italian American Tragedy of the U.S. Housing Collapse by Stephen C. Simms (2015, Feb).** Available on amazon Kindle.

- **Anishinaabemowin Curriculum by Stephen C. Simms (2015, July)** (Grand Traverse Band of Ottawa and Chippewa Indians (Traverse City, MI)-one year curriculum teaching native Americans their own language of Anishinaabemowin-learned it, planned it, taught kids the language.
- **G.R.E.A.T Burger Essay Workshop by Stephen C. Simms (Current book: 2017).**

Hopefully, you see by now that I am committed to student education, Writing growth, and Community involvement after sixteen years in the field. I am not just peddling some get-rich Writing scheme. This thing works, and it works big-time!

Trust me when I tell you that if my students could make it so can yours. I actively created this GREAT Burger book at a struggling school with large class sizes. Later, I tested it out at a public magnet school. Therefore, the activities, assignments, and bell ringers contained in this book were made to maintain easily frustrated students' focus.

You have to be a 'mass motivator' to your students, and not show an ounce of 'give-up' for this to work. Also, you have to remain committed to planning ahead with this book-20 minutes per class session. The techniques won't work as well if you don't do your homework using this manual. So read ahead and then implement them.

I am confident that students and teachers have enough resolve to get through this 15-16 week program. If you remain faithful to its contents I guarantee you fantastic improvement in your students' writing skills!

So let's get started.

References

Editorial Board. (2015, Sep.). A-PARCC-alypse Now: Dismal but honest results from new statewide test. *Chicago Tribune.* Retrieved from http://www.chicagotribune.com/news/opinion/editorial/ct-parcc-illinois-test-edit-0921-20150918-story.

Rado, Diane. (2015, Sep.). Most Illinois Students fall short on new PARCC tests. *The Chicago Tribune.* Retrieved from http://www.chicagotribune.com/news/ct-parce-results-met-20150916.

Tyre, Peg (2012, Oct.). The Writing Revolution. *The Atlantic* Retrieved from http://www.theatlantic.com/magazine/archive/2012/10/the-writing-revolution/309090/.

Wexler, N. (2015, Sep.). Why Americans Can't Write. *Washington Post.* Retrieved from http://www.realcleareducation.com/2015/09/25/why_americans_can039t_write_34118.html.

CHAPTER 1 | The Early Years

Allow your minds to travel backwards in time to the simpler skeleton imparted to our third and fourth grade learners in elementary school. There was a tidy, little introduction explaining three reasons why the more naïve essayists were writing. Then, each body paragraph would cite each of those pedantic three reasons with somewhat limited proof. Ultimately, the Conclusion paragraph served as a mirror-image of the Introduction. If you were lucky, a solitary sentence of insight might show up at the end of this structure. These were the minimal standards universally expected, and this strategy was applied for all grade-schoolers.

During those tender years, many elementary instructors did tremendous jobs demonstrating the standard parts and functions of paragraphs. They aptly used diverse 'burger models' of their own while prudently preparing their students. The scores of their grade level's standardized Writing tests were seemingly all-important! Nonetheless, many of those self-same educators would be utterly shocked that their teen-aged former pupils' repertoires never changed. No secondary system of creative, inspiring writing strategies enhanced their earliest methods; basically no growth!

If these teachers could be the proverbial 'fly on the wall' or state Writing test graders, their jaws might drop in disappointment. Somewhere within their beings these promoters of *continuous improvement* would wonder for hours on end. The nagging question gnawing at them would basically be 'why do my former scholars still write this way?' Why are 7th, 9th, and even 10th graders continuing their 4th grade writing models, instead of more mature, suitable ones? Of course, no guilt could be tossed at their feet because their writing drills were grade-level appropriate! Yet, some of them might even consider bearing a burden of shame. Instead, another follow-up question should soon surface. 'What have my students been learning about Writing since the fourth grade?' Then, they might inquire 'What of more creative Introductions, vividly detailed Body paragraphs, or unpredictable Conclusions?' That is another goal in this book and several techniques shall be meticulously lain out in due course.

\-

Here's my story...

There I finally was, after struggling to finally finish my Bachelor of Secondary English Degree in 2004-2005. A callow, but expectant gentleman who eagerly decided to give one of South Florida's mega high schools a try! Its 3,000 student population was a true melting pot of many cultures and ethnicities which I believed should be celebrated. Soon, I discovered that our English department was quite committed to education even though the recent state Writing scores were not so reflective of it.

An undeniable undercurrent of frustration was masked beneath the 'keep it positive' mantra. Muttered comments back and forth, rolled eyes, and defiant postures nearly heralded the 'real deal'. Our weekly meetings were very colorful. Back then, many of my co-workers, some of the hardest workers in Florida, felt demoralized! They knew that they were working extremely hard, but our charts and graphs were often a metaphorical slap in the face. This was mainly due to the dubious and unpopular labeling of students' efforts by the Florida Comprehensive Assessment Test (FCAT). Also, these professionals weren't so content with the "No Child Left Behind' initiatives.

Midway through that school year my eyes came open to shocking inequities. Shortly thereafter, the veneer of 'high expectations equal high achievement' was at least temporarily tossed aside. All 'newbies' or teachers fresh out of college heard about the variety and magnitude of our woes. These revelations made increasing our school's Reading and Writing scores appear to be a near impossibility. All of this came to a head for me on the day of Midterm Essay Exams.

I had jitters that Tuesday, hoping that I would do everything just perfectly. I sat down and took roll right after the tardy bell rang. Surely this was the occasion that every student would thoughtfully craft their best paragraphs of the year. I publicly announced this confident statement as an emotional incentive. Then, I proceeded with handing out of materials to these typical ninth graders. A last bit of advice; use your planning sheets as your guides. They were under way.

After grading that first set of essays, I regrettably understood that my work was cut out for me. It confirmed much of what my cohorts had been repeating all along; no quality, no imagination. Notwithstanding there were several precious glimmers of success but more than 50 to 55 percent earned a C, C-, D+, or D score. At this point, I was still very idealistic and did not believe in assigning F grades. So, my curve for most of those classes was shamefully large. It seemed that my predicament was commonplace for most English teachers. What do you do when so many students seemed to give it 'the old college try', but still fail?

Of course, I eagerly located the Chairperson of English and showed the samples to her. I insistently bickered about the recurrence of the simplest errors. Why couldn't students spell one or two syllable words? Where in the world was their sense of grammar, blah-blah-blah? This was when I considered that my lofty bar of accomplishment for our writers was set too high. I know some reader is thinking how could he say that? You should expect great work from every learner regardless or his or her race, money, or faith! But that was no longer realistic at this point.

The stylish, astute lady confided in me that we had the one of the largest English as a Second or Other Language population in our region. These ESOL students were often being pacified and appeased about their language barriers. Supposedly, if you showed a movie in English and put on the Spanish subtitles the students would improve their speaking skills. Ironically, the kindly chairperson reassured me that this was only a marginal cause of our deteriorating scores. We couldn't blame them for our failure!

We were educating around **20-25 percent of Level Ones and Level Twos**. By the way, this is FCAT-speak for lower Reading comprehension students. Most of these were American born pupils who should have a rudimentary grasp of the English language. Yet the bulk of them were truly resistant to reading books or any other material. In fact, getting through the first novel with my 9th graders was just like pulling teeth. That was even though it was a high-interest teen fiction novel called 'Forged by Fire' by Sharon Draper. I would even read one or two chapters with the students, and ask them to read one chapter at home. Most of the class would enjoy the novel since it was very relevant to their own backgrounds. Then, we took a quiz on Chapter Three. Maybe twenty to thirty percent would actually read the text and pass the comprehension quizzes. They simply had poor work habits that reinforced their lower reading skills.

In addition to that, there was another apathetic segment to address; these were the 'often absent' bunch. I would estimate this portion of learners to be **10-15 percent**. Many were dealing with major family and legal problems; no time to actually attempt improvement. These cases included youths who were devastated by early teen pregnancy, or sometimes physically or emotionally abusive parents. In other instances, promising Black and Hispanic boys tragically dropped out of our institution. Some had to help their single, struggling mothers pay rent or the electric bill. Boys had to try and become men way before their times. Reasonable percentages of these future leaders were sadly sucked into crime and the penal system. Others had to abandon their educations a year or two before graduation so they were robbed.

Worse than that, many teenage girls had to become caretakers, maids, and babysitters. This cheated these promising girls because some mothers could no longer afford daycare for their siblings. These absent students would never read the novels because they never had to time to do so. My head was spinning as I sat there and took stock in the many barriers and barricades. Our high-schoolers had experienced so much trauma and tragedy in such brief lifespans. This was attested to by some of the clothes they wore. Similarly, vulgar music and videos they were patterning their lives after were claiming student after student.

By my own estimation, that only **left some instructors with a population of 50 to 55 percent of 'salvageable, teachable minds'.** They were the stereotypical kids who were somewhat motivated, came to school daily, and attempted each assignment. Many of us rationalized that we needed to do the best we could with these 'slimmer pickings'. And even though we fought tooth and nail for 'the good kids', our approach was definitely proven wrong by the data.

Deep within our mindsets, we had become too jaded about the suffering students' abilities to turn their grades around. We forgot about believing in miracles and comebacks. Many of us had subconsciously begun writing-off and counting out youngsters who were in dire need of our moral support most. These chronic 'screw ups' needed our uplifting interaction even though their manners left a lot to be desired. These 'nobodies' were seeking our confidence in their abilities to remove their own doubts. At the very least, these 'undesirables' awaited that one humorous joke or teachable moment. It would make or break their decision to come to school the next day or simply stay home.

Instead of opening ourselves up to all, some instructors had become shaped by their educational environment. (Ironically, we were hired to shape or mold our students into greater contributors to society). Instead, some of us did the unthinkable. We made writers complete essays when they had limited know-how, and we frequently doled out passing scores. Sadly, this was even though it was apparent that the writings themselves were substandard. That unjustifiable *'paper mill'* where everybody passes for simply completing an essay, proved detrimental. Those unearned grades promoted a sense of entitlement and reduced the likelihood of valuable revisions/corrections.

Nothing was changing, and the chasm between the better and mediocre writers was widening right beneath our noses. Please take this as a friendly admonition from someone who has experienced it first-hand. Teaching around the misguided pupils who were counting on us the most was horribly unfair and ignoble. Every single student was our responsibility and should've been handled compassionately. They were to be trained as if he or she were our own sons and daughters. That year, we barely maintained our FCAT 'C' score and were once again lulled into the false sense of security. The following school year our school score dropped to an FCAT 'D' score. Not enough of us had taken the time to care for all learners. Corporately, we hadn't dared to be all of our students' keepers!

Meanwhile, I had seen enough. The ultimate lesson had become apparent. There was no way I was going to pretend like everything was satisfactory when it came to Writing. It was not only my opportunity to do something. I had a real responsibility to make *every* _single writer in my class the best_! Or, at least I would try for a reasonable enough period of time. Likewise, I'm sure that there were many teachers echoing my new stance at our school. Writing had to be put into the forefront of my lesson plans and curriculum. After all, it was the gateway to the other subjects and eventually a pathway into worthwhile careers.

I began regularly coming to my job even on Saturdays to grade extra papers; this was even though I wasn't being paid. As a single guy, there were no obstacles holding me back, and it was my obligation to be there. Most times, I'd meet my English chairperson there, too. I remember just how hardworking and truly reflective she was about her students' experiences as well. It was during many of these off-days that I began planning the next writing steps. Also, I spent hundreds of 'extra unpaid hours' reflecting upon gradually propelling my learners toward writing excellence. How could I incorporate many of the strategies from my continuous improvement courses? Oh, if I could just improve their sense of Style, vocabulary, and voice! These were amongst my earlier angsts and musings.

This was not meant to depress or discomfit anyone. It was meant to portray a more authentic picture of what Middle and High School teachers deal with daily. I wanted to personally indicate how much I identify with English educators and their tedious plights. They have to become miracle workers who nearly believe in the impossible, and have to retain unshakable perseverance. This is what it takes to achieve noticeable, class-wide writing score improvement. A year-long burden that is invisibly lugged around on educators' shoulders was the reality. Many days ended with stress headaches, fatigue, despair; and only a stiff drink or deep garden tub soak could allay them.

What needed to happen was something bigger than I had ever conceived possible before. Naturally it would require a tremendous personal sacrifice for me to turnaround so many writers at once. Several issues had to be addressed in any system that I came up with to solve it:

- It had to provide a quick planner since many students suffered from test anxiety and hence writer's block.
- Students had to be shown that there were many different sentence types and punctuations to make essays unique and expressive.
- The guide had to show them how to improve their verbs, adjectives, and adverbs to a more mature level. This would allow their ideas to be taken more seriously when written.
- This handbook needed to demonstrate color-coded, sentence-by-sentence instruction which gave the purpose and function of each sentence in every paragraph.
- It had to provide a greater sense of Style during the opening and closing paragraphs to distinguish it from the pedantic, boring essays of the past.

- The writing tutorial had to also include examples of Elaboration. This highest level of expression could only be obtained by including Facts, Reasons, Incidents, Examples, and Statistics. (After all what is a G.R.E.A.T. Burger without F.R.I.E.S.)?
- It needed an easily understandable Checklist to examine if each paragraph met the standards of G. R. E. A. T. which stands for Grammatically correct, Repetition Free, Expertly Supported, Adjective/Adverb Filled, and Transition Packed. (Peer assessment was essential in this part sense another student could more easily find a writer's mistakes.)
- It had to offer an authentic reward that students craved and were willing to work towards at the end of the schoolyear. In my case, it was a Burger King Whopper sandwich for every single student if we got a 95 percent passing rate. (You have to choose your own reward).
- Student papers had to be preliminarily evaluated by at least one state standardized writing rubric as practice writing exams. This was done at least twice.

After more than six years, this program came together in a complete, simplified, and effective way. I recommend that every single Writing tutor, English teacher, English professor, or struggling writer get this book today! Not only they could avail themselves but English as a second language students could too. The grammatical review is also ideal for urban students, rural writers, and remedial pupils. Even traditional students who could stand to spice up their essays could benefit from this essay workshop. It can be done in one classroom, a grade level, or frankly all grades from sixth to twelfth. In any case, it would cause students to reconsider the elements that make compositions stand out. School districts might consider buying sets of this book for struggling schools to spark creativity in their writing.

CHAPTER 2 | Vocabulary Enrichment

You improve writing with a consistent diet of Reading! Writing teachers must offer high-interest readings of different genres to motivate readers. Most of them are already geared up for the Internet Age, and they use technology better than adults. As a result, these tech-savvy learners would be exposed to new sight words and vocabulary terms. Not only that, but this process would take place in formats that appeal to them. (Feel free to read portions of this section to your students).

For silent reading, allow students to bring in Manga, picture books, Hip Hop magazines, romantic novels (grade appropriate), and even Comic Books. Public schools should even allow e-books and electronic book readers on the premises. It should not be such a far-fetched idea to openly embrace 21st century learning and all that it entails. As long as readers experience the print, reflect about it in their journals, and gain new vocabulary terms.

The Reading-Writing Connection is one that every student should understand. Just think about it! Billionaire Ross Perot started his company with $1,000 and he applied for a grant to expand his company. He had to convince the government to support it; now it's a five billion dollar business. Clearly, persuasive leaders like Bill Gates could sway others around them that their newest innovation is feasible. This is why he is the richest man in the world; $60 billion dollars! Oprah Winfrey began as an avid reader. Then, she became a great writer, journalist, and television reporter. Now, the icon is the richest television woman with an astounding three billion dollars. Her own television network, (OWN), highlights positive stories and accomplishments of ordinary people.

Think about renowned and successful authors Stephen King, Tom Clancy, and James Patterson. Ponder J.K Rowling--an out-of-work teacher--responsible for the world renowned Harry Potter series. These seven or eight books have created a multi-billion dollar empire because she dared to transmit her imaginative story skillfully. Now, students can hardly wait for the thicker books to be physically placed on the shelves. They are all fervent readers who became stylistic writers, and could effectively communicate their ideas to mass audiences. It was not necessarily about the level of education either.

Tens of thousands of marketers, advertisers, or account executives appeal daily to the sensibilities of others. They employ different styles of persuasive discourse and expository expression to earn million dollar accounts, humongous bonuses, etc. Even major Rappers and recording artists like Master P, Sean 'P. Diddy' Combs, & Baby Face have incorporated their businesses. They successfully run their own music production companies. Obviously, they need the Reading-Writing connection to assess whether they are being cheated or receiving a fair deal. This is why rap producer Master P is worth an estimated $600 million dollars (2010).

Earlier in U.S. history, thousands of slaves secretly learned to read so they could overcome bondage. For decades, slave-masters outlawed reading because they knew education meant freedom. These plantation owners, farmers, and businessmen knew that keeping slaves in the dark about events occurring around them was key! 'Not knowing' would keep these bondservants or subservient chattel. Thank goodness people like Sojourner Truth, Frederick Douglass, and W.E. B. Du Bois disobeyed the 'mandates of ignorance'. Essentially, illiteracy was such an oppressive weapon that Negros caught reading received the death penalty! The previously mentioned former slaves fled north before slavery was ended. They just had to take advantage of Reading and Writing in pursuit of Happiness. The short and simple fact is that 'everyone must read or their futures will be limited!'

Moreover, if you're not reading, you are not growing emotionally. People typically have needed to hold onto some encouraging word, idiom, speech, scripture, poem, or passage. These enlightened 'bon-mots'—*good words in French*--have invariably come from books of different genres. Treasured sayings and maxims were much more powerful than the letters that composed them. They became 'emotional fuel' for downtrodden hearers to defiantly struggle on despite amazing odds. I am sure that every student has heard at least one inspirational speech that has lifted their spirits. Maybe, they were at a funeral, wedding, group/club meeting; it doesn't matter the location.

In fact, each teacher should ask his or her students to write down the ten most successful people they know. (Make sure that they exclude sports players since the chances of becoming professional athletes are less than one percent). They could have heard of his or her success story on television, in movies, as employees of corporations, etc. Almost all of them will have a way with words. Either they read very well, speak quite effectively, or draft truly persuasive writings. (You could use this teachable moment to have them research three people's biographies via the Internet). They would analyze the candidates' education, writing ability, or love of literacy). From this research, I am positively certain that they will yield at least one result. Namely, most successful individuals are overwhelmingly passionate writers and communicators!

Defiantly rescue literature resistant children by telling them how futile life would be without reading! I charge you interfere in their lives (as they are right now)! Be bossy, persistent, even ornery about it because you may save them with your pointed words; still literacy at work! Remind the pupils that they are being prevented from growing, learning, comparing their lives to story characters, remaining hopeful, and absorbing valuable lessons from history. Ask them 'why make the same mistakes that others have already been through?'

Then, introduce them to engrossing storylines like the Giver, The Hobbit, etc. Introduce teen novels like: The Outsiders, Monster, Tears of a Tiger, Copper Sun, Slave Narrative of Frederick Douglass, Forged by Fire, Born Confused, Shabanu, Kite Runner, etc. There are too many titles to name here. You'll make their lives better despite their resistance. Later, their diffused anger will be replaced with sincerest gratitude. I got a little emotional and may have rambled but I felt it necessary.

Additional steps thorough teacher take to improve literacy/vocabulary in class:

1. They don't just read short stories all year, but they include at least 3-4 high interest teenage novels throughout the school-year.

It is important that teachers not limit their students by refusing to embrace the larger story pattern. Meaning, the Five Elements of a Storyline should be analyzed from novels' breadth as well. These, of course, include the Introduction, Rising Action, Climax, Falling Action, and the Resolution. Obviously, they are present in every story. Yet when you read an entire novel with students, you'll notice a greater grasp of these elements and their functions. This is especially correct when the instructor is highly interactive because the learners will be up for the challenge. Meaning, they should ask students questions, have them put themselves into characters' shoes, annotate their novels, etc. Moreover, it is a mistake to rush through these novels without thoroughly processing the themes, topics, and complex emotions in the pieces. This is why novels should be slowly unfolded over **6-8 weeks.** A well prepared teacher would assign at least 8-10 imaginative assignments during this interval. (Here is a sample of those diverse and creative assignments off the top of my head:)

- a.) Crossword puzzles dealing with Characterization (Ch. 1-2)
- b.) Critical essay responses as a particular character (Ch. 3)
- c.) Fill-in-the-blank quizzes (Ch. 4)
- d.) Cloze paragraph quizzes with (Weekly vocabulary word banks)
- e.) Make a rap/song about 7-8 events that happened in (Ch. 5) (16-20 rhyming lines) = Two grades, (in-class performance & writing according to given format) = One grade each.
- f.) Assign selective underlining/ margin notes (through text, a test taking skill)

g.) Apology Letter to (hurt, comatose, deceased, or hospitalized) character expressing regret and adding three ways he/she could have prevented the mishap. (Mid-book)

h.) After quizzes, Scavenger Hunt to find the answers of the 10 questions in the text; then selective underline/margin note these answers (class wide activity).

i.) Write a Diary entry/text entry explaining the recent five developments in a particular chapter and their significance to the plot. (Falling Action)

j.) Devise a three pronged plan to get enemies to reconcile. Explain the Who, What, When, Why, and How this plan's three steps will take place. (Resolution)

k.) Create a board game including four characters from the story. It must include authentic happenings from each character's lives. Furthermore, it should contain some bonus spaces, and losing spaces on the game board. Teach a peer to play and, then demonstrate it in front the class for 5-7 minutes. (Culminating activity)

Yearly, I create these activities from scratch or find a wonderful resource that delves deeply into the themes of a novel. You could simply go to the local Educational bookstore- Get Smart, Barnes & Nobles, etc. and purchase 'Novel Ties'. This wonderful series of workbooks contains worthwhile assignments for every grade level and many different novels. These can also be purchased at online websites like Amazon.com, Borders.com, and BarnesandNoble.com.

2. Utilize several types of Word Walls in your classrooms to help build vocabulary.

Many times, secondary teachers believe that the use of Word Walls is arcane or something mostly for elementary teachers. That is absolutely not the case however. Even 8th graders, 9th graders, and 11th graders must be absolutely inundated with new words to increase their vocabularies. Therefore, these words are written clearly on the board and left there all week. In my last classroom, my tenth graders experienced new Vocabulary Words from every direction:

a.) **Ten Weekly Vocabulary words** (6 from novel or short story)/4 words from (Weekly Gr., Latin, & Anglo/Saxon Roots list A-Z); quizzed each week using a two/ three cloze paragraph format. All 10 words are done in Vocabulary Maps because they build relationships with the words themselves.

Word Map Example

Complete sentence **definition** of new vocabulary word.	**Picture This:** A drawn representation of the word's definition; (a hieroglyph).
Two sentences using the word in the proper context without changing it.	**Synonym** of the vocabulary word.

b.) **Affable Affixes Chart** = 16 common affixes, (8 prefixes & 8 suffixes) When there is spare time, allow students to look up somewhat challenging words that begin with the prefixes. (Preferably three or four syllable words)
Purpose: To demonstrate etymologies and word families of the most common prefixes and suffixes of the particular grade level and/or one above.

c.) They must be words that no more than 50 percent of the students can define.

d.) Student writes down the definition of the word, a sentence using the word, and the definition of the prefix (given by teacher).

e.) Student places the sticky, white paper labels with the new words beneath the correct prefix.

f.) Student dictates what classmates will write in their notebook section called Vocabulary Enrichment. (4th section in our binders).

g.) Every twenty words we have a test. After there is one white paper label beneath all sixteen affixes and then a second one beneath the first four affixes. Then, there is a test based on the meaning of the affixes and clues/scenarios when the twenty words would be appropriate.

h.) I even utilized my space theme by hanging spaceships, comets, and planetoids from the ceiling using plastic hooks. Contained in them are more vivid adjectives, & better words.

3. 60 to 70 percent of your graded, displayed papers should be Writings; this places emphasis on it in your classroom. Thumb tack those poems, scripts, essays, and research papers up proudly hailing outstanding achievements.

4. It is a teacher's duty to regularly re-teach Grammar & Style elements on a daily basis. This is crucial in Middle and High School in order to refocus these writers. The importance of the elements of language cannot be overstated. Some schools have devised their own daily bell ringers to address this concern. Afterwards, your students will writer clearer, well defined drafts.

This next chapter presents purposeful 'grammar re-teaches' in exciting, interactive ways. Hopefully, your learners will find these forty-five 10-minute exercises helpful and will actively participate. You'll find that that we took three breaks during the twelve week format. Likewise, it was my intention to maintain interest by including some out-of-the-box assignments. I am confident that both you and your pupils will find this section pragmatic, and refreshing.

Enjoy Chapter 3 and review the provided answers with your students everyday!

CHAPTER 3 | Grammar Bellringers

BELLRINGER # 1 - MONDAY

In the past, you might have been taught that a noun is described as a *person, place, or thing.*

However, there is a more powerful definition that does a better job of encompassing a noun's different aspects.

The better definition:

Noun = *person, place, thing, idea, or event.*

DIRECTIONS: Read the following sentences and circle all nouns. Then, label each noun beneath the circles by their functions. (Write person, place, thing, idea, or event).

1. My brother Christopher was exceedingly overwhelmed by his surprise birthday party.
2. Aunt Tina's attitude was so acrimonious that nobody visited her hospital room!
3. When was Angela going to tell her professor that she was an expert on the Theory of Relativity?

Answers

Example # 1:

1. Brother - describes a person's position in a family   (**person**, common noun)
2. Christopher - gives person's exact name   (**person**, proper noun)
3. party - event   (**event**, common noun)

Example # 2:

1. Aunt - describes a person's position in family   (**person**, common noun)
2. Tina - provides exact name of person   (**person**, proper noun)
3. room - provides the location of the person   (**place**, common noun)

Example # 3:

1. Angela – provides a person's exact name   (**person**, proper noun)
2. Professor - describes a person's position   (**person**, common noun)
3. Theory of Relativity - describes a scientific concept   (**idea**, proper noun)

BELLRINGER # 2 - TUESDAY

Typically, a **common noun** is a general word that can mean **more than one** person, place, or thing. (That is why these remain lowercase).

> For instance: Those students should study harder for their Biology exam!
> (**students** could mean five, ten, or even one hundred learners).

> For example: Working together makes a difference to most teammates
> (**teammates** could mean two, thirty, or thousands in one group).

On the other hand, a **proper noun** includes the name of a specific person, place, thing, idea, or event. (That is why these are always capitalized).

> For instance: Sheila was not about to be disrespected by anyone!
> (Sheila is the name of a specific person, it should be capitalized.)

> For example: Susan, Mark, and Kelly are study buddies for Geometry.
> (Susan, Mark, Kelly are all specific person's names, capitalize them).

DIRECTIONS: Read the following sentences below, and identify each noun as either a proper noun or a common noun. Do this by underlining it and then writing CN or PN beneath each noun.

1. Since it is raining so hard I refuse to attend the Yankees playoff game.
2. Then, why should John contribute to the cause of Alzheimer's disease?

- -

Answers

1. **Yankees** describes a specific team or group of people.   (proper noun)
2. a) **John** describes a specific name of a person.   (proper noun)
   b) **Alzheimer's** is specific name of a thing (disease)   (proper noun)

BELLRINGER # 3 - WEDNESDAY

Pronouns are words that replace nouns.

Therefore, pronouns replace the names of persons, places, things, ideas, and events.

> For instance: David is an intelligent young mathematician who studies Calculus.
> **Ask this**: who is David?
> Answer: He is an intelligent young mathematician who studies Calculus.

Therefore, **he** is the proper pronoun replacement of David.

DIRECTIONS: Read the following paragraph below and replace the underlined proper and common nouns with the **best personal pronouns** (I, my, me, mine, his, him, your, yours, he, she, our, hers, it, its, or her).

> Stan had no idea that Stan accidentally slipped Stan's English homework into the stack of Math papers. Suddenly, Mrs. Washington collected them, and there was no way that he could pass tomorrow's English essay without his assignment. Sadly, Stan could not recall the research questions that Stan's paper required but Stan could not meet Mrs. Washington in time either. Stan and I's opinion was that Stan would have to do better on the next test.

Answers

Stan had no idea that **he** accidentally slipped **his** English homework into the stack of Math papers! Suddenly, Mrs. Washington collected them, and there was no way that he could pass tomorrow's English essay without his assignment. Sadly, Stan could not recall the research questions that **his** paper required, but he could not meet **her** in time either. **Our** opinion was that Stan would have to do better on the next test.

BELLRINGER # 4 - THURSDAY

Demonstrative pronouns are this, that, these, and those.

Sometimes these demonstrative pronouns are called the four 'th's'

DIRECTIONS: In the paragraph below, read each sentence carefully. Then, apply the best demonstrative pronoun on the correct line. (Use each demonstrative pronoun only once).

Last Thursday, Principal Johnson firmly announced "_____ students who are interested in joining the National Junior Honor Society should report to the auditorium".

A few of _____ individuals quietly exited our homeroom class after their names were called for attendance. Afterwards, Mr. Thibault strongly encouraged more of us to sign up for _____ prestigious organization. Upon hearing how passionate he was about _____ elite group, I decided to join as well.

\---

Answers

The optimal solutions for the paragraph above are as follows:

1. **those**
2. **these**
3. **this**
4. **that**

BELLRINGER #5 - FRIDAY

One of the most effective means of ensuring that the subject is not repeated over and over in a paragraph is called the **Pronoun-Antecedent Rule.**

The Pronoun-Antecedent rule holds:

1. **All pronouns have antecedents.**

   Antecedents = proper nouns that can be replaced by a pronoun.
   Since *Ante-* = before,
   antecedent = noun before its pronoun replacement

   John is a proper noun that can be replaced by the pronouns: he, his, and him.

2. **Replacement pronouns (and synonyms) should be used instead of simply repeating the noun in paragraphs.**

DIRECTIONS: Examine the following paragraph for redundancy (or repetition) of the proper nouns. Now choose from personal pronouns: (he, she, her, our, its, its, we, their, & his); and correct the underlined proper noun repetitions.

Example 1: Sharon was definitely outraged when <u>**Sharon**</u> heard the horrible news. Lady Gaga had cancelled <u>**Lady Gaga's**</u> concert in Raleigh! Sharon had paid for <u>**Sharon's**</u> tickets four months prior, and actually had front row seats. So, <u>**Sharon**</u> would rather not receive a refund but wished Lady Gaga would simply reschedule <u>**Lady Gaga's**</u> concert date.

Answer

Sharon was definitely outraged when <u>she</u> heard the horrible news. Lady Gaga had cancelled <u>her</u> concert in Raleigh! Sharon had paid for <u>her</u> tickets four months prior, and actually had front row seats. So, <u>she</u> would rather not receive a refund but wished Lady Gaga would reschedule <u>her</u> concert date.

Name: _____

Period: _____

Date: _____

Grammar Quiz # 1: NOUNS & PRONOUNS

1. The best definition of a noun is a word that describes a _____, _____, _____, _____, or _____. **(20 point question)**

2. Circle the nouns in the following sentence and label their functions (from the above five underlined categories). **(20 point question)**
    Mary and John wanted to be the first to announce their Green project of recycling older cellular phones.

3. Yours, mine, his, her, she, and ours are examples of _____. **(20 point question)**

4. Use the four demonstrative pronouns to properly complete the following sentences. **(20 point question)**
    Example: _____ holiday, called Veteran's Day, was created for _____ soldiers who defend our country. Therefore, we must remember _____ their sacrifices make it possible for us to enjoy _____ unique Democratic freedoms.

5. Using the pronoun-antecedent rule, correct the following paragraph so it clearer. **(20 point question)**
    Cedric read an interesting article expressing that texting and driving increases the likelihood of car accidents. _____ realized that many of _____ older friends were guilty of this crime. Thus, Cedric made it a priority to warn _____ friends not to text and drive. Or, _____ would instantly refuse to ride in the same car for _____ own safety sake. Cedric knew this move might make him lonelier, but it was a chance he'd take.

Answers

Grammar Quiz # 1

1. The best definition of a noun is a word that describes a <u>person</u>, <u>place</u>, <u>thing</u>, <u>idea</u>, or <u>event</u>. **(20 point question)**

2. Circle the nouns in the following sentence and label their functions (from the above five underlined categories). **(20 point question)**
   Mary and John wanted to be the first to announce their Green project of recycling older cellular phones.

   Mary = (person, proper noun)
   John = (person, proper noun)
   project = (thing, common noun)
   Phones = (thing, common noun)

3. Yours, mine, his, her, she, and ours are examples of _____ _____.
   (20 point question)
   <u>Personal Pronouns</u> include I, my, **mine**, you, your, yours, he, him, **his**, **she**, **her**, hers, it, its, we, us, our, **ours**, they, them, their, and theirs.

4. Use the **four demonstrative pronouns** to properly complete the following sentences. **(20 point question)**
   Example: <u>This</u> holiday, called Veteran's Day, was created for <u>those</u> soldiers who defend our country. Therefore, we must remember <u>that</u> their sacrifices make it possible for us to enjoy <u>these</u> unique Democratic freedoms.

5. Using the pronoun-antecedent rule, correct the following paragraph so it is clearer. **(20 pt. question)**
   Cedric read an interesting article expressing that texting and driving increases the likelihood of car accidents. **He** realized that many of **his** older friends were guilty of this crime. Thus, Cedric made it a priority to warn **his** friends not to text and drive. Or, **he** would instantly refuse to ride in the same car for **his** own safety. He knew this move might make him lonelier, but it was a chance he'd take.

Notice how much better this paragraph sounds by simply changing Cedric's name (the proper noun) into appropriate pronouns.

We could create even more variation of Cedric's name by using **synonymous phrases** such as: the young man, this concerned student, or the safety conscious passenger instead of 'he'.

Remember that these grammar bellringers usually take the first five to ten minute of class. They set the pace for the class period; so stick to this valuable behavioral management tool.

1. Let these bellringers provide you plenty of time to take attendance, handle admit slips for absences/tardies, and other matters before addressing your students. Then, you can focus on the corrections. (Typically these are collected in one section of a folder, and they take 7-10 minutes to complete.)

2. It is recommended that you have a volunteer go to the smartboard, chalkboard, or white board and answer the bellringer daily after 6-8 minutes. This should be done to prevent the loss of control of your classroom noise level.

3. Similarly, there should be some type of credit system for participation in place. Or, students should understand that there will be a weekly grammar quiz on the items you've presented as bellringers.

WEEK # 2

BELLRINGER #6 - MONDAY

Verbs are simply words that either express action or condition.

For example: I <u>run</u> with my dog every morning. *(run is a verb because it shows action)*

For example: We <u>stayed</u> inside since it was <u>raining</u>. *(stayed is a verb, it showed action)*
(raining is a verb, weather condition)

There are five types of verbs, and the first type is called an **Action Verb.**

1. **Action Verbs** - tell what a person, place, thing, idea, or event is doing.
   Example # 1 The little girls were <u>quarreling</u> over whose doll was prettier!

DIRECTIONS: Read the sentences below and <u>identify the action verbs</u> by underlining them. Which aspect of a noun does each action verb describe?

My cousin Thelma could wait no longer! Alas, she wanted to know whether her flute audition piece qualified her for the All County Marching Band. She made it!

Answers

1. wait – action verb, wait describes the action of a <u>person</u>; **(My cousin Thelma)**
2. know –action verb, know describes the action of a <u>person</u>; **(she)**
3. qualified—action verb, qualified describes the action of a <u>thing</u>; **(flute audition piece)**
4. made- action verb, made describes the action of a <u>person</u>; **(she)**

BELLRINGER # 7-TUESDAY

The second type of verb is called a **Linking Verb.**

Linking verbs - tell what a person, place, thing, idea, or event is; and uses the verb form 'to be'

'To be' verb forms include: **is, am, are, was, were, seem, be, being, been, and become.**

Example # 1 Shelly <u>was</u> a novice at the sport of lawn darts.
Example # 2 My grandparents <u>are</u> both retired.
Example # 3 That abandoned building <u>is</u> dilapidated!

DIRECTIONS: Read the following sentences and <u>underline the linking verb</u> in each sentence.

1. Did you know that Nancy Pelosi had become the first female Congress majority leader?
2. Rosa Parks did not seem fearful as the bus driver asked her to leave her seat.
3. Dr. Martin Luther King Jr. and Reverend Jesse Jackson were prominent Civil Rights leaders during the 20th century.
4. Sandra Day O'Connor was the first female Supreme Court Justice ever!
5. In November 2010, President Obama and Congressional Majority Leader John Boehner are promising a new spirit of unity in American politics.

Answers

1. '**become**' should have been underlined in Sentence #1.
2. '**seem**' should have been underlined in Sentence # 2.
3. '**were**' should have been underlined in Sentence # 3.
4. '**was**' should have been underlined in Sentence # 4.
5. '**are**' should have been underlined in Sentence # 5.

BELLRINGER # 8-WEDNESDAY

Helping Verbs have two or more words that 'assist' the main verb in its overall meaning.

For example: My son <u>is going</u> **swimming** today.

You'll notice how the two verbs 'is + going' assist the main verb **swimming** in its overall meaning.

So, *is going swimming* puts the action into the future tense and makes sense together.

For example: Those chores <u>should have been</u> **done** already!

Notice that the three verbs '<u>should</u> + <u>have</u>+ <u>been</u>' assist the main verb **done** in its overall meaning.

So, *should have been done* puts the action into past tense and makes sense together.

DIRECTIONS: Analyze the following sentences and identify the helping verbs by circling them.

1. I will be meeting my family in Miami for Christmas Break this year!
2. Should we have been listening to their private conversation?
3. It is hard to believe that any of those judges would have been fair.

Answers

1. Two verbs 'will be' should be circled in Sent. 1; they assist **meeting** in its overall meaning.
2. Two verbs 'have been' should be circled in Sent. 2; they assist **listening** in its overall meaning.
3. Three verbs 'would have been' should be circled in Sent. 3, they assist **fair** in its overall meaning.

BELLRINGER #9-THURSDAY

A **gerund** is a verb that functions like a noun.

1. Gerunds name activities, behavior, state of mind, or state of being.
2. Gerunds and may be modified by adjectives.

This seems like too much to digest but can be easily determined by asking one question:

Does this action, mental state, or condition behave like a thing or event?

For example: I love **skiing**!

Its –ing ending reveals that it is an action, but it also is the name of an activity ('event' of a noun). Thus it is a **verb** that acts like a **noun.** *Meaning it is a gerund.*

For example: **Lesson planning** is a necessity for all teachers!

Since lesson planning ends in –ing it is considered an action, yet it is the name of an activity = ('event' of a noun). Thus, it is a **verb** that acts like a **noun.** *Meaning it is a gerund.*

DIRECTIONS: Read the following sentences and indicate gerunds by underlining them.

(Remember to stick with the definition of a gerund precisely).

1. Anthony is fishing.
2. Fishing is exciting!
3. I have a boring P.E. teacher.

Answers

1. Since 'fishing' ends in –ing it is considered a verb, but it functions as a verb instead of a noun in this sentence. **Don't underline fishing. No gerund in this sentence.**
2. Since 'fishing' ends in –ing it is considered a verb, and it functions as a noun or (an event within the definition of a noun). **Therefore underline 'fishing'= gerund.**
3. Since 'boring ends in –ing it is considered an adjective, and it functions as an adjective in this particular sentence. **Therefore, don't underline 'boring'. No gerund in this sentence.**

BELLRINGER # 10 - FRIDAY

From yesterday's bellringer, we observed that some verbs ending in -ing do function as nouns, usually called gerunds.

Yet, there are some occasions when verbs end in –ing, but behave like either a 'verb' or an 'adjective'. These are called present participles.

a.) **Present Participles** are typically from the verb 'to be' and **indicate an action that is incomplete.**

Using yesterday's exercises:

Example 1: Anthony is fishing.

Consider that 'fishing' is a verb that ends in –ing, but it functions like a continuing action. Therefore, fishing is a **verb** that behaves like a **verb**, (not a noun).

So, 'fishing' in this case is a **present participle**.

Example 2: I have a boring P.E. teacher.

Consider that 'boring' is an adjective ending in –ing, but it functions like a description. Thus, boring is an adjective (not a verb), that acts like an adjective, (not a noun).

So, 'boring' in this case is a **present participle**.

DIRECTIONS: Read the following sentences carefully and <u>circle each present participle</u>.

1. Susan was studying for her Biology test.
2. Kid Rock is a fascinating Hip Hop entertainer!
3. Rapping became my favorite musical activity last year.

Answers

1. 'studying' is a verb ending in –ing, & indicates an incomplete action).
   Circle 'studying' because it is a present participle.

2. 'fascinating' is an adjective ending in –ing, that functions like a description.
   Circle 'fascinating' because it is a present participle.

3. 'rapping' is a verb ending in –ing, but it functions like a noun (event).
   Do not circle 'Rapping' because it is a gerund, (not a present participle).

Name: _____

Period: _____

Date: _____

Grammar Quiz # 2: VERB TYPES

DIRECTIONS: Match the underlined terms in the following sentences on the left with their proper rationale. Simply write the correct capital letter in front of each sentence.

Sentences	Grammatical Rationale
_____ 1. Terrance <u>was</u> silly!	A. action verb about verbal feud
_____ 2. Charlotte <u>should have finished</u> her lunch by now.	B. gerund praising retail sales
_____ 3. <u>Reading</u> is a fundamental skill.	C. linking verb on boys' state of mind
_____ 4. We have an <u>exhilarating</u> band director!	D. present participle, describing person
_____ 5. Stephanie <u>is</u> shopping.	E. helping verbs about an appetite
_____ 6. <u>Shopping</u> is awesome.	F. gerund about modern tunes
_____ 7. My cousins Ralph and Andre <u>seem</u> nervous	G. linking verb about a boy's attitude about their SAT scores.
_____ 8. The young artists had been <u>squabbling</u> all	H. linking verb, a girl's favorite action day long!
_____ 9. <u>Rapping</u> is my favorite musical activity.	I. gerund applauding literacy
_____ 10. Sheila <u>will</u> become an attorney eventually.	J. helping verb, teen's future dream

----

Answers

Grammar Quiz # 2

Sentences	Grammatical Rationale
G 1. Terrance <u>was</u> silly!	A. action verb about verbal feud
E 2. Charlotte <u>should have</u> finished her lunch by now.	B. gerund praising retail sales
I 3. <u>Reading</u> is a fundamental skill.	C. linking verb on boys' state of mind
D 4. We have an <u>exhilarating</u> band director!	D. present participle, describing person
H 5. Stephanie <u>is</u> shopping.	E. helping verbs about an appetite
B 6. <u>Shopping</u> is awesome.	F. gerund about modern tunes
C 7. My cousins Ralph and Andre <u>seem</u> nervous	G. linking verb about a boy's attitude about their SAT scores.
A 8. The young artists had been <u>squabbling</u> all	H. linking verb, a girl's favorite action day long!
F 9. <u>Rapping</u> is my favorite musical activity.	I. gerund applauding literacy
J 10. Sheila <u>will</u> become an attorney eventually.	J. helping verb, teen's future dream

WEEK # 3

BELLRINGER #11 - MONDAY

Vivid adjectives are one of the most important building blocks in the writing process. This is why we will do a rather extensive study on these.

Adjectives are words that describe a person, place, thing, idea, or event.

To determine whether a word or term is an adjective one need only ask the following three questions:

a.) What kind?
b.) Which one?
c.) How many?

For example: What kind of party is your sister having?
Answer: She is having her *twelfth birthday* party.

1. twelfth is an **adjective** since it answers **'which one'**?
2. birthday is another **adjective** since it answers **'what kind'**?

For example: How many Crayola crayons did your brother Saul stuff into the box?
Answer: He only found *five* or *six broken* crayons!

1. five is an **adjective** since it answers **'how many'**?
2. six is an **adjective** since it answers **'how many'**?
3. broken is an **adjective** since it answers **'what kind'**?

DIRECTIONS: Examine the following fragments. Label each adjective with the question it answers beneath it. What kind? Which one? How many?

a.) ...a difficult question to answer   c.) ... a sweet victory like this one

b.) ...four burning candles on the cake   d.) ...empty promises and a dozen roses

----

Answers

a.) ...a **difficult** question to answer
(what kind?)

b.) ...**four burning** candles on the cake
(how many?) (which one?)

c.) ...a **sweet** victory like **this** one
(what kind?) (which one?)

d.) ...**empty** promises and a **dozen** roses
(what kind) (how many?)

BELLRINGER #12 - TUESDAY

Pronouns can be used as <u>adjectives</u> when they come before a noun in a sentence.

For instance:

> Pronoun: I want a slice of that!
> Adjective: I want a slice of <u>this</u> delicious <u>cheesecake</u>.
>   adj.   noun

Thus, we can label the *demonstrative* pronoun 'this' as an adjective because it is describing a noun (the cheesecake) indirectly, and it <u>came before the noun</u> 'cheesecake'.

(delicious would be the next adjective in the sentence, after 'this')

DIRECTIONS: Choose the <u>pronouns that can be used as adjectives</u> in the following sentences. Then, provide the reason why based on the above definition.

1. I positively can't wait to try those chocolate chip cookies.
2. Can you believe that insensitive brute?
3. Are these two juvenile delinquents ever going to grow up?

Answers

1. **those** is a demonstrative pronoun that:
   a.) describes the noun 'cookies'
   b.) 'those' is positioned **before** the noun cookies

   Therefore, 'those' is a pronoun that can be used as an adjective.

2. **that** is a demonstrative pronoun and it:
   a.) describes the noun 'brute'
   b.) 'that' is positioned **before** the noun 'brute'

   Therefore, 'that' is a pronoun that can be used as an adjective.

3. **'these'** is a demonstrative pronoun that: a.)   describes the noun 'delinquents'

                                            b.)   'these' is positioned before the noun

Therefore, 'these' is a pronoun that can be used as an adjective.

BELLRINGER # 13-WEDNESDAY

There are special occasions when **adjectives can also be used as articles**.

There are only three main articles to consider are: **a, an,** and **the.**

(These are very general description words that barely answer the question "how many?" The response is <u>always singular</u>:)

Example 1: I would like to sit down and read a book.

('a' barely answers the question 'how many?' but you can easily tell that 'a' means one book) = an article.

Example 2: Are you ready for 'the' Honors Chemistry Exam?

('the' barely answers the question 'which one?' but you can easily observe 'the' means one chemistry test) = an article.

DIRECTIONS: Examine the following poem carefully, underline the articles, and provide the noun that each represents singularly.

A phoenix is a hearty bird,
with an attitude of endurance,
it can never be counted out;
soars above adverse influence.

She lifts her neck against the odds
because suffering's end is in sight;
and emerges from fiery depths
a more powerful fowl in flight!

(Stephen C. Simms)

Answers

Line 1: 'The' should be underlined and it represents <u>one</u> phoenix.
Line 1: 'a' should be underlined and it represents <u>one</u> hearty bird.
Line 2: 'an' should be underlined and it represents <u>a single</u> attitude
Line 3: None
Line 4: None
Line 5: 'the' should be underlined and it represents <u>one</u> set of numbers called 'odds'.
Line 6: None
Line 7: None
Line 8: 'a' should be underlined and it represents <u>one</u> more powerful fowl.

BELLRINGER #14-THURSDAY

An intriguing skill that every student should grasp is the ability to distinguish whether a word is an adverb or an adjective (by definition).

We know that **ninety-five percent of all adverbs** are actually *adjectives that end in 'ly*. Adverbs explain **Where? When? How? How Much? To What Extent?**

> **Example #1:** The girl was a swift runner.
> **You'd ask:** How did the girl run?
> **Answer:** add the adjective **swift** + **-ly** ending = **swiftly**; ***swiftly* is an <u>adverb</u>** since it explains 'how?'.

However, a writer must be careful that he or she correctly determines if the (adjective + -ly ending) word is actually an adjective or adverb. Remember, adjectives answer **What kind? Which one? How Many?**

> **Example #2:** Hugh was considered Jerry's best friend.
> **You'd ask:** How did Hugh behave towards Jerry?
> **Answer:** add the adjective friend + -ly ending = **friendly**; ***friendly* is an <u>adjective</u>** since it describes 'what kind' of person (noun)?

This is a case where an -ly ending word is not an adverb, but an **adjective**.

DIRECTIONS: Scrutinize the following sentences carefully, and determine if the -ly ending terms are either an adjective or an adverb. Explain why for each one?

1. The <u>ugly</u> mutt scared many cats away as it limped down the street.
2. Toddlers who begin reading <u>early</u> are <u>widely</u> known to excel in Language Arts.
3. On November 8, 2010, a runaway rocket <u>rapidly</u> ascended into Californian airspace!
4. The <u>chilly</u> Michigan War Museum displayed many colorful fighter jets from World War II.

Answers

1. <u>ugly</u> describes a *'thing'* which is a noun; therefore ugly is an **adjective**.
2. a) <u>early</u> describes *'when'* the action will take place; thus it is an **adverb**.

    b) <u>widely</u> describes *'to what extent'* did others know; thus it is an **adverb**.
3. <u>rapidly</u> describes *'how'* the rocket ascended; therefore it is an **adverb**.
4. <u>chilly</u> describes a *'place'* which is a noun; therefore it is an **adjective**.

BELLRINGER #15-FRIDAY

There are other **adverbs** that do not have an –ly ending but do meet its definition.

For example: The clarinets came in <u>too</u> soon, this was before the oboes were done.

In this case, 'too' describes an action; **it is an adverb.**

For instance: We broke the previous attendance record at our school <u>today</u>!

In this case, 'today' describes 'when?'; **it is an adverb.**

For example: We turned <u>right</u> onto Bienvenue Road.

In this case, 'right' describes an action of turning; **so it is an adverb.**

DIRECTIONS: Analyze the following sentence fragments. Then, determine if the underlined words are adjectives or adverbs. Explain why for each?

1. ...but hopefully she will make the right decision
2. ...sometimes Aaron changes his fickle mind suddenly
3. although April often settles her disagreements over there.

Answers

1. **right** describes a type of 'thing' (a decision = noun); it is an **adjective**.

2. a) **sometimes** describes 'When?'; thus it is an **adverb**.

   b) **fickle** describes a type of 'thing' (a mind = noun); thus it is an **adjective**.

3. a) **often** describes 'when?' an action happens; therefore it is an **adverb.**

   b) **over there** describes 'where?' an action happens; therefore it is an **adverb**

Name: _____

Period: _____

Date: _____

Grammar Quiz # 3: ALL ADJECTIVES, ADVERBS, & ARTICLES!

DIRECTIONS: Answer the multiple choice items by **clearly writing a capital letter on the provided lines.**

_____ 1. **Find all adverbs:** "We will gradually address grammar rules that are often missed by most students today".

    a.) gradually, often, missed   c.) will, gradually, most, missed

    b.) gradually, often, most, today   d.) none of the above

_____ 2. **Provide the rationale of each adverb from the above sentence respectively.** (Use the answer from question # 1 to select **the proper grammatical rationale for each adverb in order.**)

    a.) To what extent? When? How much?   c.) To what extent? When? How much? When?

    b.) When? How much? How many?   d.) How much? When? Where?

_____ 3. **Select the proper grammatical rationale for adjectives in the next sentence.**
"Two years ago, President Barak Obama was challenged with a plummeting stock market!"

    a.) How many? Which one? What kind? What kind?   c.) When? Which one? How? What kind?

    b.) How much? What kind? Which one? Where?   d.) none of the above

_____ 4. There are also adverbs that do not end in –ly. Identify these adverbs in the following sentence.
There is seldom a case when the Board of Directors will flat-out condone coworker harassment!

a.) is, will, condone

c.) a, the, will

b.) case, board of directors, coworker

d.) seldom, flat-out

_____ 5. The simplest way to **'create' an adverb** is by adding _____ to _____.

a.) adjective + -ly

c.) noun + -less

b.) gerund – (ing)

d.) verb + -ly

_____ 6. **Articles** barely answer the question _____; and it is always singular!

a.) 'What kind?'

c.) 'Where?'

b.) 'How many?'

d.) 'Which one?'

_____ 7. **Choose articles** from the following choices:

a.) this, that, those, these

c.) the, a, an

b.) too, much, often

d.) this, their, our

_____ 8. The **pronoun antecedent rule** demands that a writer _____.

a.) replace a proper noun with a pronoun

c.) switch a common noun with a synonym

b.) exchange a pronoun with a proper noun

d.) transfer a common noun with a pronoun

_____ 9. Clearly underline the demonstrative pronoun in the following sentence only: (one word only)
Do you actually expect me to wear these dingy socks today?

Answers

Grammar Quiz # 3

DIRECTIONS: Answer the multiple choice items by **clearly writing a capital letter on the provided lines.**

____B____ 1. **Find all adverbs:** "We will gradually address grammar rules that are often missed by most students today".

    a.) gradually, often, missed   c.) will, gradually, most, missed

    b.) gradually, often, most, today   d.) none of the above

____C____ 2. **Provide the rationale of each adverb from the above sentence respectively.** (Use the answer from question # 1 to select **the proper grammatical rationale for each adverb in order.**)

    a.) To what extent? When? How much?   c.) To what extent? When? How much? When?

    b.) When? How much? How many?   d.) How much? When? Where?

____A____ 3. **Select the proper grammatical rationale for adjectives in the next sentence.**
"Two years ago, President Barak Obama was challenged with a plummeting stock market!"

    a.) How many? Which one? What kind? What kind?   c.) When? Which one? How? What kind?

    b.) How much? What kind? Which one? Where?   d.) none of the above

____D____ 4. There are also adverbs that do not end in –ly. Identify these adverbs in the following sentence.
There is seldom a case when the Board of Directors will flat-out condone coworker harassment!

    a.) is, will, condone   c.) a, the, will

    b.) case, board of directors, coworker   d.) seldom, flat-out

___A___ 5. The simplest way to **'create' an adverb** is by adding _____ to _____.

    a.) adjective + -ly   c.) noun + -less

    b.) gerund – (ing)   d.) verb + -ly

___B___ 6. **Articles** barely answer the question _____; and it is always singular!

    a.) 'What kind?'   c.) 'Where?'

    b.) 'How many?'   d.) 'Which one?'

___C___ 7. **Choose articles** from the following choices:

    a.) this, that, those, these   c.) the, a, an

    b.) too, much, often   d.) this, their, our

___A___ 8. The **pronoun antecedent rule** demands that a writer _____.

    a.) replace a proper noun with a pronoun   c.) switch a common noun with a synonym

    b.) exchange a pronoun with a proper noun   d.) transfer a common noun with a pronoun

__these__ 9. Clearly underline the demonstrative pronoun in the following sentence only: (one word only)

Do you actually expect me to wear these dingy socks today?

WEEK # 4
INFORMAL ASSESSMENT WORKSHEETS

Right now, it is critical to 'mix it up'! We would not want you, the teacher, or your students, to be lulled into a sense of routine. So switching gears in order to break up the monotony is necessary!

This week of Informal Assessments was designed to specifically reflect upon what pupils have learned in the prior three weeks. Also, it was a chance for the learners to just have some fun with it.

These exciting, hands-on activities will include the following:

1. Adverb Advertisement (Spirit Week or Homecoming Dance)
2. Dead Words Eulogy (Actors Mourn Dead words, Teacher eulogy)
3. Forbidden Island of Dead Words (Students construct mural)
4. 'Dead Words I Would Change' Jam (Create/perform song)

Suggestion:

(Grade the Adverb Advertisement, and 'Dead Words I Would Change').
Then, you have your two grades per week minimum required by many school districts.

Name: _____

Date: _____

Activity #1: Announcing Your Homecoming Dance
(Learning Modality: Tactual)

INSTRUCTIONS: Attempt to include at least four or five ' –ly' adverbs in this announcement of the most important dance of the year. Be sure that it is convincing and grammatically formal for your teenage audience (no slang or text spelling). It should also mention the appropriate dress, night's theme, starting/ending dates & times, and crowning of king/queen. (Several volunteers should read these aloud for their classmates).

Activity #2: Dead Words Eulogy
(Learning Modality: Aural)

The misleading monacre of this exercise might evoke mental pictures of student boredom and depression. However, this activity can be both quite informative about sentence expansions, and engrossing.

I normally use this exercise in the fall around Halloween so that the class can keep with the season. Be sure to follow the directions below since it takes about two days to set up this activity.

DIRECTIONS:

1. Day 1: Mini-lesson/bellringer on Dead words—(replacing overly used adjectives and verbs that do not adequately describe nouns).

Sample list of Dead Words

Overused adjectives: good, nice, fair, bad, happy, sad,
Overused adverbs: too, fast, quickly, very, etc.
Other Overused terms: get, wanna', woulda', coulda' shoulda', ask, 'cause, etc.

(There are a hundred more of these dead words that should be buried and forgotten!)

Day 1: Pass out small square 2 × 2 inch pieces of paper.

- **Personalize:** Ask students to consider five Dead words that they personally overuse while writing essays (write them on the front of paper)—(10 minutes)

- **Think-Pair-Share:** In groups of two or three, have each student assist the other with finding three better synonyms for each dead word. (Dictionaries and thesauruses are welcome in this exercise, if team members can't come up with the synonyms themselves) (15 minutes)

- **Decision Time:** Ask members in each group to decide which two words on all their lists are the most commonly used. (3 minutes)

- **Whole Class Review:** Spokesperson of group tells entire class their two dead words, and the three better synonyms that they used to replace each one. (7-10 minutes)

- **Closure:** Have all students walk up to a 'coffin-like' or jack-o-lantern receptacle, place their small pieces of paper in it.

- **Homework:** Wear black or dark clothing, and bring white handkerchiefs if possible.

2. Day 2—Set up your room; pretend the front of your classroom is a place where the officiator would give a eulogy.

   a.) Place chairs around the front of class in a semicircle
   b.) Put the podium in the front.
   c.) Slide a chair in front of the podium
   d.) Place empty mini-coffin or jack o' lantern
   e.) Put 6-7 mini-snickers on podium (hidden from sight)

- **Bellringer:** explains the rules of the Eulogy (5 minutes)

   a.) Pull small papers from coffin; hand them out to students. Then, quietly gather in the hallway.
   b.) Play somber music from CD player for the funeral's beginning.
   c.) Use handkerchiefs; roleplay 'mourning relatives' of dead words as you enter the room.
   d.) No screaming, falling onto floor, but make the mourning believable.
   e.) (5 min procession): slowly walk in, drop your dead words into coffin.

- **Dead Words Teacher Eulogy**: (15 minute prepared speech provided on next page)

He or she pretends to be a middle aged, Southern preacher, rabbi, or priest as they read from the script. *(Throw out the candy when students repeat "I will change today!" This occurs two of three times.)*

Make sure you perform this ceremony towards the end of the period because students might not want to do anything else after it.

Dead Words Eulogy

Dearly beloved,

We are gathered here to mourn those tired words whose day has finally come.

That is why you all have traveled from miles around it was just to see them off.

For so many years, the 'words that should not be spoken' lingered into our daily conversations. But that was okay, they were only meant to be used when we were six, seven, or eight years old.

Our parents looked on in awe; yet they knew that we would eventually let them go. That's why we'd comment "what a nice car" when a visitor dropped by. Or, we'd reply "this food tastes good" as if we did not have the ability to describe it as "scrumptious" "delectable" or "delicious".

Grandma and mama still peered at us hoping "oh it's just a phase; he or she will grow out of it". But we clung to these simple adjectives resisting the growth that should come to all vocabularies.

We turned eight, nine, ten, and even eleven; without any change. (How many know that we must all change in order to grow? I said "How many know that we must all change in order to grow?" Yet it did not happen!

Instead, we physically matured two, three, and even four years; but those 'words that were on a respirator' kept creeping into our formal writings. That's right, we did the unthinkable.

We tragically shoved "good, bad, happy, sad, fine, and okay"—words that belonged in a toddler's book--right into our most formal writings; essays.

*It really wasn't our fault; these worn-out terms seemed easier than allowing our vocabularies to grow; allowing our thoughts to become more sophisticated. Come now—who would say "she **said** he was wrong" when they could more colorfully offer "She vigorously **denied** his misguided statement".*

But now we know that these banal terms were just a cop-out; just a path of laziness that made us sound uneducated in essays. And all of us in this room absolutely knew that we needed to do something about it—Am I right about it?

It is time to bring our minds up and set our sights higher! We can no longer afford to be embarrassed by our own remarks in speeches & writings.

-Instead of saying 'sad', why not depressed, melancholy, somber, or bemused...
-And Why not replace 'bad' with horrendous, negative, or regrettable
-How about switching 'very' with quite, tremendously, truly, or even fully.

I encourage you to change today... *(throwing snickers)*

-Replace said with "stated, remarked, refuted, or argued" and your day will be brighter.
-Bring a smile to your teacher's face; write down 'requested & inquired' instead of asked.
-Complement someone you care about with "you look spectacular, that dress is splendid, that suit fits like a glove, or your shoes are quite fashionable" Never say that's cute... ***I encourage you to change today...*** *(throwing snickers)*

And when you change these words and transform your vocabularies, readers and hearers all around you will respond. They will embrace all that you have to share with them.

Everyone repeat these phrases after me:

To dead words we all proclaim:

ashes to ashes,
dust to dust,
remain stranded on Forbidden Island,
for we have learned to Trust

in our abilities to grow
and express in a mature way
with eager minds ready
we gladly release you today.

Amen
(applause)

– Stephen C. Simms Sr.

Make sure you forewarn the students that they have to say "I will change today." This happens immediately after you prompt them by yelling "I encourage you to change today". That's how they receive the mini-snickers or other candy prizes.

This is a pretty cool lesson to record on the video camera as well. Have a student who is a proficient writer work the camera. Train him or her how to use it (left and right adjust, pan inward, pan outward, and when to stop/start the record button). Doing so will ensure a quality recording of this Dead Words eulogy.

Activity # 3: Island of Forbidden Words
(Learning Modality: Kinesthetic-Artistic)

Most students never lose their child-like zeal of drawing, cutting, coloring, and pasting original artwork. A handful of your learners might be rather skilled artists upon closer inspection.

Here is an opportunity for those kids who learn through the kinesthetic domain to shine. You'll be surprised at the untapped talent just sitting out in those rows of desks and chairs.

I recommend that this Dead Words Mural be at least 6 feet by 6 feet, preferably 8 feet by 10 feet. The purpose of such an imposing word wall mural is so that the words are prominently displayed as a major classroom learning system. Then, writers could actively use it when they are drafting essays.

Once the learners construct this mural, they should add more terms to every two or three weeks or so. Words should only be added as they discover more banal words, and replacements for them.

The Forbidden island of Dead words should consist of:

1. *One large tree in the center with many droopy limbs. Some of the brown, yellow, and reddish leaves are being blown from it.*
2. *The one-foot tall landmass at the base of the tree should be somewhat barren.*
3. *It can have some beige or brown sand in spots with some patches of grass.*
4. *It should contain with 3-5 interspersed headstones saying "RIP".*
5. *Two or three Black birds, ravens or crows with red eyes, should be on the ground or on top of the tombstones.*
6. *Orange, yellow, and reddish leaves should have 25-40 Dead Words inscribed onto them. They should be falling off of the tree and on the ground to represent their obsolete nature.*
7. *On the other hand, the green leaves that remain on the treetop should be the better synonym replacements. This visually indicates that only the more vivid, descriptive terms deserve the right to remain living. Add three or four gray clouds on the wall above the mural for realism as well.*

Supplies:

- *Approximately 25 sheets of white construction paper*
- *5 packs of Markers*
- *3-4 packs of Color pencils*
- *2 packs of Sticky tack or 2 packs of double sided mounting squares*
- *10 sharpened Pencils*
- *5 Scissors*

INSTRUCTIONS

Day One: (Tracing the outline of the Mural—**Last 40 minutes of period/block**)

a.) If you have 6-7 periods a day: split up the outlining process. Allow the first three periods to focus on the outline of the island's land: tombstones, ravens, sand, grass, and some orange, yellow, reddish oak tree leaves.

(If you have block scheduling, allow the first block to concentrate on the island's landmass. The second and third blocks will create the tree, its limbs, the clouds, and the sun)

1. Tape four to five pieces of construction paper together on the backside of them. They will eventually fit on the wall smoothly as one large piece.

2. After 5-10 minute verbal collaboration, three or four students can begin tracing the one foot tall landmass on four or five pieces of construction paper.

    a.) Who will trace slanted tombstones?

    b.) Who will sketch the ravens?

    c.) Who will draw the grass and specks of sand.

    d.) What else should be on the landmass?

    (Small group): Ask about three or four skillful artists who will take about (30 minutes) to complete their parts (on the floor). Allow them to wallow and color on the floor like they're children, because they still are. That is, provided that nothing is exposed because of shorter or risqué clothing.

3. Whole class Instruction: (At the same time), the other 15-20 seated students should begin cutting out two five-inch oak leaves each from portions of 5 construction paper sheets. They would use pencils to trace their leaves, and color pencils to lightly shade red, orange, or yellow. Then, they could write in two of their personal dead words. (15 minutes)

4. Whole class Instruction: Afterwards, the 15-20 seated students can use thesauruses or guess at least two replacement synonyms for their dead words. These are preferably three or four syllable words. Then, they can record them in a dry erase board list. (10 minutes)

5. Whole class Instruction: Have them trace two more five inch leaves from the scraps of the 5 pieces of construction paper. Also, use three more sheets of construction paper, and then cut them out for the next class period. (5 minutes)

6. Closure: Have each student read two new synonyms on the board and tell the class which Dead word they replace using the following sentence. (10 minutes)

    The better, more vivid synonym is _____ and it always replaces the dead word _____.

Leave these connected sheets on the floor so students can see their progress. (Please forewarn the students not step on the wall-worthy sketch.)

Day Two:

1. (Periods 3 & 4; or 2nd Block)—Last 45 minutes. The class can now focus on the roots and trunk of a mighty oak tree.

   (Although these trees are not as typical as palm trees, the idea necessitates that you have enough voluminous limbs. Then, you could effectively display many more vivid, descriptive terms at the top of the tree).

2. Assign three or four skilled artists at the beginning of the period. (Quickly explain their tasks of making the roots and developing the trunk in pencil only! This instruction should happen after attendance is taken, while other students are completing bell ringer). (Entire Task: 30-40 minutes).

3. Tape four construction sheets together vertically on the backs of the sheets.

4. Three or four artists should strategize the roots (four or five roots should intrude/overlap into the top-center of the forbidden island) (5 minutes)

5. Review the idea of *finding better synonyms* for the Dead Words, and its importance in earning higher writing scores. (5-7 minute discussion).

6. Introduction of interactive game: (Three minutes)

   Whenever there are dull adjectives in sight,
   Wherever simple adverbs come to light,
   Don't pretend there's nothing you can do,
   It's time to play "Winning Words Review"
   I'm your host/(ess) _____,

   We're about to use our imaginations, an
   egg-timer, and our teamwork to win
   fabulous prizes...

   The rules are:

- There will be two teams. (Left side vs. Right side of the room).
- Only members of one side may be recognized; blurt out when the answers come to mind.
- A contestant from each team will come up and pull a leaf from the container. Then their teammates will come up with as many 2 to 4 syllable words to replace them within the time limits
- Each side will have five rounds to win the game.
- Both teams will be given: 30 seconds for the first 2 rounds, 20 seconds for the third round, 10 seconds for the fourth & final rounds.

Now, it's time to play, 'Winning Words Review!!!'
(Game length: 15-20 minutes)

Materials:

- Egg-timer
- Team recorder (writes words on sheet of paper)
- Score keeper: (person gives points for every different word during each time period).
- Two sheets of construction paper
- Two pens/markers
- Leaves (with Dead Words on them)
- Container or hat: shuffle leaves inside of it.
- Five candy prizes: buy a bag of mini-snickers or kit-kat bars for the best player of each round. (Ask the winning side who contributed the most words and take a hand vote!)
- Grand prize: one movie ticket/card

Note: the winning team should choose the most valuable player (MVP) based upon how many responses the teammate provided. Then, the teacher must make a tremendous ado about the MVP's accomplishment. (Link the champion's ability to improve their writing vocabulary)

(Forewarn your neighboring teachers the day of this activity because it will be pretty loud. You can warn the players from the outset not to be too loud; but it probably won't work. Nonetheless, you should not feel guilty about this noisiness. This is especially since you are actually inducing your learners to be more creative).

While the game is going on:
(Differentiated instruction)

6. Two artists should trace the roots carefully so that the five horizontal sheets (across the bottom) and the four vertical sheets (going upwards from the center) can overlap effectively.

7. Two other sketchers can begin tracing the trunk from the bottom up. (Remember the bottom of the trunk should begin at about 10 inches to a foot across in width, and slowly become slimmer to about 7 inches). Eventually the height of the entire trunk should reach at least 5-6 feet above the baseboard.

8. Perhaps one of your artists could draw a 5-7 inch owl hole in the center of the oak; another owl standing on an outer branch would also bring out the realism of the piece.

After the game occurs:

9. Hands-on activity: Color 10 yellow, 10 orange, 10 green, and 10 reddish leaves. (Make sure that they lightly color in these leaves so that the words that they'll write in will be visible). **(10 minutes)**

10. Now, your students already know the dead words that were listed. They should **think up two more dead words** that they often 'abuse' in their essay writing which have not been mentioned. Then, they should record these on their 10 yellow, 10 orange, and 10 reddish leaves. **(10 minutes)**

11. Clean up and collect all of the newer leaves that contain the latest dead words on them. **(5 minutes)**

   • Per(s) 5 & 6 or Block 3: **(Last 45 minutes)** The task ahead consists of adding realistic looking branches of the treetop. They should be jagged, and proportional to the trunk and the rest of the tree. Also, including a sun and three or four clouds would make the word wall even more authentic.

12. Bellringer: Write down better synonyms list from board. **(5 minutes)**
   Choose 4 students to continue working on the treetop, sun, and clouds. They should begin immediately with these sketches:

   1. **Tape six or eight construction pages together in one large rectangular shape to sketch the treetop. It should be three to four construction papers across and stack a matching construction paper atop of each one.**
   2. **Place the attached paper onto the floor and begin sketching.**

13. Review the idea of *finding better synonyms* for the Dead Words, and its importance in earning higher writing scores. **(5 minute discussion)**.

14. Play "Winning Words Review" **(25 minutes)** Give this period the extended version since it is the end of the day. Instead of 5 rounds, 7 or even 9 rounds would be an exciting way to end the day. Moreover, your students won't forget the concept of more vivid synonyms either. (This time, use 2nd period's dead words to find newer synonyms. Have students write them on the green leaves as they win points.)

15. Hang it up **(Last 10 minutes)**: Have sketching students carefully place and tape up the treetop, sun, & clouds. Then, aesthetically place the last of the synonym replacement leaves onto the tree or falling towards the ground. Obviously, 'the keepers' stay on the tree, the banal words fall to the ground.

— The End —

Activity # 4: 'Dead Words I Would Change' Jam
(Learning Modality: Musical)

The most recent research corroborates that African Americans, Hispanic Americans, and Native Americans tend to learn well when participating in a musical modality. It also reflects that they work better in learning groups. I concur, but believe that nearly everyone loves to sing and dance and perform. This activity allows each individual student the opportunity to stand on their own efforts and build confidence while presenting.

Since our last activity was about a Forbidden Island. It seems only fitting that we use one of the most famous tunes involving an Island. You've probably heard the Gilligan's Island theme music before. This will be the tune around which we shall develop our lyrics.

You can download a clean copy, (one with no lyrics), of the Gilligan's Island theme on YouTube.com. Also, you must play the actual song/video for classwide inspiration by going to www.gilligansisle.com/theme.html.

DIRECTIONS:

1. Provide your students with a chorus about the Forbidden Island. (optional)
2. Instruct students to find better, more vivid synonyms for their three most commonly used dead words.
3. Fit the three and four syllable synonyms into the rhythm and notes of the song.
4. Every other line should rhyme. Rhyme Scheme: abab or abcb
5. Practice in front of a mirror at home at least four to five times at home
6. Perform the song in front of your peers.

See the sample song below. I use the thesaurus and also my memory just like the song suggested. It lead me to form the following Sample Chorus and Sample Verse. You'll note that the sample Verse has black text. These are the synonym replacements of the word 'kinda'. Note that the first four lines of the sample Verse are two syllable replacements; the last four lines of it are three & four syllable replacements.

Sample Chorus:	On a for-bid-den is-land,
	I'd throw dead words a-way
	replace them with some better terms,
(8 lines)	and sing them un-til day.
	Count-ing on my me-mo-ry;
	a the-saur-us I would search
	for useful, vivid adjectives,
	bury dead words in the dirt.
Sample Verse:	Instead of blurting 'kinda'
	'Sort of' would suffice
	'Partly, rather' work quite well
(8 lines)	'sometimes' is just fine.
	Correct spelling of kinda'
	k- i- n- d- o- f-,
	or edit it 'to some extent';
	'in a way' might help.

Sing this for your students to the Gilligan's Island theme and they should easily get the task.

Good luck on your exercises, and remember to limit each poetic line to a comparable amount of syllables. The most ideal amount is between 5 to 6 syllables because <u>lines of a poem are not sentences</u>, but intentional, descriptive phrases and/or fragments.

Create Your Own 'Dead Words' Jam!

Re-Cap of this Assignment's Expectations:

Part A: You'll create an 8 lined Chorus,
5-6 syllables each line, &
every other line's end word rhymes.
This poem must fit the Gilligan's Isle theme.

Part B: You'll create an 8 lined Verse
5-6 syllables each line, &
every other line's end word rhymes
This poem must fit Gilligan's Isle theme

This can be an awesome presentation opportunity! Students can make about 5-10 copies of their lyrics so pairs or trios of learners can sing their chorus together. Then, the learner could have an interactive performance. All students sing each learner's Chorus to Gilligan's Isle theme. Then the writer sings his/her Verse, and the entire class sings that Chorus again. This is an easy Presentation grade: one grade on fitting the criteria of the Song, another grade on class performance. Students will love it!

Another suggestion: Make a television show like 'Spectacular Sing-A-Long' where students compete for the most imaginative and well performed song! You can even put it on video if you are completing National Board certification, or wish to capture it for future classes.

WEEK #5
VARIATION OF PUNCTUATION

BELLRINGER #16-MONDAY

In formal essays, evaluators have come to expect **'freshness of expression'** from learners who earn upper scores. Part of this is determining a less repetitive means of punctuating sentences. In turn, a more dynamic sense of the writer's abilities would be displayed.

Variation of punctuation, one of the most obvious ways to bring diversity of expression, is often avoided by essayists. They defiantly stick with periods or 'comma sentences to death'. The result tends to be robotic, colder phrases that can bore an audience. Hopefully, this lesson will assist in changing that tendency.

DIRECTIONS:

1. Review the selected 9 punctuation marks, functions, & examples in the three column table below.
2. Next, draft a 'text message' to your best friend about the steps you've taken to prepare for your sister or brother's 15th birthday party.
3. The 'free write' should be no longer than 10 lines long, and should include all nine punctuation types from the table below. (15 minutes).

Punctuation Types	Functions	Examples
Period =.	closes out a complete thought; either informative statements or passive commands	Let's go. (pas. command) It is hot outside. (info. statement)
Question mark =?	concludes an inquiry that is a complete thought	Why not? (complete inquiry) Haven't you heard from Emma? (complete inquiry)
Exclamation point =!	shows joy, anger, excitement, yelling, shouting, or aggressive commands	Stop it! (aggressive command) I can't believe you won! (joy/excitement/yelling)

Comma =,	Separates elements in a sentence, Separates informal salutation, Separates two comp. thoughts	She likes tan, red, & blue. (elements) Dear Aunt Sharon, (salutation) We won, and we must fight on. (two complete thoughts)
Semi-colon =;	Connects two complete thoughts so closely related, they belong in one sentence.	Mary's dog is very hyperactive; it won't stop barking or sit still. (closely related, two complete thoughts)
Colon =:	Used after a word introducing a quote, example, explanation, or a formal salutation.	Mama always said: "haste makes waste." (quote) Dialogue: two people sharing thoughts (explanation) Dear CFO Jones: (formal salutation)
Dashes = --	Indicates an interruption you want to draw attention to.	Other colors--red and blue--are also popular car hues. (interruption w/ colors)
Quotation Mark = " "	Includes exact text from a source	According to Webster's, "nouns are a person, place, or thing." (exact quote)
Parentheses =	Used like commas to contain further thoughts or qualifying remarks about a topic/definition	John and Jane (who were actually half brother and sister) both have red hair. (qualifying remarks)

(2011, What are the Fourteen Punctuations in English Grammar? www.YourDictionary.com)

BELLRINGER # 17: YOU ARE THE EDITOR-IN-CHIEF!

DIRECTIONS:

1. Pretend that you are the Editor-in-chief of a major newspaper in your area.
2. Read the following news article carefully.
3. Insert *at least seven different punctuation marks* in the correct places to make the piece flow smoothly and clearly.

The Bufford Bulletin

Recently several middle and high school principals petitioned the county superintendent to extend the technology ban They sought to include the phrases disruptive electronic noises and shimmering LCD screens in school legislation. Meaning, hi-tech disturbances tweets blaring rings musical compositions were updates. Defiant students all around the campus of West Garvey High were absolutely outraged enough was enough Many student body members wanted to ask when would the administration stop stripping them of their rights According to Webster's Dictionary Freedom was the first amendment right for citizens to express themselves Protests walk-outs and letters to the principal could work something had to be done soon The best way for learners to deal with a crisis when civil rights are blatantly stolen is to go home and exhale.

Explanations of Each Punctuation

Sent. 1 = Comma behind transition 'Recently', **period** or exclamation to end complete thought. The fact that several principals contacted the Superintendent indicates a level of excitement. Or it can be taken as an informative statement.

Sent. 2 = **Colon** belongs behind 'phrases' since it is the word introducing a quote. Single or double **quotation marks** belong around the phrases "disruptive electronic noises and shimmering LCD screens". This is because they are the specific phrases from the principals who happen to be a source.

Sent. 3 = **Comma** behind transition 'meaning'. **Dashes** could be used to surround tweets, blaring rings, musical composition since it is an intentional disruption to bring attention to specific noises. Or, a writer could use the parenthesis around this same group of words since they provide qualifying remarks about the definition.

Sent. 4 = The complete thought of the sentence actually ends at 'outraged'. Yet the final phrase 'enough is enough' was so closely related that these thought belonged together. This is the reason for the **semi-colon** after 'outraged'. Of course, the students were frantically upset which proves excitement, so the sentence should end with an **exclamation mark**.

Sent. 5: The subtle clue is that the student body members wanted to 'inquire', a better adjective for ask. This means that the sentence should certainly end with a **question mark**.

Sent. 6: A transition 'According to Webster's Dictionary' should end with a comma; or colon since it the word introducing a quote.

Sent. 7: Commas help list different items/elements in a series. This is the reason for Protests, walk-outs, and
We connect 'something must be done' with a semi-colon since it relates so closely to the first part of it. Ends in an exclamation showing how upset students are to consider the previous list.

Sent. 8: The phrase 'when civil rights are blatantly stolen' is a further thought of this incident. It must have **parenthesis.**

The Bufford Bulletin (with correction marks)

Recently, several middle and high school principals petitioned the county superintendent to extend the technology ban(. or !) They sought to include the phrases: "disruptive electronic noises and shimmering LCD screens" in school legislation. Meaning, hi-tech disturbances--tweets, blaring rings, musical compositions--were updates. Defiant students all around the campus of West Garvey High were absolutely outraged; enough was enough! Many student body members wanted to inquire when the administration would stop stripping them of their rights? According to Webster's Dictionary: "Freedom was the first amendment right for citizens to express themselves." Protests, walk-outs, and letters to the principal could work; something had to be done soon! The best way for learners to deal with this crisis (when civil rights are blatantly stolen) is to go home and exhale for now.

BELLRINGER #18: VARIATION OF SENTENCE STRUCTURES (A)

DIRECTIONS: Review the following directions aloud with class during the first five minutes, then allow students to complete the exercises below in 6-8 minutes.

THE FOUR TYPES OF SENTENCE STRUCTURES:

The four types of sentence structures include simple, compound, complex, and compound complex.

Simple Sentences

A simple sentence contains one independent clause.

> For example:

1. Coach Madison supported Louis and the team.
2. Becky and Louis left town on Friday morning.

Compound Sentences

A compound sentence contains two or more independent clauses, jointed by a coordinating conjunction (and, but, or, so) or a semicolon.

> For example:

1. Mr. and Mrs. Banks supported Louis, but Mr. Jasper criticized his emotional outburst.
2. The small town was in an uproar; their team had been defeated.

Complex Sentences

A complex sentence contains one independent and one or more dependent (subordinate) clauses.

> For example:

1. Because the coach acted unfairly, Louis refused to play with the team.
2. The class performed the one act play which Marion had written.

Compound-Complex Sentences

A compound-complex sentence combines two or more independent clauses and at least one dependent (subordinate) clause.

> For example:

> Although our team feared the opposition, they played exceptionally well, and they almost won the game.

(2011, The Four Types of Sentences, www.Digication.com)

DIRECTIONS: From the aforementioned definitions and examples, identify the types of sentence below. Are they simple, compound, complex, or compound-complex sentences?

> **Helpful Hint:** [Try underlining the independent clauses once and double underline the dependent clause]

1. Mark stole my purse, and I went to my teacher, who redressed the problem.

2. She promised to improve the work environment; about time!

3. Vicky decided to redress the problems that she had created between her friends and she tried to make amends with them because she missed talking to them.

(2011, The Four Types of Sentences, www.Digication.com)

Answers & Explanations

1. <u>Mark stole my purse</u>, and <u>I went to my teacher</u>, who redressed the problem.

   'Mark stole my purse' is an independent clause

   'and' is a coordinating conjunction from FANBOYS

   'I went to my teacher' is an independent clause

   'who redressed the problem' is a dependent clause.

   By definition, a <u>Compound-Complex sentence</u> combines two or more independent clauses and at least one dependent (subordinate) clause. That is what this sentence structure happens to be.

2. She promised to improve the work environment; 'about time!

    'she promised to improve the work environment' is an independent clause.

    'about time' is a dependent clause.
    the independent clause and the dependent clause are separated by a semi-colon.

    By definition, a <u>Complex Sentence</u> contains one independent and one or more dependent (subordinate) clauses.

3. Vicky decided to redress the problems that she had created between her friends and she tried to make amends with them because she missed talking to them.

    'Vicky decided to redress the problems that she had created between her friends' is an independent clause.

    'she tried to make amends with them because she missed talking to them' is the other independent clause.

    The two independent clauses are not conjoined by any punctuation like a semi-colon, but they are jointed by a coordinating conjunction 'and'

    By definition, a <u>Compound Sentence</u> contains two or more independent clauses, jointed by a coordinating conjunction (and, but, or, so) or a semicolon.

BELLRINGER # 19: EXTRA PRACTICE - FOUR TYPES OF SENTENCE

DIRECTIONS: Identify the following sentences by underlining the independent clauses once and the dependent clauses twice. Are they compound, complex, simple, or compound complex?

1. When he made some inflammatory comments, he tried to redress the situation, but he made it worse.

2. I felt badly, but I redressed the nonsense by giving her a hug.

3. The customers were much happier when the owner redressed the problem with the food.

(2011, The Four Types of Sentences, www.Digication.com)

Answers with Explanations

1. When he made some inflammatory comments, he tried to redress the situation, but he made it worse.

    'When he made some inflammatory comments' is a dependent clause

    'he tried to redress the situation' is an independent clause,

    'he made it worse' is an independent clause.

    Both independent clauses are joined together by a coordinating conjunction.

    By definition, a <u>Compound-Complex sentence</u> combines two or more independent clauses and at least one dependent (subordinate) clause. That is what this sentence structure happens to be.

2. I felt badly, but I redressed the nonsense by giving her a hug.

    'I felt badly' is an independent clause.

    'I redressed the nonsense by giving her a hug' is an independent clause

    'and' is the coordinating clause joining the two independent clauses together

    By definition, <u>Compound Sentences</u> contains two or more independent clauses, jointed by a coordinating conjunction (and, but, or, so) or a semicolon.

3. The customers were much happier when the owner redressed the problem with the food.

    This is one long independent clause which is the equivalent to a Simple Sentence.

    By definition, a <u>Simple Sentence</u> contains one independent clause.

BELLRINGER # 20: VARIATION OF SENTENCE STRUCTURES (B)

Loose Sentence, Periodic sentences, & Periodic Interruptive Sentences

---

DIRECTIONS: Review the following definitions and examples with your students at the beginning of class. Then, allow them to create one Loose sentence, one Periodic Sentence, and one Periodic Sentence.

THE LOOSE SENTENCE: This sentence is a basic statement with a string of details added to it.

Basic statement: *The teacher considered him a good student.*
Loose sentence: *The teacher considered him a good student, steady if not inspired, willing if not eager, responsive to instruction and conscientious about his work.*

(Ask yourself 'how do I shrink this sentence form to 15 words or less?)

THE PERIODIC SENTENCE: In this sentence, additional details are placed before the basic statement. Delay, of course, is the secret weapon of the periodic sentence.

Basic statement: *John gave his mother flowers.*
Periodic sentence: *John, the tough one, the sullen kid who scoffed at any show of sentiment, gave his mother flowers.*

Basic statement: *The cat scratched Sally.*
Periodic sentence: *Suddenly, for no apparent reason, the lovable cat scratched Sally.*

(The second Periodic sentence fits the GREAT Burger requirement while the first does not).

THE PERIODIC (INTERRUPTIVE): In this sentence, additional details are added inside the basic statement:

Basic statement: *Love is blind.*
Periodic sentence: *Love, as everyone knows except those who have not been afflicted with it; is blind.*

(This periodic sentence does fit the GREAT requirement of 15 words or less per sentence. I like the interruptive form of periodic sentence).

(2011, Loose & Periodic Sentences,http://www.azed.us/students/languagearts/ la68lessons/2la68s/sentences.html)

Be careful while creating examples these advanced forms of sentence variations. (Each of these sentences should be fifteen words long or less; meeting GREAT Burger requirements).

DIRECTIONS: Draft an appropriate example of the Periodic Sentence, Loose Sentence, and the Periodic Interruptive Sentence from the Basic Statements provided below.

> **Helpful Hints:**
> 1. avoid too many dependent clauses (15 words or less)
> 2. use vivid adjectives or details to better describe the main statement.
> 3. make sure your clauses are directly related to the main statement's traits.

1. Shelly is going to Disney World. (Loose Sentence)

2. Rick was nervous about his Civics test. (Periodic Interruptive)

3. Why don't Western and Middle Eastern countries get along? (Periodic Sentence)

Answers with Explanations

1. Shelly is going to Disney World. (Loose Sentence)

   Example response: Shelly is going to Disney World, an exhilarating outing, next Tuesday, and she can't wait!

   (This Loose sentence has two additional details about Shelly's trip but still manages to be 15 words or less).

2. Rick was nervous about his Civics test. (Periodic Interruptive)

   Example response: Rick, the Algebra student who worked late last night, was nervous about his Civics test.

   (This Periodic Interruptive subtly tells you this student didn't get a chance to study. Now he's nervous. It also fits within the GREAT burger requirement of 15 words or less). This structure is the same as an appositive sentence in this example. It is a sentence which the definition is provided between subject and predicate.

3. Why don't Western and Middle East countries get along? (Periodic Sentence)

   Example response: Why, many people wonder, some others debate, don't Western and Middle Eastern countries get along?

   (This Periodic Sentence pushes the main statement to the end of the sentence, while offering two additional statements before it. It manages to do so with 15 words or less).

(2011, Loose & Periodic Sentences,http://www.azed.us/students/languagearts/la68lessons/2la68s/sentences.html)

Now you are armed with at least 6 different types of sentence, and 10 types of punctuation. This powerful arsenal of choices will allow writers to greatly vary their sentences. So, their writings can lose the routine, predictable aspect.

WEEK # 6
OTHER SENTENCE SKILLS

BELLRINGER #21: AVOIDING COMMA SPLICES (BACKWARD SENTENCES)

Many beginning writers are not careful enough when they try to vary their sentences. Sometimes, they put commas in awkward places in their sentences.

Comma Splices: (also known as backwards sentences), are an example of common comma misuse. It occurs when a writer transcribes the entire predicate, then places a comma, and afterwards writes down the complete subject.

Lots of times, these syntactical errors show that the writer is a(n) English as a Second or Other Language (ESOL) or Limited English Proficient (LEP) learner. This may very well be the proper position of the grammatical elements in their native language; especially the romance languages. So these comma splices must be vividly demonstrated and permanently corrected.

Teachers: I'd advise you to bring in the latest Star Wars compact disc. Then, play a five-minute scene of Master Yoda speaking to the rest of the Jedi. Then ask then what is wrong with his speech pattern. *(Teachable Moment)* Obviously, Master Yoda, the little green alien, would vocalize awkward expressions like:

a.) "strong with you, the force of the universe is" = predicate (comma) subject
b.) "in grave danger, Luke Skywalker may be" = predicate (comma) subject
c.) "of the Clone Wars, Perhaps this is the beginning" = predicate (comma) subject
d.) "take over the Senate, Chancellor Palpatine is attempting to" = predicate (comma) subject

---

DIRECTIONS: Present the previous **four Comma Splices** to your students and have them correct the order of the words. Since they are backwards sentences the answers should be relatively easy.

Correct Answers

a.) The force of the universe is strong with you.

b.) Luke Skywalker may be in grave danger!

c.) Perhaps, this is the beginning of the Clone Wars.

d.) Chancellor Palpatine is attempting to take over the Senate.

BELLRINGER #22: PARAGRAPH 'PATCH-UP' GAME

A 'great rule of thumb' for determining if there is a comma splice is the **30/70 rule**. I came up with it myself. In essence, having to place 30 percent or more of a sentence's 15 words before a comma reveals that it is a 'backwards sentence'. Therefore, we can infer that **transitional phrases** can only be five words or less. That phrase in front of the sentence that you place a comma behind should be no more than five words.

Anything more basically guarantees that you should invert the sentence. Take the phrase that is six words or more and replace it at the end of the sentence.

For instance:

(Backwards sentence)   During my Summer vacation last July 18th, we unexpectedly left early.

(Corrected sentence)   We unexpectedly left early during my Summer vacation last July 18th.

This actually has double transitions in the first clause. Trans 1: during my summer vacation, Trans 2: Last July 18th. *All I did was exchange the Predicate with the Subject, and remove the comma between them.*

DIRECTIONS: Read the paragraphs below and fix all comma splices in them as you rewrite each.

      For all of my closest family members, Summer break is usually a source of exhilaration. To me, a feeling of persistent nervousness gradually overtakes my inner being. Then, a myriad of thoughts cross my mind like 'what am I going to wear?' As I begin packing my designer luggage, my mental list typically unravels. One would imagine that I would pre-plan what will be taken; paper and pen help. Instead of last minute packing, my better choice would likely be taking a week! More time would allow me to split up my clothing and I would probably grab everything. Instead of resisting this reasonable checklist, during my next trip I will use these suggestions.

Answers

Summer break is usually a source of exhilaration for all my closest family members! To me, a feeling of persistent nervousness gradually overtakes my inner being. Then, a myriad of thoughts cross my mind like 'what am I going to wear?' My mental list typically unravels as I begin packing my designer luggage. One would imagine that I would pre-plan what will be taken; paper and pen help. Instead of last minute packing, my better choice would likely be taking a week! More time would allow me to split up my clothing and I would probably grab everything. During my next trip, I will use these suggestions instead of resisting this reasonable checklist.

(Use a timer, groups, and a reward to see which group fixes it fastest; they win the five-ten minute game!)

BELLRINGER #23: DANGLING MODIFIERS—ANOTHER REASON TO AVOID LARGER TRANSITIONAL PHRASES!

Dangling Modifier: When we begin a sentence with a modifying word, phrase, or clause, we must make sure the next thing that comes along can, in fact, be modified by that modifier. When a modifier improperly modifies something, it is called a "dangling modifier."

Confusion	Changing the oil every 3,000 miles, the car seemed to run better.
Repair Work	Changing the oil every 3,000 miles, Fred found he could get much better gas mileage.

The car did not change its own oil so 'it' is not responsible for itself running better! That is why confusion exists in the first example. Since a 'person' is responsible for changing the oil, then a person (Fred) must be the specific noun that is modified by modifier. **(See repair work).**

Then, this 'backwards sentence' can be remedied even further by switching the predicate with the Subject, and removing the comma.

GREAT Correction: **Fred found he could get much better gas mileage changing the oil every 3,000 miles.** (It is more straightforward and decreases the likelihood of dangling modifiers).

There is one neat way to remember if a sentence has the correct modifier throughout its structure. Simply ask yourselves one question: Is the same person or group that completed the action responsible for the results?

DIRECTIONS: Correct the following confusing sentences that may have 'dangling modifiers' by providing the GREAT Corrections. *(Hint: 'Who completes the action?' Inanimate objects don't complete actions.)*

1. Pipe-cleaning the valves weekly, the trumpet sounds better than ever!
2. Searching Uncle Jim's couch pillow cushions each visit, I supplement my allowance.
3. Sprinting one mile every morning, a body can burn calories more efficiently.

Answers

1. Jack's trumpet playing sounds better than ever from pipe-cleaning his valves weekly. ('Jack' could be any proper noun to replace the trumpet in this dangling modifier sentence).
2. I supplement my allowance while searching Uncle Jim's couch pillow cushions each visit. (Backwards sentence easily corrected by changing Subject & Predicate order; remove comma.)
3. Sheila can burn calories more efficiently by sprinting one mile every morning. ('Sheila' could be any proper noun to replace 'a body' in this dangling modifier sentence).

(2011, Modifier Placement, http://grammar.ccc.commnet.edu/grammar/modifiers.htm)

BELLRINGER # 24: MISPLACED MODIFIERS

Basic Principle: Modifiers are like teenagers: they fall in love with whatever they're next to. Make sure they're next to something they ought to modify!

Misplaced Modifier: Some modifiers, especially simple modifiers — only, just, nearly, barely — have a bad habit of slipping into the wrong place in a sentence. (In the sentence below, what does it mean to "barely kick" something?)

Confusion   He barely kicked that ball twenty yards.

Repair Work   He kicked that ball barely twenty yards.

EXPLANATION: The word 'kick' implies that a footballer uses a foot to violently knock a ball away. So what does 'barely (violently knocking a ball away) mean? Absolutely nothing!

Barely & **Violently** are absolute opposites which *cancel out* the meaning of the noun 'kick'. Thus, 'barely' cannot modify 'kick'!

Therefore, a better placement of 'barely' would be the actual distance since it describes the limitation of the action. He kicked the ball barely twenty yards. (It properly describes an action = definition of an adverb)

DIRECTIONS: Please determine if the following sentences have misplaced modifiers and then correct them.

1. Shanice only completed one-half of her Winter packet.
2. Jarod skillfully sang 'Auld Lang Syne' during the New Year's Program
3. Kevin barely scratched the surface of the tension between his girlfriend and I!
4. Actually, my grandmother just died a year ago.

Answers

1. 'Only' incorrectly modifies the verb 'completed'. Shanice completed only one-half of her Winter packet.
2. 'Skillfully does correctly modify 'sang'. Therefore, it is correct!
3. In this case, 'barely' correctly modifies the verb 'scratched'; this is true even though 'scratched the surface' is a figure of speech.
4. 'just' incorrectly modifies the verb 'died' as we learn later in the sentence. Actually, my grandmother died just a year ago. Just modifies 'the period of time' better than the verb 'died'.

(2011, Modifier Placement, http://grammar.ccc.commnet.edu/grammar/modifiers.htm)

BELLRINGER #25: SQUINTING MODIFIER

A third problem in modifier placement is described as a **"squinting modifier."** This is an unfortunate result of an adverb's ability to pop up almost anywhere in a sentence; structurally, the adverb may function fine, but its meaning can be obscure or ambiguous.

For instance, in the sentence below, do the students seek advice frequently or can they frequently improve their grades by seeking advice? You can't tell from that sentence because the adverb *often* is "squinting" (you can't tell which way it's looking). Let's try placing the adverb elsewhere.

Confusion

Students who seek their instructors' advice often can improve their grades.

Repair Work

Students who often seek their instructors' advice can improve their grades.

Repair Work

Students who seek their instructors' advice can often improve their grades.

Both of the **Repair Work examples** are correct because they separate the two verbs into two distinct clauses. Then, the adverb is specifically placed in front of either 'seek' or 'improve'. This step removes the ambiguity of the sentences so that the meanings are crystal clear!

DIRECTIONS: Analyze and correct the following sentences containing squinting modifiers.

1. What you say *often* you will accept as the truth.
2. Instructors who cancel classes *rarely* are reprimanded.
3. We agreed *at our first meeting* to dissolve the old procedures.

Answers

1. What you <u>often</u> say you will accept as the truth. (or) What you say is what you will <u>often</u> accept as the truth.
2. Instructors who <u>rarely</u> cancel classes are reprimanded. (or) Instructors who cancel classes are <u>rarely</u> reprimanded.
3. We agreed <u>at our first meeting</u> to dissolve the old procedures. (or) We agreed to dissolve the old procedures <u>at our first meeting</u>.

These answers are correct since the underlined adverbs actually do modify the verbs after them.

G.R.E.A.T. Burger Essay Workshop: A Helpful Advice for Students in Writing Essays!

70

WEEK #7
THE LONG FORGOTTEN SKILL OF EXPANSIONS

BELLRINGER #26

Elementary teachers tried their darndest to ensure that their 2nd, 4th and even 5th graders' sentences would improve. They sought for our syntactical patterns to mature—'I love cats.' versus 'I really like calico cats!' What they were doing was methodically maturing our sense of Voice. They expected us to tweak babyish language patterns by including simpler adjectives, adverbs, and transitions. This was a central tactic to demonstrate Writing growth in 3rd and 4th graders, especially during their standardized tests.

Elementary instructors' advice was and still is very cogent. Sixth, eighth, tenth, or twelfth grade writers cannot afford to take this skill lightly. The days of conversational or chatty style in essays must end, and formal drafting must be reinstituted.

Today's essayists must reclaim their imaginative ideas and resist robotic drafting. In its place, they should incorporate the unexpected and a freshness of expression. Complex transitions, adjectives, and adverbs are the 'crucial stitches in the tapestry of compelling expression'. They are the essential seasoning of the GREAT Burger and tools writers must use more regularly.

DIRECTIONS: Read the slightly immature sentences below. Then, carefully add one complex transition, -ly adverb, and adjective in the correct position. This should properly enhance it.

1. I heard the grandfather clock strike five!
2. Marsha could win the fifty yard dash.
3. Jonathan Swift was the author of 'A Modest Proposal'.
4. Teachers challenge their students.

> *Remember: Transitions are 5 words or less at the beginning of a sentence followed by a comma. Complex adjectives describe nouns very specifically, and complex adverbs describe action or times quite well.*

Answers

1. Suddenly, I heard the antique grandfather clock loudly strike five!
   (Complex Trans.)   (Comp. Adj.)   (Comp. Adv.)

2. Likewise, Marsha could possibly win the tougher fifty yard dash.
   (Complex Trans.)   (Comp. Adv.)   (Comp. Adj.)

3. Actually, Jonathon Swift is the only author of the renowned essay "A Modest Proposal".
   (Complex Trans.)   (Comp. Adv.)   (Comp. Adj.)

4. Overall, teachers should regularly challenge their unmotivated students.
   (Complex Trans)   (Comp. Adv.)   (Complex Adj.)

BELLRINGER #27: RELATIONSHIP BETWEEN SUPPORTING DETAILS AND EXPANSIONS

TS = **Topic Sentences:** provide the main idea of paragraph.

SD = **Supporting Details:** back up writer's stance on subject.

EXP = **Expansions:** offer the most specific causes or proof.

What writers need to understand more clearly is that Supporting Details (SDs) and Expansions (EXPs) are closely related. Supporting detail 'backs up the writer's stance on a subject'. Expansions are needed to further justify why the writer feels the way he or she does.

An **expansion** should: Clearly provide **a very specific cause** for one's stance. Or, it should openly express **proof why the writer's stance is the correct one.**

Examine the following examples:

Prompt: Describe an ugly dog and the features that make it an eyesore.

elephant- (SD)   **Big, droopy** ears cover **both** sides of its face.

(EXP)   Therefore, they look like **floppy** wings placed **closely** to its body.

Notice: This EXP 'openly expresses proof' that the dog is ugly. (It agrees that writer's stance is the correct one).

Prompt:	Describe the gracefulness of a flamingo and how its features exhibit this virtue.
flamingo- (SD)	**Thin, flexible** <u>legs</u> support this natural beauty.
(EXP)	**So**, they **confidently** saunter across **rugged** riverbeds without fear of tipping over.

Notice: This EXP is a 'very specific cause for the flamingo's gracefulness'-(main cause why the stance is true).

DIRECTIONS: Read the next two supporting details and provide EXPs. One should be 'a main cause', the other should 'openly express proof'

Prompt:	I could easily pass any test offered at school.
(SD 1):	Basically, my strategy is to prepare my mind without mentally exhausting it.
(EXP 1):	_____.

(Hint: Choose a difficult subject's test and specifically offer a main strategy that helped you pass it)

Prompt:	I can attend the college of my choice if I improve my grades right now.
(SD 2):	Instead of relying on loans, I could wisely prepare myself to contend for scholarships.
(EXP 2):	_____.

(Hint: Openly express proof about one of your relatives who received a scholarship after working hard).

Answers

(EXP 1): One 90 percent score came after using index cards to review my theorems for Geometry.

(EXP 2): My cousin Steve, who studied two hours daily, actually went to Junior college for free.

BELLRINGER # 28: EXPANSIONS IN A PARAGRAPH

Understand that Topic Sentences, Supporting Details, and Expansions are also related in another quite important way. They generally set the mental scene of a paragraph from general to specific. A <u>Topic Sentence</u> is an overall statement, a <u>Supporting Detail</u> further breaks down the topic, and <u>Expansions</u> vividly show specific causes or provide specific proof (of the topic).

Read the simplistic paragraph below:

"The Ugly Dog"

The dog next door is really ugly. It has a big knot on his head that is red. It also has sores on its ears that he scratches. This is why this canine looks ridiculous.

TS = **Topic Sentences:** provide the main idea of paragraph.

SD = **Supporting Details:** back up writer's stance on subject.

EXP = **Expansions:** offer the most specific causes or proof.

GREAT Burger Three Expansion Introduction:

"The Ugly Dog"

TS The dog next door appears as ugly as can be! (SD 1) You see, a large, scabby lump stands at the top of his head. EXP 1 It is obvious that someone viciously struck him hard with a rock or stick. (SD 2) Also, infected sores ooze just behind both ears. EXP 2 They are constantly torn open as the irritated beast scratches them. (SD 3) Oddly, the left rear leg hangs five inches shorter than the others. EXP 3 He lost the bottom part of it to surgery after an accident. CS Certainly, the sight of this pitiful canine makes the toughest bystander want to ignore his existence.

a.) Do you see how the expansions (in blue) offer very specific causes or proof?

Ask yourself if each EXP is the cause or proof of the previous Supporting detail. Then write it on the provided line.

EXP 1: _____   EXP 2: _____   EXP 3: _____

Answers:

EXP 1: Very specific cause   EXP 2: Very specific proof   EXP 3: Very specific cause

BELLRINGER #29: INCORPORATING EXPANSIONS IN PARAGRAPHS.

There is no single or most correct method of building a paragraph although there are many recommended forms. I prefer to stick with the common accordion paragraph or chain paragraph methods. They show direct relationships between each sentence in a paragraph which visually makes sense to most readers.

Consider the following Three Expansion paragraph:

"The Ugly Dog"

TS The dog next door appears as ugly as can be! SD 1 You see, a large, scabby lump stands at the top of his head. EXP 1 It is obvious that someone viciously struck him hard with a rock or stick. SD 2 Also, infected sores ooze just behind both ears. EXP 2 They are constantly torn open as the irritated beast scratches them. SD 3 Oddly, the left rear leg hangs five inches shorter than the others. EXP 3 He lost the bottom part of it to surgery after an accident. CS Certainly, the sight of this pitiful canine makes the toughest bystander want to ignore his existence.

(TS + SD 1 + EXP 1 + SD 2 + EXP 2 + SD 3 + EXP 3 + CS) = is mainly based upon the accordion paragraph model in which I have added Expansions denoted EXP 1, EXP 2, and EXP 3. From this model, a writer can quickly discern several traits. This paragraph, like every other has around eight sentences; time out for 'microwave' paragraphs. Consider the following paragraph again.

Moreover, one observes that this paragraph begins with a Topic Sentence (TS). Then, it is followed by a Supporting Detail (SD 1) which reveals a bit more. Afterwards, the writer specifically reveals an (EXP 1)-which either is a 'detailed piece of proof' or 'a specific justification' why the previous SD 1 was true'. Secondly, you will notice that there is another Supporting Detail (SD 2) and then (EXP 2) expands (SD 2)'s premise even more. Similarly, SD 3 brings up a third issue and EXP 3 elucidates SD 3's position with a personal example as well.

This eight sentence format contains specific, imagery filled information that send the reader right into the middle of the action! Expanded sentences or expansions almost always have at least one: adverb, adjective, and transition!! They provide the richness of wording (or Diction) that proves you have really thought about an essay prompt.

DIRECTIONS: Have each student create their own Three Expansion Introduction paragraph based on this prompt. (Hint: no more three reasons! Now, you must use three very specific expansions after your SDs).

> "My favorite role model is _____ because he/she has several commendable traits".

(Then, the teacher should have two students to read their Intros aloud after 10 minutes; if students are still unsure, instructors could demonstrate the process on the smartboard. Then, learners could try again for homework).

(OPTIONAL) BELLRINGER #30: REVIEWING THREE EXPANSIONS PARAGRAPH (PART TWO)

Well today is the last day of the week and we wouldn't want to begin a new chapter of exercises. I recommend revisiting the Three Expansion Introduction prompt from yesterday.

Gauge the trend:

a.) If half or more students did not get it: take this time to try it again! Have one or two volunteers read their paragraphs. Then, the teacher could write out the paragraph, and explain how each sentence is related. Trial and error is your friend in paragraph writing.

b.) If most of your students got it then you could go onto the following Prompt #2. The idea is that if they have the grasp of the information they can apply it again.

Prompt # 2:

Read: Pretend that you are Mr. Green--a Biology teacher--that has recognized how creative a student of yours is. As a result, you gladly entered him/her into 'Tomorrow's Innovators' contest with a grand prize of $25,000 scholarship.

Think: Silently choose a peer whom you believe is quite creative and diligent when it comes to her/his classes.

Explain: Draft a three Expansion Introduction recommendation (as Mr. Green) that provides this peer's scholarly qualities. Then, include three Expansions (or specific examples when this learner has used these qualities to excel in different academic subjects/exams).

Prompt 2-Answer

TS I have personally known Yesenia for two school-years; an impressive Earth Science and Biology student! **SD 1** During this period, she has truly proven herself to be conscientious in her study habits. **EXP 1** Yesi turned in two outstanding Science projects that easily won second and third place. **SD 2** Also, the pupil's record of hardly missing homework assignments in Math, Science, or English is admirable. **EXP 2** I carefully gathered this insight from discussions with several teachers this year. **SD 3** Most noteworthy, this unconventional thinker absolutely possesses a knack for 'thinking outside of the box'! **EXP 3** This 'uniter' brokered a workable solution for a Middle East tension debate that she'll mention. **CS** Without reservation, Ms. Lopez deserves to be considered as a candidate for Tomorrow's Innovator's Contest.

Wouldn't you want your own recommendation to read like this one! How much of a chance would you believe you'd have to be a finalist? This Paragraph meets the GREAT Burger standard! It includes three adjectives, three adverbs, and three transitions. All sentences are 15-16 words or less, and it includes specific proof (EXPs) of Yesenia's academic traits.

Did you notice that I adhered to the 'Repetition Free' portion of GREAT? I did not repeat Yesenia's name over and over again. Instead, I obeyed the pronoun-antecedent rule which told me to use pronouns, other names, and descriptions of Yesenia instead. As a result, I managed to complete the entire Introduction paragraph without 'parroting her name'. (see underlined words above) Repetition is the enemy of a GREAT Burger Essay!!!

WEEK # 8
LET'S MIX IT UP!

Hopefully, your perseverant writers have readily absorbed these skills like a sponge up to this point.

Congratulations, for battling on this far. When you question them about the material they should be responding quicker and more accurately. Now would be the perfect time for a break so that your essayists can reassess what they have learned. They also need a breather for the final set of bell ringers that begin next week.

During this week, we will review sentence variation, punctuation marks, Supporting detail-Expansion relationships, Comma Splices (or backwards sentences), and modifiers.

Of course, these tasks will be offered in much more informal and interesting activities. See for yourselves just how fascinating developing language skills can be.

DECIPHERING GREAT WRITING ADVICE

DIRECTIONS: Pretend that this is a secret message your teacher scribbled on a piece of paper just before you took your standardized Writing test. He/she was probably a bit worried about it, and wanted to give you an 'extra boost'.

Now use the code key below to 'carefully unscramble' that cogent writing advice (from Weeks 5-7). Write in all capital letters during this fifteen minute exercise!

Code Key

Q = 1	A = 2	Z = 21	S = 12	X = 22	W = 3	D = 13	C = 23	E = 4
R = 5	F = 14	V = 24	T = 7	G = 15	Y = 9	H = 17	B = 25	U = 10
J = 18	N = 26	I = 6	K = 19	M = 16	O = 8	L = 20	P = 11	

__ __ __ __   __ __ __ __ __ __ __   __ __ __ __

12 17 8 3   5 4 2 13 4 5 12   9 8 10 5

__ __ __ __ __ __ __ __ __ !

4 22 11 4 5 7 6 12 4

___ ___ ___   ___ ___ ___   ___ ___ ___ ___ ___ ___
10 12 4   7   17 4   11 5   8   11 4   5

___ ___ ___ ___ ___ ___ ___ ___ ___   ___ ___ - ___ ___
11 20 2 23 4 16 4 26 7   8 14   20 9

___ ___ ___ ___ ___ ___ ___ . ___ ___ ___ ___ ___ ___ ___ ___ ___ ,
2 13 24 4 5 25 12   23 2 5 4 14 10 20 20 9

___ ___ ___ ___ ___ ___   ___ ___ ___ ___ ___ ___ ___ ___ ___
23 5 4 2 7 4   4 22 11 2 26 12 6 8 26 12

___ ___ ___ ___   ___ ___ ___ ___ ___ ___ ___ ___   ___ ___ ___
9 8 10 5   2 10 13 6 4 26 23 4   23 2 26

___ ___ ___ ___ ___ ___ ___ ___ . ___ ___ ___ ___ ___
4 26 24 6 12 6 8 26   2 24 8 6 13

___ ___ ___ ___ ___ ___ ___ ___   ___ ___ ___ ___   ___ ___ ___ ___ ___ ___
12 8 10 26 13 6 26 15   20 6 19 4   16 2 12 7 4 5

___ ___ ___ ___ ; ___ ___ ___ ___   ___ ___ ___ ___ ___
9 8 13 2   7 10 5 26   7 17 4 12 4

___ ___ ___ ___ ___ ___ ___ ___   ___ ___ ___ ___ ___ ___ ___ ___ ___
25 2 23 19 3 2 5 13   12 4 26 7 4 26 23 4 12

___ ___ ___ ___ ___ ___   ___ ___ ___   ___ ___ ___ ___ ___ ___
2 5 8 10 26 13   2 26 13   5 4 16 8 24 4

___ ___ ___ ___ ___ ___ .
23 8 16 16 2 12

GRAMMAR & PUNCTUATION—(WEEKS 5-7)

DIRECTIONS: Use the bellringers, and exercises from (Weeks 5-7) to complete this crossword puzzle.

ACROSS	DOWN
2. contains thoughts/qualifying words	1. He barely ran ten yards.
6. separate words, greetings,& thoughts in paragraphs	2. Include she, her; instead of repeating Sara
8. uses exact text from sources	3. Conjunction type of FANBOYS
9. joins two related complete thoughts	4. Adverb doesn't modify closer verb
11. adverb confuse sent meaning	5. Most specific causes or proof
13. shows yelling, joy, or commands	7. Basic statement with added details
14. 1 indep., 1 dep.clause & semi-colon	10. Has 2 indep. & 1 dep. clauses
15. the 'enemy' of a GREAT essay	12. Give emphasis to interruptions
16. has subject,(definition), pred.	
17. phrases only five words or less	
18. form: predicate (comma) subject	
19. GREAT sent. word-limit, ends run-ons	
20. addt'l words before basic statement	

Created by Puzzlemaker at DiscoveryEducation.com,4/27/2011

Grammar & Punctuation--(Review Weeks 5-7)

Answers

Note: two word answers do not have spaces between them in the puzzle above.

_____   _____

ACROSS

2. contains thoughts/qualifying words	parentheses
6. separate words, greetings,& thoughts in paragraphs	commas
8. uses exact text from sources	quotation marks
9. joins two related complete thoughts	semi-colon
11. adverb confuse sent meaning	squinting modifier
13. shows yelling, joy, or commands	exclamation
14. 1 indep., 1 dep.clause & semi-colon	complex
15. the 'enemy' of a GREAT essay	repetition
16. has subject,(definition), pred.	interruptive
17. phrases only five words or less	transitions
18. form: predicate (comma) subject	comma splice
19. GREAT sent. word-limit, ends run-ons	fifteen
20. addt'l words before basic statement	periodic

DOWN

1. He barely ran ten yards.   misplaced modifier
2. Include she, her; instead of repeating Sara   pronoun-antecedent
3. Conjunction type of FANBOYS   coordinating
4. Adverb doesn't modify closer verb   dangling
5. Most specific causes or proof   expansions
7. Basic statement with added details   loose sentence
10. Has 2 indep. & 1 dep. clauses   compound-complex
12. Give emphasis to interruptions   dashes

Created by Puzzlemaker at DiscoveryEducation.com

G.R.E.A.T. Burger Essay Workshop: A Helpful Advice for Students in Writing Essays!

82

REFLECTIVE WRITING: (DAYS 3-5)

As stressed in other places, reflective writing is an essential aspect of learning growth. We use it when recalling events from novels and short stories, relating ourselves to characters, and interacting with fresh experiences. Teachers allow students 10 minutes for the paragraphs each day. Then, spend 5 minutes to share two or three of them.

Over the next three days, the writing students should deeply reflect upon at least three grammar or writing elements they have learned. (Perhaps, the review has merely refreshed their memories on the proper way to perform a particular skill).

DAY 3: Provide a newer/reviewed skill that you found important for strengthening your writing. Draft a paragraph about it, using an actual example, the definition, how it differed from what you previously thought, and how you will employ it better in the future. (Be sure to use your 3 adverbs, 3 adjectives, and 3 transitions so the reader can digest these six to eight sentences smoothly).

DAY 4: Identify another grammar rule that you found helpful (i.e. 30/70 rule, 5 words or less transition rule, fifteen words per sentence) and state it clearly for your audience. 1. Compare how you use to handle sentences with large transitions with this method. 2. Share how conforming to this method would improve the overall flow or essence of your paragraphs. (Be sure to include your 3 adverbs, 3 adjectives, and 3 transitions so the reader can understand clearly).

DAY 5: In the past, most learners have been stuck in a rut. Meaning, they only incorporate two or three types of sentences in their essays. Name at least two new types of sentence you've learned about and why you had not used them before. Then, instruct your audience on how to use these with clear examples. There should be at least two 'for instance' transitions with clear EXPs in this one. (Be sure to use your 3 adverbs, 3 adjectives, and 3 transitions so the reader can fully appreciate these seven sentences).

WEEK #9
MONDAY AND TUESDAY

BELLRINGER # 31-32 HISTORICAL REVIEW INTRODUCTION PARAGRAPHS

Try turning back time just before your current situation!

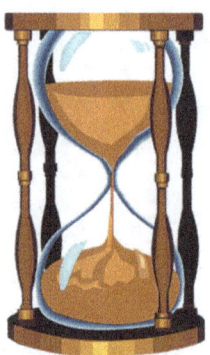

During Week #7, the Three Expansions paragraph was illustrated in a sentence by sentence format for ease of use. Over the next two weeks, I will personally share four more ideal introductions that I was taught. They were instilled in my writing repertoire from high school years, throughout my collegiate experience, and even as an English teacher. (These have been around for many years before me but they are still advantageous over the three reasons introductions).

I have found the following four introductions to be particularly engrossing and eye-catching. What is more, 'top buns' of an essay sufficiently hook readers' attention spans. Essentially, the 'well-enthused grader' must continue reading the body paragraphs. They certainly must determine what 'all the hoopla' was about in the introductions. That is how a writer knows that he or she has drafted a successful <u>attention grabbing</u> intro.

Have you ever heard the adage, "those who do not remember past mistakes are doomed to repeat them?" In some ways, a <u>historical review introduction</u> allows a reader to replay the particular events that unfolded before reaching the stance. It sequentially answers the question "what led up to your present stance on this issue?"

DIRECTIONS: *Consider the following prompt and respond to it using a historical review introduction*

Prompt: Recently, a few student skirmishes and injuries at two high school football games caused Principal Evans to enact a ban. Last Friday, he has 'outlawed' both I-phones and I-pads at school athletic functions. Respond to his decision providing specific evidence to back up your stance.

Historical Review Intro:

TS At 7:00 PM, one of the greatest division rivalries was brought to a new level at a home game! SD 1 Ninety-nine percent of spectators were corporately cheering, booing, waving flags, or otherwise engaged. EXP 1 Unfortunately, two petty freshmen came to the all-important event with wrong motives—impressing their friends. SD 2 One supposedly cool 'geek' named Trevor was displaying several 'apps' to his buddy Jonathan. EXP 2 Then, sophomore Jeffrey—attempting to reach his seat only fifteen feet away—squeezed past Trevor. SD 3 His motion accidentally knocked the Google cellphone twenty feet into the mud beneath our bleachers. EXP 3 Suddenly, pushing and shoving gave way to blows, both youngsters showing how terribly they fought. SD 4 (Optional) The principal rightfully punished the two with indoor suspensions, and then over-reacted about others' rights. CS Therefore, I am deeply opposed to this technological ban because of two irresponsible students' actions!

Note: This paragraph provides a sequential account of the details that led up to the writer's stance.

This structure has nine sentences, but yours can have as few as seven or eight sentences.

This paragraph is very specific including names, actions, 3 adverbs, 3 transitions, and 3 adjectives.

This attention grabbing structure makes the reader want to read on.

Now I would like for you to try it over the next two days using two different persuasive prompts provided below.

DAY 1:

Prompt 1: Because of budgetary cutbacks, many middle and high school boards have considered phasing out Physical Education and Home Economics altogether. Consider how this will impact the lives of teenagers you know. Then, draft a historical review introduction providing the events that led up to you stance. (No three reasons intros).

TS: _____, _____.
SD 1: _____. EXP 1: _____,
_____. SD 2: _____.
EXP 2: _____, _____.
SD 3: _____. EXP 3: _____,
_____. CS: _____.

DAY 2:

Prompt 2: A minority of health conscious parents were very vocal in a PTA meeting last week. They were suggesting that the health food machines were a great start. Also, students should not be allowed to eat so called 'take-out' foods like pizza or submarine sandwiches during lunch. Provide a historical review introduction illustrating the events that led up to your stance. (No three reasons Intros)

TS: _____!

SD 1: _____, _____.

EXP 1: _____. SD 2: _____,

_____. EXP 2: _____.

SD3: _____, _____.

EXP 3: _____. CS: _____,

_____.

Be sure to include dialogues or conversations in your allusions to make them even more believable. Remember, they don't have to be true, they must be convincing.

Historical Review Intros

(Sample Answers)

DAY 1:

Prompt 1: Because of budgetary cutbacks, many middle and high school boards have considered phasing out Physical Education and Home Economics altogether. Consider how this will impact the lives of teenagers you know. Then, draft a historical review introduction providing the events that led up to you stance. (No three reasons intros).

TS Sweaty students were suddenly called back inside of their locker rooms one Thursday afternoon. SD 1 Puzzled athlete Miguel Gomez inquired, "why are we dressing in, there is still half an hour to go?" EXP 1 The totally frustrated PE coach blurted "there will be no more racquetball, basketball, or football!" SD 2 Instantly, the teenager responded "what do mean by that?" EXP 2 He refused to give me the details while slowly dragging his feet into his office. EXP 3 The question was still nagging me. SD 3 During this final period, a cowardly hand-out informed us that PE had been suspended. EXP 3 Stripping our rights seemed not only unfair but un-American as well. CS Therefore, I am definitely opposed to this hasty removal of physical fitness from students' academic experience.

> Note: none of this ever happened to me; I made the entire story up including the names. Doesn't this introduction make you want to read the body paragraphs? Notice how the Closing sentence provides the stance clearly.

DAY 2:

Prompt 2: A minority of health conscious parents were very vocal in a PTA meeting last week. They were suggesting that the health food machines were a great start. Also, students should not be allowed to eat so called 'take-out' foods like pizza or submarine sandwiches during lunch. Provide a historical review introduction illustrating the events that led up to your stance.

TS I cannot actually believe that a minority of 'health nuts' prevailed over common sense! SD 1 Initially, parents started out with a positive platform: stock junk food machines with healthier choices. EXP 1 Then, sixty percent of my peers and I fully supported their anti-obesity efforts. SD 2 Next, the total elimination of choice on any type of food they considered unhealthy was overboard! EXP 2 Many of my counterparts turned against these 'health bullies'; maintaining a balanced diet was preferred. SD 3 Now, these controversial protesters are even complaining about entrees most Americans love. EXP 3 Specifically, removal of pizza and submarine sandwiches might push many students to boycott cafeteria food altogether. CS Thus, the administration should overrule this latest crusade to restrict students' dietary choices.

> Note: ad hominem (or attacking the man/group) is not normally permitted. (Health nuts and health bullies were not so abrasive terms though). Examine how this story explains each policy push of some zealous parents up to the stance of the writer.

WEEK # 9
WEDNESDAY AND THURSDAY

BELLRINGER #33-34: ANECDOTE INTRODUCTION PARAGRAPH

Isn't this picture absolutely adorable and totally ridiculous at the same time?

Have you ever made a comical mistake, partook of an awkward accident, or actually stumbled or fell?

In so many ways, we are forced not to take life and its happenings so seriously. Every now and then, we reconsider our personal foibles and chuckle at them. This smile, chuckle, or hilarious outburst is the emotion that we will purposefully attempt to evoke. You have heard these funny intros at family gatherings, your workplace, over dinner, amongst friends. No doubt you would recognize them instantly.

ANECDOTE INTRODUCTIONS are more appropriately considered *ice-breakers*. They unexpectedly disarm the tension or (expectation of three reasons) of a table reader during standardized tests. They deliver an amusing or entertaining opening to essays on top of offering something better than the alternative!

DIRECTIONS: *Consider the following prompt and respond to it using an anecdote introduction*

Prompt: Recently, a few student skirmishes and injuries at two high school football games caused Principal Evans to enact a ban. Last Friday, he has 'outlawed' both I-phones and I-pads at school athletic functions. Respond to his decision providing specific evidence to back up your stance.

    TS The wackiest event happened during our divisional rivalry playoff game last Friday! **SD 1** An arrogant freshman was showing off his I-pad II to a classmate named Jonathan. **EXP 1** While focusing on the game, as everyone else was, he had not noticed the staggering sophomore. **SD 2** Jeffrey clumsily squeezed through these buddies accidentally bumping it into the mud below the bleachers. **EXP 2** Five surrounding observers burst into obnoxious laughter as the teenager looked down in horror. **SD 3** One sassy spectator commented, "I'll bet he'll watch the game now!" **EXP 3** He did not know how he would actually show his face in class on Monday. **CS** Thus, the comical episode was about as bizarre as Principal Evans' decision to ban our gadgets.

> Note: An Anecdote introduction is just like writing a funny historical review with a clear Clincher Sentence **(CS)** at the end. Yet, their purposes are dramatically different.

  a.) Notice how the **TS** always provide the set up: The (funniest, wackiest) event occurred on my way to (where)!

  b.) **SD 1**: Where were you and who were you with?

  c.) **EXP 1**: Un-careful action that will cause the accident happens.

  d.) **SD 2**: Comical accident, incident, foible, etc.

  e.) **EXP 2**: Reaction of the onlookers who witness accident (laughter, falling down, etc)

  f.) **SD 3**: Verbal jab/comment made by a sassy, irreverent onlooker.

  g.) **EXP 3**: How the accident victim felt afterwards.

  h.) **CS**: Explains your stance in spite of this comical experience.

Again, none of this never happened; we just skillfully made it up to go along with the prompt. It does not have to be true; it must be believable, and a bit funny or quirky.

Anecdote Introduction paragraph steps:

a.) Notice how the **TS** provides the set up: The (funniest, wackiest) event occurred on my way to (where)!

b.) **SD 1:** Where were you and who were you with?

c.) **EXP 1:** Un-careful action that will cause the accident happens.

d.) **SD 2:** Comical accident, incident, foible, etc.

e.) **EXP 2:** Reaction of the onlookers who witness accident (laughter, falling down, etc)

f.) **SD 3:** Verbal jab/comment made by a sassy, irreverent onlooker.

g.) **EXP 3:** How the accident victim felt afterwards.

h.) **CS:** Explains your stance in spite of this comical experience. *(sometimes anecdote structure varies).*

DAY 3:

Prompt 1: Because of budgetary cutbacks, many middle and high school boards have considered phasing out Physical Education and Home Economics altogether. Consider how this will impact the lives of teenagers you know. Then, draft an anecdote introduction providing the events that led up to you stance. (No three reasons intros).

TS Finally, my persistent mother convinced me that home economics was even a course for football jocks! **SD 1** I cautiously enrolled thinking that it couldn't hurt to learn a few recipes. **EXP 1** By October 2010, I'd readjusted my mindset and totally accepted the idea of becoming a culinary master. **SD 2** Here was my shot to create the perfect souffle' and impress my teacher. **EXP 2** Then, my chance to carry out this dream was ripped from my grasps rather suddenly. **SD 3** Sadly, November 5th was the traumatic date when Mrs. Kennedy's spirits and my tasty dish were both deflated! **EXP 3** She frankly added that the school board took her job to save money. **CS** Obviously, my blood was boiling over this waste of time and the dismissal of a veteran teacher! **(Note: SD 3 bittersweet, yet partly comical).**

DAY 4:

Prompt 2: A minority of health conscious parents were very vocal in a PTA meeting last week. They were suggesting that the health food machines were a great start. Also, students should not be allowed to eat so called 'take-out' foods like pizza or submarine sandwiches during lunch. Provide an anecdote introduction illustrating the events that led up to your stance. (No three reasons Intros)

TS I experienced the weirdest dream the night before returning from Spring Break! **SD 1** Initially, my eyes swept around the cafeteria during lunch, and spotted some awkward occurrences. **EXP 1** It was quite easy to notice that everyone's trays had the same exact foods on them. **SD 2** This lack of selection transformed our lunchroom into a seventy-percent filled prison. **EXP 2** Students actually began avoiding lunch altogether rather than accepting their bland gruel. **SD 3** Another disturbing trend was the noticeable segregation from learners whose parents railed against food choice. **EXP 3** These kids were mainly viewed as losers whose parents had no lives of their own to ruin. **CS** Overall, I truly believe this will be students' eventual reactions to such an ill-considered decision**.**

> Note: paragraph shows the 'oddest' dream using phrases seventy percent filled prison, bland gruel, lives of their own to ruin.

WEEK #9
FRIDAY

BELLRINGER # 35 PERSONAL TESTIMONY INTRODUCTION (20 MINUTES)

Lots of students may recall testimonies or testimonials from their religious services. Some writers in your classroom will recognize this as one of the most popular advertising techniques on television! Everywhere you look, you see either paid actors or unpaid spokespersons of products. They always claim that their product is superior and that it will work lightning fast. Let's have fun with this one since it's the last day of the week.

Activity I:

    a.) (Set your timer for 5 minutes)

    b.) Instruct learners to draw two columns on a piece of paper: one for Product name and the other for spokesperson claims.

    c.) Fill it in with the requested information

    d.) Have the winner and the runner-up to read their list of products, spokesperson claims.

For example:

Nutrisystem = product,   I lost weight and kept it off = spokesperson claim

Shark Mop = product,   cleans many surfaces quickly = spokesperson claim

Activity II: Personal Testimony Introductions are unique in that they begin with an original stance in its first sentence. Then, the second sentence admits that something life-changing happened. After that, the writer exclaims that their opinion is now opposite of what it was in the third sentence. Sentences 4-6 (What was the last straw?) Give the sequential details that solidified this change of stance. Then, the Clincher sentence reaffirms the new stance.

a.) Have your students make a small three column notes chart in their notes.

b.) Head each column: Original stance, Life-changing occurrence, Newer stance

c.) Instruct students to listen to the song for an original stance, life-changing occurrence, and newer stance.

d.) Play YouTube video on smart-board, 70's classic "I will survive" by Gloria Gaynor. Google the song at http://www.youtube.com/watch?v=ZBR2G-il3-I

e.) Only play the first 1 minute and 25 seconds (1:25) of the video and song. This segment of the video clearly displays the three transitions effectively.

Answers should be similar

Original Stance	Life-changing Occurrence	Newer Stance
Gloria was scared to live without a man.	Gloria spends several nights recalling his cheating/abuse.	Gloria no longer needs an abusive man to define her.

Now let your students try piecing each sentence of the Personal Testimony together from the previous three column notes chart into the template of a paragraph below.

Prompt: Mrs. Gloria Gaynor refused to accept her cheating husband's behavior, and would seek happiness elsewhere. Inform us about the process that led her to this decision. (Use Personal Testimony Intro.)

First sentence: provides original stance in its first sentence.

Second sentence: admits that something life-changing happened.

Third sentence: writer exclaims that their opinion is now opposite of what it was.

Sentences 4-7 (What was the last straw?) Give the sequential details that solidified this change of stance.

Clincher sentence reaffirms the new stance.

Solution should be similar

TS Gloria used to be absolutely terrified about living without any man at all! SD 1 Then, a truly painful but life-changing recollection of Jeff's infidelity and torture woke her up. EXP 1 From then on, she vowed never to depend upon an unfaithful spouse to fulfill her life. SD 2 It became crystal clear that the cheater didn't even respect his wife. EXP 2 Unbelievably, he had the nerve to brazenly invite his mistress to their home, suspecting nothing. SD 3 However, Mrs. Gaynor returned home to collect her money and found them together. EXP 3 This was an affair that she would surely never recover from, and refused to try. CS Instead of remaining bitter, Gloria would first recuperate and find a genuine gentleman to love.

Let's examine it closely:

a.) **TS**: gives original stance—*Gloria used to be afraid of living without a man.*

b.) **SD 1**: mentions that something life-changing happened—*recalled Jeff's cheating, torture.*

c.) **EXP 1**: provides readers with her newer stance—*she no longer needed an abusive man!*

d.) **SD 2**: What was the last straw? (detail # 1)—*Jeff showed his intense disrespect for her.*

e.) **EXP 2**: What was the last straw? (detail # 2)—*he invited his mistress to (their) home.*

f.) **SD 3**: What was the last straw? (detail # 3)—*Gloria unknowingly catches them kissing.*

g.) **EXP 3**: What was the last straw? (detail # 4)—*she refuses to forgive him or work it out.*

h.) **CS:** Clincher sentence affirms newer stance—*Gloria would heal and look for great guy.*

Did you see how the sentences aligned with the previous template?

It wasn't very difficult; it should have felt like natural story-telling. Also, you should notice how the <u>first 3 sentences were simply switching your opinion</u>. Then, <u>the next 3-4 sentences simply justify why you switched to your new stance</u> in a sequential story. The Clincher verifies your newer stance.

Allow a few students to recite their paragraphs aloud. You could actively edit them so that everyone will get what each sentence should contain. Please review this paragraph so that every learner gets it.

WEEK #10
MONDAY

(BELLRINGER #36--OTHER FACTORS INTRODUCTIONS)

Other Factors Introduction: Obviously, we learn about our world mainly through electronic gizmos these days. Newspaper articles, internet magazines, evening news, specific channels, and even internet correspondences deliver new data on a daily basis. So we must embrace Kindles, I-pads, I-pods, MP 3 players, Blue ray disc players, and other innovative devices.

Therefore, it is a reasonable extension to use these 'information outlets' to sound more official in introductions. This is mainly accomplished since they are presumed to be reputable sources. Most people would not argue with a news channel's findings. *(Yet, the writer knows that they made up the source's findings only to prove their stance).*

Here are the steps of Other Factors Introductions:

a.) **First sentence**: drafter logically retells where he or she gathered the information

b.) **Second sentence**: how the news was specifically presented and his or her initial reaction

c.) **Third sentence**: Further deliberation about the outcome of the story.

d.) **Sentences Four-Six**: Specifically, what you did in response?
Or, how this decision will personally impact your life and/or your peer's lives?

e.) **Clincher sentence**: Affirm your stance on this particular issue.

Example 1:

Other Factors Introduction: (News item)

TS On Cable Network News (CNN), they recently broadcast a special on drastic state budget cuts! **SD 1** I became even more concerned when the newscaster mentioned overhauling education. **EXP 1** Absurdly, one school board commissioner callously suggested removal of Physical education and Home economics. **SD 2** I couldn't believe what I'd seen and immediately sat down to write my school board members. **EXP 2** My fingers frantically jotted down six reasons that cutting these two classes would backfire. **SD 3** When mom entered our home, I swiftly showed her my spirited response; she approved! **EXP 3** I felt such a sense of accomplishment in rapidly responding to this potential injustice. CS: Therefore, I am absolutely opposed stripping our schooldays of these classes; vital to social interaction.

Note: Couldn't you see just how sequential this story or (introduction) was? Sentences 1-3 revealed the station, controversial issue, and the unsettling statement of a school board member. Sentences 4-7: provide your immediate reaction and the steps you carried out to protest the statement. Sentence 8: reaffirms your stance for your readers clearly.

Now it's your turn.

DIRECTIONS: Use the prompt below and construct an Other Factors Introductions (News item) based on the template.

Prompt: Recently, a few student skirmishes/injuries at two high school football games caused Principal Evans to enact a ban. Last Friday, he has 'outlawed' both I-phones and I-pads at school athletic functions. Respond to his decision providing specific evidence to back up your stance. (Hint: Use the school's loudspeaker or a school board notice sent home to parents as the Other Factor).

Here are the steps of Other Factors Introductions:

a.) First sentence: drafter logically retells where he or she gathered the information

b.) Second sentence: how the news was specifically presented and his or her initial reaction

c.) Third sentence: Further deliberation about the outcome of the story.

d.) Sentences Four-Six: Specifically, what you did in response?
Or, how this decision will personally impact your life and/or your peer's lives?

e.) Clincher sentence: Affirm your stance on this particular issue.

TS:_____. SD 1:_____,
_____. EXP 1:_____.
SD 2:_____, _____.
EXP 2: _____.
SD 3:_____, _____.
EXP 3:_____. CS:_____,
_____.

Sample Answer

TS My mother stood there in shock while reading the hand-out I received during last period! **SD 1** Apparently, our over-protective administration was going to coddle us high-schoolers out of even more enjoyment. **EXP 1** Specifically, the North Carolina agency had done away with PE and Home Ec. over night! **SD 2** Something had to be done about this travesty immediately so mom scheduled an appointment downtown. **EXP 2** That Friday morning, the furious lady stepped into the Superintendent's office to personally scold him. **SD 3** He nervously showed her the disastrous figures and how broke the state was. **EXP 3** Yet, she wasn't convinced that this was the only feasible alternative. **CS** Then, mama regrouped still certain that our stance was correct; pupils needed those two classes!

> Note: *Examine the many ways we were able to say 'mom' with constantly repeating the same words. (See each underlined word). That was how we adhered to the Repetition Free rule. Also, we limited the number of 'I's—a frequently repeated word—by using my and me as substitutes.*

BELLRINGER # 37: TUESDAY (ANOTHER TYPE OF OTHER FACTORS INTRODUCTION):

With the advent of small screen or portable television I sought to expand coverage of Other Factors, Now it includes mobile TV phones, I-phones, android phones, e-notebooks, and even Satellite Television. All you need to do here is just mention the latest device you were using just once in this paragraph.

This Other Factors Introduction works the same way as the previous one:

Here is the pattern:

a.) First sentence: drafter logically retells where he or she gathered the information

b.) Second sentence: how the news was specifically presented and his or her initial reaction c.) Third sentence: Further deliberation about the outcome of the story **(& mention the source device).**

d.) Sentences Four-Six: Specifically, what you did in response?
Or, how this decision personally impacted your life and/or your peer's lives?

e.) Clincher sentence: Affirm your stance on this particular issue.

DIRECTIONS: Using the prompt below, create an Other Factors Introduction answer the following prompt.

Prompt: Everyone has a vacation they will never forget. Recall the most enjoyable trip you've had in a long time. Then, persuade an audience that this would be your greatest trip ever.

TS:_____, _____.

SD 1:_____.

EXP 1:_____, _____.

SD 2:_____.

EXP 2:_____, _____.

SD 3: _____. EXP 3: _____,

_____. CS: _____.

Sample Answer

Other Factors Introduction: (Mobile TV)

TS On the Travel Channel, the most unforgettable commercial about Orlando, Florida caught my attention! **SD 1** Emerald waters were reflecting the golden sun, and this reminded me to savor life's pleasures. **EXP 1** Then, I watched as a multi-colored Calypso band played tropical music; truly eye-catching! **SD 2** Vivid pictures on my mobile television screen actually reminded me of Caribbean paradise. **EXP 2** Of course, this was luxury without the added expense. **SD 3** So, I frugally saved my allowance every week for five months to visit this summer. **EXP 3** It was assuredly a hard-fought battle but I did it! CS: Afterwards, I toured Sea World, met new friends, and tried exotic foods down there.

BELLRINGER # 38: WEDNESDAY

'Double-Proof' Body Paragraphs

Teachers often observe the wimpiest three or four sentence structures that students turn in as paragraphs. By sixth grade, no paragraph structure should have less than six sentences. Moreover, these sentences should be expansions; containing adjectives, transitions, & adverbs.

By eighth grade, writers should accept 7-9 expansions per paragraph as the norm in any essay. The main reason for this GREAT concept is that the fuller the mental picture created, the greater the clarity of your point will be. Thus, the higher the grade will become. That is, presuming a writer is not repeating the same point over and over. Or, he/she is not rewording the same thought in that paragraph; breaking Repetition Free rule.

Therefore, utilization of GREAT Burger does away with repetitions. It does so by providing more than one specific instance for a writer to expand. In its place, writers include two (3-4 sentence) stories that prove their essay's stance in each paragraph. As a result, you can satisfy readers' craving for sufficient details to support your thesis.

DIRECTIONS: Analyze the following portion of a Quick Essay Planner that leaves three choices for Body Paragraph 1:

Subject: My favorite role model is...

TS 1: President Obama showed perseverance

EXP 1: endured racism during 2008 Pres. Race **(X)**

EXP 2: man dignified, 'birthers' claim he's not American, two years.

EXP 3: compromises with party of No (2010)

Now, you must eliminate one of the **EXPs**. Since **EXP 1** & **EXP 2** are similar, cross out **EXP 1** (see **X**).

Construct Body Paragraph 1: record the TS 1, expand EXP 2 (for at least three sentences) Then, expand EXP 3 (for at least three sentences) = at least seven total sentences. Notice: EXP 2 = 3-4 sentence mini-story, EXP 3 = 3-4 sentence mini-story.

TS 1 Initially, President Obama remarkably displayed perseverance in many instances. EXP 2 One amazing instance occurred when a radical group actually claimed he was foreign-born. They abrasively kept demanding that Barack show his birth certificate; this leader repeatedly discounted them. Tastelessy, the foremost 'birther', named Donald Trump, boisterously berated the statesman until he produced documentation. EXP 3 Another example of Obama's determination unexpectedly happened during 2010. I'm certain that the commander-in-chief was occasionally sickened by the constant 'No' votes of the majority party. Resultantly, many stalemates made it appear that he was taking care of the 'people's business'. He undeservedly paid a big price for this perception during the 2010 mid-term election.

Time to practice 'Double-Proof' Body Paragraphs: (25 minutes)

Prompt: In the past four years, gasoline prices have jumped to over $4.00. This has made it exceedingly difficult for many consumers to afford work and vacation travel. Choose an alternative fuel—electric, natural gas, hydrogen, wind, solar, or ethanol—to which our country should transition. Fully explain

DIRECTIONS: Complete the following portion of a Quick Essay Planner that leaves three choices for Body Paragraph 1. Then, eliminate one EXP with an X. Afterwards, construct a Body Paragraph using this structure as your guide.

> **Subject:** My preferred fuel form…

TS 1:

EXP 1:

EXP 2:

EXP 3:
    (X)

<u>It's as easy as a-b-c!</u>

a.) Now, fill in the diagram by first choosing your preferred form of fuel **(Subject)**.

b.) Afterwards, a general statement claiming that your fuel is advantageous belongs in **TS 1**

c.) **EXP 1**, **EXP 2**, **EXP 3** are specific examples of this fuel's benefits mentioned in the **TS 1**

d.) Eliminate the weakest of **EXP 1**, **EXP 2**, or **EXP 3**; these are the two expansions in para. 1

Then, construct this first body paragraph by including the **TS 1** and expanding the two remaining **EXPS** into two 3-4 sentence mini-stories. *(Refer to the above example for clarification).*

Answers should be similar

> **Subject:** My preferred fuel form...

> **TS 1:** Electric cars, advantageous to nation

> **EXP 1:** less cost to fill up

> **EXP 2:** convenient fill-up at home

> **EXP 3:** more stable, cost control **(X)**

<u>It was easy as a-b-c!</u>

a.) I preferred electric cars in this example but yours could be any of the other alternatives.

b.) Afterwards, a general statement claiming that your fuel is advantageous belongs in **TS 1**.

c.) **EXP 1** & **EXP 2** are specific examples of this fuel's benefits mentioned in the **TS 1**.

d.) We eliminated **EXP 3** because it was disputable; prices might rise in the future. So, we included the two remaining expansions in our body paragraph #1

Body paragraph # 1: TS 1 gives subject of paragraph, EXP 1 is a 3-4 sentence mini-story, and EXP 2 is a 3-4 sentence mini-story. This leaves us a very complete mental snapshot of **at least 7 sentences in BP 1**.

    TS 1 Absolutely, electric cars would immediately improve the United States economy! **EXP 1** The average consumer could probably save as much as $150 to $230 dollars per month. Simply put, it costs much less to produce voltage from nuclear reactors than OPEC. Oil Producing Energy Countries should certainly beware that we would no longer be at their mercies. **EXP 2** Furthermore, the public could practically eliminate time-consuming waits in lengthy fuel lines! A driver would simply plug their automobiles into inexpensive wall terminals at home. Then, the entire ordeal of searching for the lowest gasoline prices would finally be done. So, Americans could prudently funnel this extra money towards bills or their children's college funds.

> *Note: no repetitions of subject, 15 words or less each sentence, 3 adjs, 3 advs, & 3 trans; & 2 convincing EXPs).*

BELLRINGER # 39 THURSDAY

Extra Practice of 'Double Proof' Body Paragraphs

We will continue the previous prompt about alternative fuels as a secondary practice. Hopefully, your readers are grasping the hand-in-hand relationship between each **TS**, first **EXP**, and remaining **EXP** (after the weakest is eliminated).

Let's continue with the second body paragraph template. Remember to avoid writing sentences in each box; write in caveman instead. Be certain that every **EXP** actually does fit beneath its Topic Sentence.

Subject: Preferred fuel, electric cars

TS 2:

EXP 1:

EXP 2:

EXP 3:

As easy as a-b-c!

a.) Now figure out a 'second justification' why America should switch to your chosen fuel. **(TS 2)**

b.) **EXP 1, EXP 2, EXP 3** must be very specific examples of why your second justification is correct!

c.) Eliminate the weakest **EXP**: the one that is disputable or not convincing enough; (place an X beneath).

d.) Include the **TS 2**, first **EXP** and **its 3**-4 sentence mini-story, and second **EXP 3**-4 sentence mini-story.

DIRECTIONS: Afterwards, write your second body paragraph using the above template as your guide. Meaning, lengthen the TS 2, expand the first EXP to a 3-4 sentence mini-story; and then expand the remaining EXP to a 3-4 sentence mini-story.

(Body Paragraph 2 Answers should be similar)

Subject: Preferred fuel, electric cars

TS 2: electric cars, conserve environ.

EXP 1: Stops 'Big Gas' monopoly on econ. **(X)**

EXP 2: Lower airborne illnesses, allergies

EXP 3: Melting polar ice caps.

Note: we intentionally disqualified EXP 1 since it was an economic example; those belong under TS 1. Therefore, we will use TS 2, expanded EXP 2, and expanded EXP 3 to forge our 7 or more sentence body paragraph #2.

TS 2: Moreover, my preferred alternative to messy gasoline is electricity because it wisely conserves our environment. EXP 2: Have you seen an increasing number of U.S. citizens enduring allergy symptoms every year? Then, they spend tens of billions of dollars on medications; those have little to do with their conditions. In smoggier towns, vehicle pollution wreaks just as much havoc on people's respiration systems. This is evidenced by watery eyes, irritated noses, and headaches like typical allergies. EXP 3: With equal consideration, scientists have empirically studied the North Pole's shrinking ice caps. They have tragically approximated only 25 years before these masses have disappeared. However, immediate American switch to kilowatts would likely prolong the existence of these wintry lands. Soon, other nations would help buy us time to re-solidify this precious polar bear habitat.

Notice: No subject repeats, varying sentence structures, Expertly supported with data and stats. 15 word or less per sentence, at least three adverbs, three adjectives, and three transitions. Gramatically correct sentences = GREAT Burger paragraph indeed! Does your body paragraph 2 adhere as closely as this one does to the format? If so, you've done a fantastic job.

BELLRINGER # 40 FRIDAY

'Third Time's the Charm!

DIRECTIONS: Go ahead and complete the third column of the GREAT Quick Essay Planner. Be certain to exclude or eliminate potential EXPs that belong in the prior two categories.

Subject:

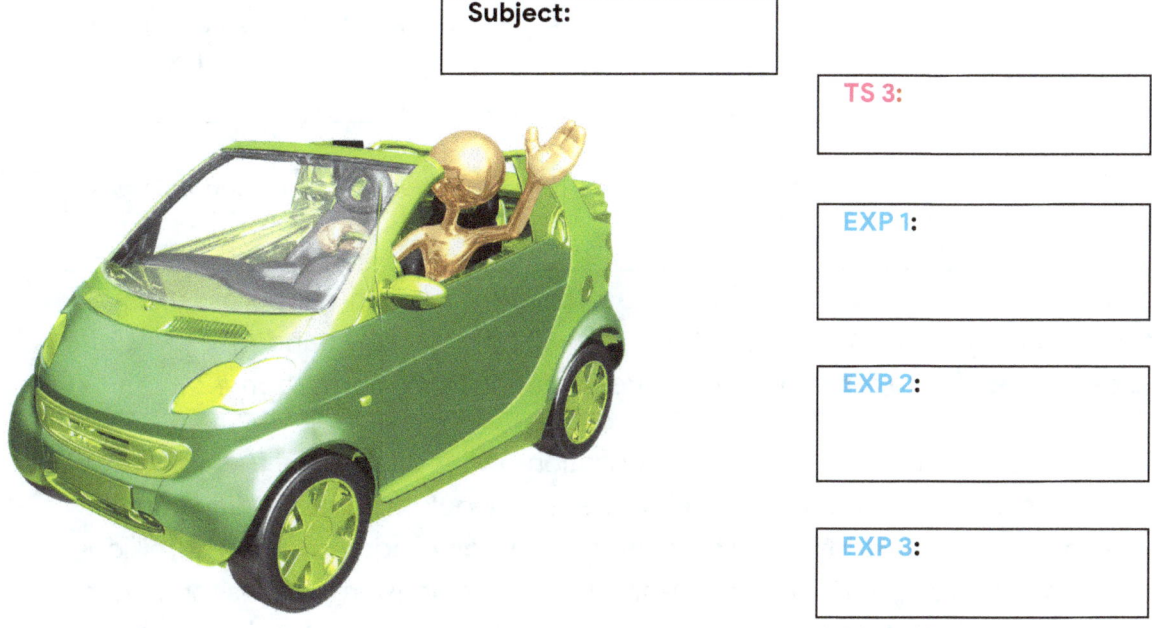

TS 3:

EXP 1:

EXP 2:

EXP 3:

As easy as a-b-c!

a.) Now figure out a 'third justification' why America should switch to your chosen fuel. **(TS 2)**

b.) **EXP 1, EXP 2, EXP 3** must be very specific examples of why your third justification is correct!

c.) Eliminate the weakest **EXP**: it is disputable, misplaced, or not convincing enough; (place an X beside it).

d.) Include the **TS 3**, first **EXP** and its 3-4 sentence mini-story, and second **EXP 3-4** sentence mini-story.

DIRECTIONS: Afterwards, write your third body paragraph using the above template as your guide. Meaning, lengthen the **TS 3**, expand the first **EXP 1** to a 3-4 sentence mini-story; and then expand the remaining **EXP 2** to a 3-4 sentence mini-story.

(Body Paragraph 3 should have similar answers)

> **Subject:** Preferred fuel, electric cars.

> **TS 2:** a new sense of freedom

> **EXP 1:** families will take more road-trips

> **EXP 2:** less gas and oil trucks crowding the road

> **EXP 3:** no choosing gas or grocery (**X**)

> Note: we intentionally disqualified **EXP 3** since it was an economic example; those belong under **TS 1**. Therefore, we will use **TS 3**, expanded **EXP 1**, and expanded **EXP 2** to forge our 7 or more sentence body paragraph #2.

    TS 3 Likewise, the countrywide utilization of this alternative fuel will foster a fresh sense of freedom **EXP 1** More parents would frequently plan spur-of-the-moment road-trips as mini-vacations. Imagine adding virtually millions more Yellowstone Park, Mount Rushmore, or Lincoln Memorial visitors! Then, these extra sightseers could actually cherish America's wonders in a personal, profound ways. Mere monuments may even increase levels of civic responsibility and national pride in our citizenry. **EXP 2** Another advantage of 'kilowatt vehicles' is directly due to the decreased consumption of fossil fuels. Drivers should gradually feel relieved that they won't have to swerve away from as many gas and oil trucks. Dramatically, that stressful emotion of apprehension could be reduced, and 'road-hogs' could relax. As a result, both passengers and operators would better appreciate their journeys as well as the destinations.

Notice: No subject repeats, varying sentence structures, Expertly supported with data and stats. 15 word or less per sentence, at least three adverbs, three adjectives, and three transitions. Gramatically correct sentences = GREAT Burger paragraph indeed! If your Body Paragraph 3 was just as detailed and vivid as this then your efforts shall be rewarded!

So, the end product of our three 'Double Proof' Body Paragraphs should be quite striking. Each structure should exhibit both a completeness of explanation and deeper compliance to grammar rules. Let's analyze how well we addressed the prompt; electric cars as the chosen alternative fuel:

TS 1 Absolutely, electric cars would immediately improve the United States economy! **EXP 1** The average consumer could probably save as much as $150 to $230 dollars per month. Simply put, it costs much less to produce voltage from nuclear reactors than OPEC. Oil Producing Energy Countries should certainly beware that we would no longer be at their mercies. **EXP 2** Furthermore, the public could practically eliminate time-consuming waits in lengthy fuel lines! A driver would simply plug their automobiles into inexpensive wall terminals at home. Then, the entire ordeal of searching for the lowest gasoline prices would finally be done. So, Americans could prudently funnel this extra money towards bills or their children's college funds.

TS 2 Moreover, my preferred alternative to messy gasoline is electricity because it wisely conserves our environment. **EXP 2** Have you seen an increasing number of U.S. citizens enduring allergy symptoms every year? Then, they spend tens of billions of dollars on medications; those have little to do with their conditions. In smoggier towns, vehicle pollution wreaks just as much havoc on people's respiration systems. This is evidenced by watery eyes, irritated noses, and headaches like typical allergies. **EXP 3** With equal consideration, scientists have empirically studied the North Pole's shrinking ice caps. They have tragically approximated only 25 years before these masses have disappeared. However, an immediate American switch to kilowatts would likely prolong existence of these wintry lands. Soon, other nations would help buy us time to re-solidify this precious polar bear habitat.

TS 3 Likewise, the countrywide utilization of this alternative fuel will foster a fresh sense of freedom **EXP 1** More parents would frequently plan spur-of-the-moment road-trips as mini-vacations. Imagine adding virtually millions more Yellowstone Park, Mount Rushmore, or Lincoln Memorial visitors! Then, these extra sightseers could actively cherish America's wonders in personal, profound ways. Mere monuments may even increase levels of civic responsibility and national pride in our citizenry. **EXP 2** Another advantage of 'kilowatt vehicles' is directly due to the decreased consumption of fossil fuels. Drivers should gradually feel relieved that they won't have to swerve away from as many gas and oil trucks. Dramatically, that stressful emotion of apprehension could be reduced, and 'road-hogs' could relax. As a result, both passengers and operators would better appreciate their journeys as well as the destinations.

(You'll agree that this composition is overflowing with proof. Each paragraph is much more powerful and persuasive than single EXP body paragraphs.)

WEEK #11
'EDIBLE EXTRAS'

BELLRINGER # 41: AFFABLE ADAGES

I surnamed this week's activities 'Edible Extras' primarily because there are some additional ingredients we need to include. These superior ingredients are the 'piece de resistance', or the 'icing on top of the cake'; (two figures of speech). Essentially, they will elevate a writer's score from very good or GREAT, to magnificent or even most memorable.

At trendier burger shops all over America they allow patrons to build their own burgers from scratch. Such establishments generously offer many more exotic toppings than lettuce, onions, pickles, and tomatoes; those associated with homemade burgers. (Bacon strips, blue cheese, pepperoncini, chili, and even fried onion rings are just a few so-called extras).

In verisimilitude, let's investigate the sheer impact that figurative language, dialogue, and interjections play. We'll identify how each special ingredient 'spices up' your GREAT burger even more. Meaning, we can make a GREAT burger TERRIFIC! Notwithstanding it takes about two or three GREAT essays to get there though.

Benjamin Franklin, illustrated below, was more than a Founding Father of the new American nation in the 1770s. This avid inventor of the lightning rod and author of Poor Richard's Almanack was acutely aware of figurative language. He intimately fathomed how they could encourage positive behaviors, and discourage negative ones. In fact, Mr. Franklin came up with many maxims to do just that, and they are still familiar today.

This 'Master of Maxims' is credited with hundreds of short, easily remembered expressions of a basic principle, general truth, or rule of conduct called maxims. Just think of a maxim as a 'nugget of wisdom'. (Definition of Maxim, www.google.com, May 16, 2011)

DIRECTIONS: In groups of two or three, read the famous maxims by Benjamin Franklin below. Afterwards, translate the valuable behavioral lesson each recommends to 21st Century language. Encourage thesauruses and dictionaries in this (15 minute activity).

1. To err is human, to repent divine; to persist devilish. _____.

2. A good example is the best sermon. _____.

3. Love your neighbor, yet don't pull down your hedge. _____.

4. A bird in the hand is better than three in the bush. _____.

5. After crosses and losses, men grow humbler and wiser. _____.

6. 'Tis easy to see, hard to foresee. _____.

7. When the well's dry, we know the worth of water. _____.

8. Little strokes fell great oaks. _____.

9. Keep your eyes wide open before marriage, and half-shut afterwards. _____.

10. Fish and visitors stink after three days. _____.

These are maxims that many writers would not readily incorporate into their essays. Each maxim's language is a bit dated, and from a more proper form of English during the late 1700s. Therefore, we should look at modern equivalents.

Let's see how well you did with these maxims made from the 18th century. I'll bet you were surprised at how many of these sayings or maxims are still prevalently spoken today. You answers should be approximately the same or very similar to mine on the next page.

DIRECTIONS: In groups of two or three, read the famous maxims by Benjamin Franklin below. Afterwards, translate the valuable behavioral lesson each recommends to 21st Century language. Encourage thesauruses and dictionaries in this (15 minute activity).

(Answers should be nearly the same)

1. To err is human, to repent divine; to persist devilish.

   Making mistakes is normal, apologizing is an admirable quality; intentionally continuing wrongdoing is evil!

2. A good example is the best sermon.

   Behaving properly is better than ordering others to do so.

3. Love your neighbor, yet don't pull down your hedge.

   Be kind to others but keep them out of your business.

   (Or) Be nice to friends but protect your own interests.

4. A bird in the hand is better than three in the bush.

   What you possess is better than what you hope to possess.

5. After crosses and losses, men grow humbler and wiser.

   The more lives lost, the more likely feuding or warring parties will compromise.

6. 'Tis easy to see, hard to foresee.

   Anyone can tease about mistakes after they happen, but it is harder to steer clear of mistakes during a trial/ temptation.

   (Or) Hindsight is 20/20.

7. When the well's dry, we know the worth of water.

   You don't really appreciate what you have until it's gone!

8. Little strokes fell great oaks.

   It may take many attempts before one gets it right.

   (Or) If at first you don't succeed, try again.

9. Keep your eyes wide open before marriage, and half-shut afterwards.

   Carefully watch for warning signs before marrying, but don't watch for each mistake afterwards.

10. Fish and visitors stink after three days.

    Guests, relatives, and/or certain situation grow tiresome after three days. Family wears out their welcome soon.

Here are several maxims that many writers would not readily remember to incorporate into their essays. (It is more likely that 5th graders and 10th-12th graders would include them). Each maxim's language is a bit dated, and from a more proper form of English during the 1700s. Therefore, we should look at modern equivalents.

Later, we will try to blend one or two of these 'older maxims' into our tapestry of words called paragraphs. Keep your eyes peeled for instances when you could replace a sentence with one of them..

BELLRINGER # 42: MODERN MAXIMS

Now let's bring these sayings into this century. What are some 'figures of speech about behavior' you've heard from relatives. Perhaps, your mother or grandfather quoted them while trying to teach you a valuable life lesson. When we say Modern Maxims we mean 'proverbs' for behavior within the last 100 years or so.

For example: *Nothing from nothing leaves nothing.*
Modern equivalent: You only get out of life what you put into it.

Maybe your great-aunt, or great grandmother taught you a memorable lesson about the value of a dollar?

For example: *A penny saved is a penny earned. A fool and his money are soon parted!* (Ben Franklin's)
Modern equivalent: Money doesn't grow on trees!

Or, your older father tried to instill values about a positive work ethic in you.

For example: *Early to bed, early to rise, makes a fellow happy, wealthy, and wise.* (Benjamin Franklin)
Modern translation: The early bird gets the worm.

DIRECTIONS: A clue will be provided about a particular maxim. Each person in the group should take turns working backwards to figure out an appropriate maxim. Items in parentheses are another clue or keyword in the modern maxim (10-15 min).

MAXIM TOPIC	ACTUAL MODERN MAXIM
1. A person always says what's right, but doesn't do it.	_____.
2. Writing a letter can produce better results than violence.	_____.
3. (mouth), If you can't handle it, don't begin the task.	_____.
4. (group of fowl), People with the same mindset hang out.	_____.

5. Experienced folks dislike doing things _____.
   differently.

6. (two foods), Resolve disputes calmly _____.
   not bitterly.

7. (farm), You'll be treated the same way _____.
   you treat others.

8. (policy), Telling lies is not the optimal _____.
   way to relate.

9. (community) Lots of folks watch over _____.
   children.

10. The toughest people make it through _____.
    difficult issues.

These maxims or **aphorisms** can be useful in Introduction Paragraphs, especially Personal Testimony Introductions. Also, Concluding paragraphs sometimes contain maxims as.

DIRECTIONS: A clue will be provided about a particular maxim. Each person in the group should take turns working backwards to figure out an appropriate maxim. Items in parentheses are another clue or keyword in the modern maxim (10-15 min).

MAXIM TOPIC CLUE	ACTUAL MODERN MAXIM
1. A person always says what's right, but doesn't do it.	You should practice what you preach.
2. Writing a letter can produce better results than violence.	The pen is mightier than the sword.
3. (mouth), If you can't handle it, don't begin the task.	Don't bite off more than you can chew!
4. (group of fowl), People with the same mindset hang out.	Birds of a feather flock together.
5. (canine)Experienced folks dislike doing things differently.	You can't teach an old dog, new tricks.
6. (two foods), Resolve disputes calmly not bitterly.	One catches more flies with honey than vinegar.
7. (farm), You'll be treated the same way you treat others.	What ever you sow, you will also reap.
8. (policy), Telling lies is not the optimal way to relate.	Honesty is the best policy.

9. (community) Lots of folks need to watch over children.	It takes a village to raise a child. (African proverb)
10. The toughest persons make it through difficult issues.	Only the strong will survive. (Or) 'Survival of the Fittest' (Or) When the going gets tough, the tough get going.

This second batch of maxims should be much more familiar than the first which are normally taught in fifth grade. These seem to apply more to the daily lives of present friends, relatives, and acquaintances. Therefore, a drafter would be truly apt to jot a few into a paragraph to sound 'folksy'. Specifically, that person's sense of Voice would seem more personable—he or she would 'sound' gregarious.

Most everyone, especially table readers, absolutely idolize a people-person's writing. This is so because they have a relatively unique style. Verily, inclusion of these familiar maxims bodes well for those looking to score higher in the 'freshness of expression' category. This desirable grouping always earns one of the higher two scores; they are that anti-robotic writer.

BELLRINGER #43: DIALOGUING

Dialoguing is another advanced writing technique that regularly adds credibility to written statements. That is why it is often included in police reports, court hearings, novels, comic books, and even student referrals. This practice authenticates an account by exploiting actual quotes, unique syntactical structures, and emotional inflections. Then, that story proffers a much clearer and believable mental depiction of unfolded events.

Read the two following excerpts about the same topic and answer the following questions:

1. Which statement sounds richer or more complete?
2. Which statement reads more convincingly?
3. Which statement drives the main idea home better?

DIRECTIONS: Just examine the two paragraphs below that are crafted around the same exact topic. Then, answer the three previous questions.

Prompt: Hand-held electronic devices are constantly evolving and can quickly become obsolete in months. Consider the major reasons why you purchase new devices or stick to the older ones. Then, provide detailed justifications for the stance you have chosen.

Intro. Paragraph 1: Over the past decade, constant improvements in hand-held devices have prevented me from purchasing 'smart devices'. I intentionally stuck to my trusty old, touch screen cellphone popular in the year 2000 instead. Admittedly, my conscience was willing to limit thousands of so-called apps to a handful. This is partially due to the hefty prices. Meaning, new-coming electronic fads seem to have larger and larger costs. In addition, 'the next best thing' always seemed to be around the corner. Our U.S. recession of 2007 and common dollar sense often shove my wallet back into my pocket. Ultimately, my budget cannot afford to follow every single electronic trend advertised on television.

This is not a bad paragraph spelling out the author's apprehension to buy newer handheld devices for fear of owning obsolete ones. This A-/B+ paragraph lacks a deeper relationship or connection with the topic. It lacks an experiential or historical element convincingly linking an author to his stance; it is still somewhat general though!

Intro. Paragraph 2: One autumn evening, my father and I bravely lined lawn chairs in front of Best Buy. "Sit down son, it's going to be a long night" was his ardent request. Our insatiable hunger for the $799 I-phone was apparently shared by 300 other customers. Dad was not about to let them block us from this latest status symbol. Merely three months later, we were in for one of the rudest awakenings ever! "Dad get in here, you won't believe this" I loudly ordered. As he entered, his nervous reply "what's all the fuss about?" was soon explained. Our expressions dropped into frowns as Christmas commercials bragged about the I-phone's slashed price, now $399. Then, our mutual vow became to never purchase electronic gadgets when they are initially introduced!

This A+ response is GREAT-er simply because it is a personal testimony intro which 'authenticates' the stance.
The dialogue adds the right amount of personal touch to accentuate the main idea. (See blue highlights).

BELLRINGER # 44: INTERJECTIONS

Interjections: are short, succinct bursts of emotional reaction that amplify an author's reaction to his or her audience. Usually, these single words, fragments, or short sentences uncover the heart of a matter. Ex(s): Hurray! Awesome! Yipes! This is ridiculous! That was incredible!

Example # 1: If you just won the Publisher's Clearinghouse Sweepstakes, you wouldn't blabber "isn't it wonderful that I won't have to work again!" You wouldn't have the time to react like this.

Instead, you'd excitedly voice your near delirium with the following: Wow! OMG! This is unbelievable! I must be dreaming! Are you kidding me? Get out! Ahhhh! No way!

From those interjections, onlookers would instantly comprehend that something fantastic and unexpected just happened. Such brief screams of excitement jar attention away from external happenings to the emotions of the speaker. They abruptly prompt the reader as if to say 'hey everyone, listen up!'

DIRECTIONS: Let's examine how much more emphasis is placed upon the main idea by including two or three interjections in yesterday's dialoguing paragraph.

(Blue writing = dialoguing, red writing = interjections)

One autumn evening, my father and I bravely lined lawn chairs in front of Best Buy. "Sit down son, it's going to be a long night" was his ardent request. Our insatiable hunger for the $799 I-phone was apparently shared by 300 other customers. Dad was not about to let them block us from this latest status symbol. Merely three months later, we were in for one of the rudest awakenings ever! "Dad get in here, you won't believe this" I loudly ordered. As he entered, his nervous reply "what's all the fuss about?" was soon explained. Our expressions dropped into frowns as Christmas commercials bragged about the I-phone's slashed price, now $399. Then, our mutual vow became to never purchase electronic gadgets when they are initially introduced!

After placing three interjections and three pieces of dialogue, here is our end product:

"Phew!" was all my weary body could utter. My father and I were first to line our lawn chairs in front of Best Buy. "Sit down son, it's going to be a long night" was his ardent request. I swiftly complied; it would be six more hours before purchasing the $799 I-phone! Three hundred other customers shared his enthusiasm but might soon regret their decision. "Oh man!" I grunted disappointedly, and then ordered "Dad get in here now". He entered and nervously replied "what's all the fuss about?" Christmas commercials clarified that we overpaid by $400 after only three months; "so ridiculous!" Then, our mutual vow became to never purchase electronic gadgets when they are initially introduced.

Did you see how each interjection cued your attention; hey listen up? Twice the personality and emotion were included in this paragraph. This writing seems like it belongs in a novel because of the wealth of literary devices.

It is an improvement over the previous GREAT paragraph, and would likely be scored higher on essay exams.

(Remember, GREAT Burger insists writers not stretch these intro or body paragraphs any longer than 9 sentences).

Now it's your turn. We will combine the lessons from Bellringer # 43 and Bellringer # 44 into two practice sessions. Please complete one paragraph on each of the two days.

Adding interjections and dialoguing into your paragraphs is a skill that must be practiced to further your understanding.

Below, two relevant prompts will be provided in order for you to perfect the intricate art. This first is a persuasive prompt and the second is an expository prompt. Remember, you are word artists who must be able to weave in two or three interjections and pieces of dialogue. Doing so, produces the most polished, captivating, and realistic storylines.

Prompt #1: You've heard of the old adage "you can't judge a book by its cover". Recall if there was ever an occasion where your clothing made you stand out. Provide three justifications to support or refute the adage above. (Persuasive)

TS: _____ , _____ .
SD 1: _____ , _____ .
EXP 1: _____ , _____ .
EXP 2: _____ . EXP 3: _____ ,
_____ . EXP 4: _____ .
CS: _____ .

Prompt #2: Interior design plays a more important role in people's lives than they actually realize. Pretend you won $5,000 to makeover your bedroom. Specifically name three items that you would add or fix to improve your level of comfort. Provide the rationale behind each of your choices. (Expository)

TS: _____ , _____ .
SD 1: _____ .
EXP 1: _____ , _____ .
EXP 2: _____ . EXP 3: _____ .
_____ . EXP 4: _____ . CS: _____ , _____ .

Sample responses for paragraphs:

Prompt #1:

TS The timeless adage "you can't judge a book by its cover" was recently proven true! SD 1 For a month, I'd tirelessly reviewed practice SAT items from both study guides and online. EXP 1 "Want to reschedule, hon'?" was the proctor's hasty remark but timeliness wasn't at issue. "Unbelievable!" was my muttered response. EXP 2 Next, Mrs. Flynn judgmentally pursed her lips at my mismatched socks and un-ironed dockers. I whispered "Ease up!" while confident in my concentration; so what if I looked bum-ish. EXP 3 She sarcastically quipped "good luck son"; pretty shallow because I was going to ace this test! CS Therefore, it isn't wise to prejudge folks because appearances can be deceiving.

It meets a GREAT-er standard with an adage, two pieces of dialogue, two interjections; and a very specific persuasive argument!

Prompt # 2:

TS Last Friday, I received an unexpected email message that profoundly changed my life! **SD 1** I supposedly won a $5,000 bedroom makeover from HGTV. I naturally 'flipped out' and yelled "Wow, am I being punked or what?" **SD 2** A subsequent phone call verified it; "Awesome!" this thing was for real. I loudly reassured myself. **EXP 1** Now, I could truly sleep easier with a Posturepedic bed replacing my worn-out one. **EXP 2** Builders could actually add onto my shallow closet by taking space from a nearby bathroom. **EXP 3** Getting a professional painter to design an ocean inspired mural would jar me from emotional boredom. **CS** These are several choices that would make my room more comfortable, practical, and lively.

It meets a GREAT-er standard with two interjections, two pieces of dialogue, and a very specific expository story!

Congratulations, you have completed all of the bellringers required to fully comprehend the GREAT Burger Manual. I know that they have enriched both your grammar skills and paragraph writing skills.

CHAPTER 4 | GREAT Burger Essay Manual

This next chapter presents the GREAT Burger format to your students in a clear, concise fashion. It must have taken me at least 100 hours to come close to adequately refining this manual. Admittedly, there is an ample breadth that must be covered to demonstrate this system. That wasn't the only barrier. I had to ensure that the following templates and definitions were relatively simple, which was no easy feat! A tertiary concern was keeping the length down to less than 10 pages to conserve paper at schools everywhere. Moreover, it was vital so the workbook would not prematurely scare students away.

As you move through this section, most of the subject matter should be a refresher from the twelve weeks of grammar bell ringers. Here we mainly intend to reinforce what students have already learned by reviewing it in a foreshortened version. Thus, you have to economically print this manual for every writer in your classes. So, please print the booklet as nine, double-sided pages that way students have the advantage of full-sized pages. Although they need it as an in-class an at home reference, you will have conserved paper and trees. Again, please do not print these as nineteen one-sided pages.

Lastly, you must have *the all-important chat* before you begin the writing exercises. Inform your students in a firm, friendly manner that they will be undergoing this GREAT Burger Essay workshop. Do this a week ahead. This means that you must set the ground-rules as it goes to attendance. I remember demanding that my students not miss a day for the next two weeks unless it is an absolute emergency. I further insisted that their 'emergency' qualify as an excusable admit pass.

Moreover, it is imperative that they not ask to go to someone else's classroom during your English period. My youngsters were instructed to go to the bathroom before my class. There was no excuse why they could not make it to class except authentic physical illness; not a non-serious cold. Ultimately, students comprehended that this workshop was worth about eight grades. So, in-class instruction would get them the best scores because of the peer checklists. These valuable resources would basically catch most of their mistakes before they submitted final revisions. Good luck, remain vigilant, and monitor those checklists every step of the way!

GREAT BURGER

INTRODUCTION

PARAGRAPHS

CONCLUSION

ESSAY WORKSHOP

Essay Writing Tips for Middle School, High School, and College Students!

by

Stephen C. Simms Sr.
Ph. D, Business Administration

"Organization is what you do before you do something, so when you do it, it's not all mixed up."

--*A. A. Milne a.k.a. Winnie the Pooh*

- *Would you erect a skyscraper without a blueprint?*

- *Should you bake a birthday cake without a recipe?*

- *Could you build a fence and not know the cost?*

- *Would a writer draft a novel without a layout?*

- *Should you take a vacation without travel plans?*

By now, you get my drift. You cannot precisely and effectively make anything without planning!

I can't wait to show you the GREAT Burger Quick Essay Planner. It is absolutely the reason why each GREAT paragraph is chock full of fantastic support/proof.

GREAT BURGER QUICK ESSAY PLANNER

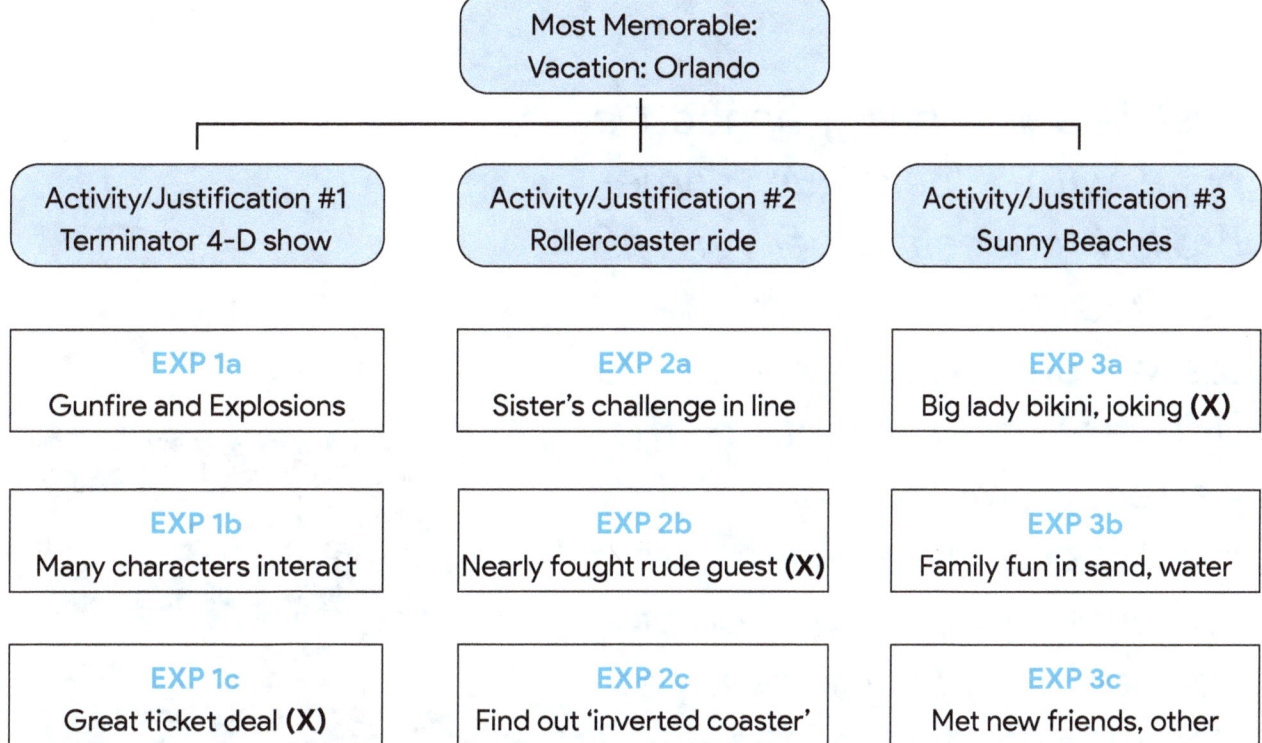

This quick essay planner becomes easier over time. First time, do it in class and take 20 minutes to see how far students get.

1. You'll notice we no longer use the words 'Three Reasons' because reasons are too simplistic.

   -That is why each one is called **Activity #1, Activity #2, Activity # 3** for Expository essays; 'What did you do?'
   -Also, they are called **Justification # 1, Justification # 2, & Justification # 3** if you are doing Persuasive essays; 'What is your specific proof?'

2. Notice that EXP 1a, EXP 1b, EXP 1c are actually very specific 'mental snapshots' of activities. The reader must be able to visualize doing it as well when you write about it in your actual essay. You use two of the three mental snapshots. Then you eliminate the weakest ones in your essays (See X). This is a **'double-proof' Body paragraph**.

3. Note: Each entry is always written in 'caveman'; YOU SHOULD NEVER WRITE COMPLETE SENTENCES IN A PLANNER! At first this planner will take around 15-18 minutes, as you work with it you will do it in 10-12 minutes.

Just imagine being handed a plate with a delicious, flame-broiled cheeseburger on it? As you take a whiff of its tasty aroma, look down at the different layers. Picture that perfect combination; a lightly toasted bun, melted cheese, ripe tomatoes, and sweet onions. You can't wait to sink your teeth into it! In like fashion, a GREAT essay manages to combine the freshest ingredients. It includes an eye-catching opening, an assortment of facts/examples, and the beefy main idea.

(Sample GREAT introduction paragraph)

Did this GREAT introduction grab your attention?

Did it make you hungry?

Every single Introduction should make a reader desire to 'digest' the rest of your essay like this!

'BURGERS 101'

<u>Let's deconstruct our delicacy!</u>

Certainly, we are aware that a Middle, High school, or College essay should contain five paragraphs:

a.) Each paragraph should contain at least 6-8 sentences.
b.) Each of these paragraphs should contain vital ingredients of the finest quality- adjectives, adverbs, and transitions.

In coming up with our ideal burger, each of us has to decide how much of each ingredient to include.

HYPOTHETICALS: (students close eyes, you describe A & B)

a.) How would you like a huge burger with half a pound of mayonnaise between the buns, and no meat at all?

This happens when a writer only mentions the superficial or vague elements of their topic. They make this mistake <u>rather than including vivid details!</u>

b.) Adding too few garnishes or condiments in our snack could make it taste as bland as hospital soup.

This happens when a writing lacks transitions, adverbs, and (adjectives greater than four letters) in every sentences. (Transitions begin every other sentence.)

Let's take a look at some GREAT examples of Introductions!

Introduction Paragraphs:

In elementary school, students are taught to list three reasons in their Introduction Paragraphs. However, that is where the typical 'three reasons' paragraphs should remain!

*Learners from middle school, through high school, and even college have many advanced alternatives. I will personally introduce you to Five Different Types of Introduction paragraph:

Three Expansions Introduction:	provides readers with three 'mental snapshots' clearly & persuasively supporting a writer's stance.
Anecdote Introduction:	an amusing or ironic story that 'breaks the ice' for the reader while still explaining the writer's stance on a topic.
Other Factors Introduction:	using allusions, television shows, news articles, (three types) magazine statistics, etc. making a case for his/her stance.
Historical Review Introduction:	retelling the events sequentially that led up to the writer's stance.
Personal Testimony Introduction:	Initially, a writer presumed one stance, until a personal experience changed their entire outlook.

Examples of Innovative Introductions

Prompt: Everyone has an unforgettable vacation. Think about the places you've visited in the past five years. Then, write an expository essay convincing the reader why this was your most memorable vacation.

Three Expansions Introduction:

It had been a truly frigid winter, and I was burnt out by schoolwork. I, like the flocks of snowbirds, could hardly wait to visit sunny Orlando! I joyfully rode the most amazing roller-coasters through tunnels and loops. My family and I awkwardly frolicked between the warm waters and sand of the beach. Then, we went shopping at trendy Las Olas Boulevard; one of Florida's most fancy malls. Therefore, this was the greatest trip we had ever experienced in our lives!

Anecdote Introduction:

The most bizarre incident happened to me on my way to Orlando, Florida! After procrastinating for days, I finally packed my large suitcase the morning of the trip. My clothes were simply shoved into my luggage without neatly folding them. As a result, I had to beg my teenage brother to sit on my bag just to properly zip it up. We unwisely arrived at the airport forty minutes before take-off; and raced for our gate! I tripped and fell alongside my suitcase about three hundred feet from our terminal. Suddenly, my Samsonite exploded sending my bathing suits and underwear flying everywhere. I was absolutely embarrassed as I lay there in the middle of a pile of clothes. Despite this minor setback, I was certainly determined to enjoy myself in beautiful Orlando, Florida.

Other Factors Introduction: (News item)

On Cable Network News (CNN), they recently highlighted several desirable activities one could enjoy in Orlando. The pristeen beaches, amazing seafood, and luxurious hotels actually hypnotized me! My mind was now dead-set on this vacation spot, and that led me to contact Travelocity. Quickly, I booked our flight, hotel, and reservations to quite exhilarating activities. My mom and dad were pretty proud that I took the initiative since they needed a breather as well. A week more of this humdrum life and we were out of here! Finally, we were greeted by the blazing sun and the humid air of Orlando!

Other Factors Introduction: (Television Commercial)

On the Travel Channel, the most unforgettable commercial about Orlando, Florida caught my attention! Emerald waters were reflecting the golden sun, and this reminded me to savor life's pleasures. Then, I watched as a multi-colored Calypso band played tropical music; truly eye-catching! It actually reminded me of Caribbean paradise without the added expense. So, I saved my allowance every week for five months to visit this summer. Then, I toured Sea World, met new friends, and tried exotic foods down there.

Other Factors Introduction: (Television Show)

Last Thursday evening, my favorite cast of Jersey Shore visited magical Orlando! The usually reserved Vinny became adventurous and tried parasailing over the Atlantic Ocean. Unbelievably, Snooki sipped on some really bright, virgin daiquiris I desired to sample through the television. Ronnie and Samantha—constantly feuding 'soulmates'—calmly sat down, and shared some exquisite Mediterranean dishes. While peering at their plates, my mouth watered intensely, and my taste buds were ready. My next move was to secure plane tickets to Orlando as soon as possible.

Historical Review Introduction:

There were merely two days until my family and I would be free for our Summer Vacation of 2006! Stumbling into the darkened den, I gladly overheard my mother Sara confirming our reservations. We were going to stay at the luxurious Wyndham Resort in Orlando. Then, she exhaled a brief sigh and loudly proclaimed that it was packing time. My sister, my dad, and I eagerly snatched our clothes from overstuffed drawers. We randomly shoved them into our suitcases, which my mom eventually repacked without criticizing us. Obviously, she felt as we did; this was truly going to be our greatest vacation ever!

Personal Testimony Introduction:

At first, this small town country boy was truly hesitant about visiting a big city like Orlando. I believed that I would be out of my element, like 'a fish out of water'. Then, my more free-spirited cousin Terrance convinced me that I would enjoy it. He promised that Sawgrass Mills, a mall shaped like an alligator, had great discounts! I played 'Devil's Advocate', and looked it up on the internet; was it everything Terrance described? Unless my eyes were deceiving me, his story checked out and that made me wonder. I pondered how many other attractions I would fondly remember. So, we drove to Orlando, and I have never regretted the trip since.

Don't these five Introduction types make you desire to 'digest' more?

Did you notice how imaginative each Introduction paragraph sounds?

1. Complex Adjectives, Adverbs, & Transitions are interwoven into each sentence (like a written tapestry).

2. Intros don't incorporate 'three simplistic reasons'. *Instead, 'three mental snapshots' allow the reader to create a mental picture of each event*: (see three Expansion Introduction sample).

3. Each Introduction does not only provide an effective hook for the reader. *Each Introduction actually became a hook making the reader want to read on.*'

SEVERAL TECHNIQUES YOU SHOULD AVOID IN THESE INTRODUCTIONS:

- Do not include a definition from a dictionary or encyclopedia; too simplistic!
- Resist including more than one question in these introductions. This method, known as the Socratic method, is usually employed to hammer out deeper, philosophical meanings. (It should not be used so the writer can avoid coming up with a bona fide introduction).
- 'Microwave' Introductions, those with one to four sentences, do not include enough sensory details. These briefer structures do not frame your argument or stance well enough. Nor do they provide a complete mental picture to 'hook the readers', so they will continue reading.

FORMATS OF THE INNOVATIVE INTRODUCTIONS

Generally, all introduction paragraphs have the same format. They include a Topic Sentence, three or four supporting details, and a Clincher sentence.

Topic Sentence (TS): provides the main idea of the paragraph.

Supporting Detail (SD): reveal some of the aspects of the topic that will be discussed.

Expansions (EXPs): these sentences are more specific causes or proof of your stance. We will use these more than supporting details!

Clincher sentence (CS): (also known as a Thesis Statement or Closing sentence) concludes the paragraph with the writer's specific stance or position on the prompt.

Now, I am going to give you a 'schematic' for each example paragraph. Remember, that writing essays affords you nearly infinite variability. I am simply providing a rough pattern of four types of Introduction paragraphs to make them easier to use. (Advice: leave your Clincher or Closing sentence at the end of every Introduction paragraph).

Three Expansions Introduction: specifically describes three activities or justifications of writer's stance.

    TS Shocking statement or Statistic about the prompt's topic! **EXP 1** A vivid, mental snapshot of your first justification or activity. **EXP 2** A vivid, mental snapshot of your second justification or activity. **EXP 3** A vivid, mental snapshot of your third justification or activity. **CS** A clear statement of the writer's stance about the topic of the prompt.

> Note: **EXP 1**-**EXP 3** stands for Expansions 1-3; they are much more specific than simple reasons.

From the previous page: My favorite vacation destination was Orlando.

My reason: I went to the beach. ('as bland as hospital soup!' Not good in an essay at all!)

My EXP 1: (the specific activity of Three Expansions Introduction):

My family and I awkwardly frolicked between the warm waters and sand of the beach.

(Can't you picture doing this in your mind?) That is why we call it a *'mental snapshot'* or an *'Expansion'*.

(**EXP 2** & **EXP 3** should be mental snapshots just like this sample **EXP 1**.

Anecdote Introduction: a humorous, awkward, or bizarre 'icebreaker' that disarms a table reader—person who grades standardized writing tests. (We're still using the Memorable Vacation prompt here).

TS The (oddest, strangest, wildest, wackiest, most peculiar **(pick one))** incident occurred on my way to (Orlando)! **EXP 1** Set-up of joke, quip, accident, or practical joke related to prompt—**(what were you specifically doing just before the incident?) EXP 2** Then, speak about the location or setting you entered before the incident occurred-**(Where were you? Who was around you?) EXP 3** Suddenly, the practical joke or accident happens; **(tell us what that was). EXP 4** Mention a **snide comment that may have been made by an onlooker** that was funny to the other witnesses, while you were embarrassed. **CS** Point out **how that person's snippy remark affected your position** on the topic.

> Note: This is admittedly an advanced technique that your students will have to practice. However, it is one of the most effective Introductions that I have included. It is certainly worth two or three attempts as the structure of these anecdote Introductions vary quite a bit. (See previous example)

(Advice: Keep the length down to no more than eight sentences!!) Intros only require moderate specificity!!!

Other Factors Introductions: Allusions of *news items, television shows, commercials, journals, etc.* may be used to further focus your readers' attention on the legitimacy of your stance).

TS Last **(day of the week)**, I was absolutely fascinated by the (news item, television show, commercial, or journal article **(pick one)**) on/in: (the Travel channel, the newspaper name, Cosmopolitan magazine **(pick one)**)! **EXP 1** I initially noticed the **(1st appealing activity or justification)** that happened (during/on /beneath/while) a beautiful, golden sunset **(weather/ time of day). EXP 2** Next, my imagination was definitely blown away when the **(2nd appealing activity or justification)** made me desire to _____. **EXP 3** The most outrageous event occurred when (a young person, group of people, family **(pick one)**) actually did **(3rd appealing activity or justification)**. I could wait no longer, and I wasn't even going to try! **Strong Transition = (Therefore, Thus, So, etc (pick one))**, my next move was to book our family's flight to sunny Orlando.

Hint: Other Factors Introduction is just like creating a three-Expansion using allusions from different sources. Just be very specific in each expansion like the previous Other Factors was, and spice it up with adjectives, adverbs, and transitions.

> Note: You could also use allusions of poetic lines, grandma's old sayings, wise idioms, song lyrics, poignant text messages or emails, and other literary forms. They could be mentioned to support your stance on a particular prompt, and they are also considered 'Other Factors Introductions'. Therefore, this is at least the **nine-in-one**, *versatile* Other Factors Introduction.

Personal Testimony Introduction: a pretty powerful method that demonstrates a person's original stance, then a life-changing event, and how that event has dramatically switched the writer's stance.

Hint: some students may relate this to a portion of religious services in a church, mosque, or synagogue. On occasion, audience members initially speak out about tough circumstances, and then something great or 'miraculous' happens. Afterwards, their 'doubtful stance' has now switched to one of 'strong belief'. (Briefly ask your students about this).

We are still dealing with the Expository 'Most Memorable Vacation' prompt.

> **TS** Transition, your original stance from the provided prompt—At first, this small town, country boy was truly hesitant about a road trip to Orlando! (**EXP 1**) How did you presume you would feel if you did the activity of the prompt? I believed that I would be out of my element, like 'a fish out of water'. (**EXP 2**) Transition, a 'life-changing event' happened to switch my previous stance —Then, my free-spirited cousin Terrance convinced me I would absolutely enjoy it! (**EXP 3**) A demonstration or evidence that the second stance is just as valid— He promised that Sawgrass Mills, a mall shaped like a gigantic alligator, really had great discounts. (**EXP 4**) What was your raw reaction to his/her convincing statement?—So, I played Devil's Advocate', and looked it up on the internet; 'everything Terrance described. (**EXP 5**) When you found the opposite stance to be correct, how did your actions also switch? I pondered how many other attractions I would fondly remember. **CS** Transition, thesis statement or Clincher sentence. Soon, we drove to magical Orlando, and I have never regretted it since!

> Note: Remember to keep these paragraphs between 6-9 sentences. If you write more you would be wasting time, and also giving away too many details. Those 'extra details' would belong in the body of the essay instead.

ADDITIONAL ADVICE

- Don't get stuck on carrying these layouts to the letter. As long as your stories are vivid, sequential, and end with your Clincher you're fine.
- Some of these Introductory paragraph types will tempt you to include every detail. Resist this idea, and limit each between 6-9 sentences.
- None of the Introduction paragraphs have to be true! They have to be convincing, and elicit believable 'mental pictures'.

YOU'RE UP NEXT AT THE GRILL!

Now you can demonstrate what you've learned thus far.

Be sure to follow the GREAT format:

- 15 words or less per sentence
- At least 3 adjectives, 3 adverbs, & 3 transitions
- Choose two of the four types of Intros, vary sentence structures

Today you will be expected to draft two different types of Introductions. You must pattern them based upon the previously provided Innovative paragraph formats.

Essay Prompt

Read: A major deal was made about a required dress code at Anthony Arnold Middle school last year as parents voted on it.

Think: Now all students must only wear three colors of polo shirts, and blue or khaki slacks. Think about how this would affect you.

Explain: Write a persuasive essay stating why you either support or oppose this new dress code. Be sure to include at least three convincing justifications to back up your stance on this issue.

Innovative Introduction Paragraph format

TS:_____. EXP 1:_____,

_____.

EXP 2: _____.

EXP 3: _____, _____.

EXP 4: _____.

CS: _____, _____.

DIRECTIONS: Complete two different Introduction Types in-class and finish them at home if necessary. Then, bring them in tomorrow and we will peer edit them using the GREAT Burger checklist.

Teachers:

a.) Please allow students to read one of each type aloud just to see if they have gotten the hang of the format. This would likely take 10-15 minutes as you complement the four writers/volunteers about the positives.

b.) Then, allow writers to switch papers, and use the GREAT Burger checklist. It is provided on the next page. Students will need a clean sheet of paper to jot down their checklist items, and whether or not each paragraph meets them.

c.) Since students are only beginners at this point you will be obliged to do a lot of verbal queuing & inspecting. To keep them on track, you recite each category and specify which areas they should be assessing. Each letter of GREAT should only take about five minutes to assess.

d.) (HAVE THEM WRITE THIS OUT—the process of doing so reinforces memory of the GREAT BURGER Essay Checklist. Writing out and assessing two Introduction Paragraphs should only take 45 minutes. (The Checklist is on the next page).

Homework: Students should go home and fix all missing adverbs, adjectives, transitions, incorrect grammar, misspellings, sentences longer than 15 words, repeated phrases, etc.

 **GREAT BURGER ESSAY CHECKLIST**

Introduction Paragraph:

_____ Does Topic Sentence begin with a shocking statement or statistic?
(yes or no)

_____ Does the 'body' of the paragraph contain either three vivid expansions or a detailed story?
(yes or no)

_____ Are the details of the story or Expansions in a logical or sequential order?
(yes or no)

_____ Does the vivid Intro end with a Clincher Sentence or Thesis that clearly defines his/her stance?
(yes or no)

_____ Grammatically (yes/no) Correct?	_____ Repetition (yes/no) Free?	_____ Expertly (yes/no) Supported?	_____ Adj. /Adv (yes/no) Packed	_____ Transition (yes/no) Filled?
__a) No misspellings	__a) Look for 'I'	__a) Facts	__a) 3+ adjectives	__a) 3+ Transitions
__b) No awkward sentences	__b) Repeated names instead of pronouns	__b) Reas./Exps	__b) 3+ -ly adverbs	
__c) Subject-Verb agreement		__c) Incidents		
		__d) Examples		
		__e) Statistics		

(If true, place checks in these subheadings)

> Note: **All subheadings must be true before you can write 'Yes' in front of G, R, E, A, or T; E must have at least three checks.** If one is incorrect, write NO. Then, peers must specifically write out whether a word is misspelled, the para. is missing a transition, if there is an awkward/backward sentence, repeating names of people or places constantly, or if it missing two adverbs.

(Fellow students are counting on your accuracy to get them a GREAT grade on their Final Intro. Revisions!) Teachers, make sure your students do not take short-cuts in order for this to work well! You must pace the room making sure students are all-in!

Body Paragraph 1, 2, & 3 Checklist:

Remember, GREAT Burger Body Paragraphs require 'twice the proof or justification' as ordinary body paragraphs! This ensures an upper standardized test score because this provides 'ample support of the writer's stance'.

_____ Does the Topic Sentence reveal the writer's first activity or justification for his/her stance?
(yes or no)

_____ Does the BP include at least two detailed stories or FRIES to support the Topic Sentence?
(yes or no)

_____ Does each detailed story or example of FRIES have at least 3 sentences in it? (Paragraph =7-9 sents?)
(yes or no)

_____ Grammatically (yes/no) Correct?	_____ Repetition (yes/no) Free?	_____ Expertly (yes/no) Supported?	_____ Adj. /Adv (yes/no) Packed	_____ Transition (yes/no) Filled?
__a) No misspellings	__a) Look for 'I'	__a) Facts	__a) 3+ adjectives	__a) 3+ Transitions
__b) No awkward sentences	__b) Repeated names instead of pronouns	__b) Reas./Exps	__b) 3+ -ly adverbs	
__c) Subject-Verb agreement		__c) Incidents		
		__d) Examples		
		__e) Statistics		

(If true, place checks in these subheadings)

Conclusion Paragraph Essay Checklist:

> Note: Great Burger Conclusion Paragraphs do not allow writers to spend three or four sentences re-hashing each justification or activity. Instead, expert writers restate their topic sentence, recap their justifications all in the second sentence, and then offer enlightened commentary on the topic. They include at least two of the four provided Conclusion techniques).

_____ Does Topic Sentence rephrase your original stance on the prompt?
(yes or no)

_____ Does 2nd sentence restate your three justifications all in one sentence?
(yes or no)

_____ Does the next three sentences use at least two types of advanced Conclusion Techniques?
(yes or no)

_____ Grammatically (yes/no) Correct?	_____ Repetition (yes/no) Free?	_____ Expertly (yes/no) Supported?	_____ Adj. /Adv (yes/no) Packed	_____ Transition (yes/no) Filled?
__a) No misspellings	__a) Look for 'I'	__a) Facts	__a) 3+ adjectives	__a) 3+ Transitions

__b) No awkward sentences

__c) Subject-Verb agreement

__b) Repeated names instead of pronouns

__b) Reas./Exps

__c) Incidents

__d) Examples

__e) Statistics

__b) 3+ -ly adverbs

(If true, place checks in these subheadings)

Note: G, R, E, A, T, must all be true without any missing components and E must have at least three yeses for all of the ingredients to add up to be a successful G.R.E.A.T. burger paragraph.

Now it's time to present the beefy Body Paragraphs 1, 2, & 3!

GREAT Burger body paragraphs contain twice 'the meatiness' (or support) of normal body paragraphs!

As you begin, it should be clear that each body paragraph is composed of three parts. They begin with a Topic Sentence, add the first selected Expansion (3-4 sentences); then add the second selected expansion (3-4 sentences) directly from your planner. Thus, Body paragraphs are at least 7-9 sentences long.

TS: _____ , _____ .

EXP 1a: _____ .

EXP 2: _____ , _____ .

EXP 3: _____ . **EXP 1b**: _____ ,
_____ .

EXP 4: _____ .

EXP 5: _____ , _____ .

(Optional CS): _____ .

Innovative Body Paragraph 1,2,3 Pattern

From the above diagram, we begin with the Topic Sentence (TS). Then, we choose the first expansion in Column A of our planner called EXP 1a. The following sentence EXP 2 simply develops the details of the previous Expansion. EXP 3 provides closure of this first mini-story. Then, EXP 1b transitions us into the second selected expansion from Column A. (We have Xed or crossed out the weakest expansion in Column A; namely EXP 1c. Afterwards, we must supply even more specific justification of EXP 1b in EXP 4. Certainly, EXP 5 finalizes the second mini-story in this paragraph. The Optional CS or Closing sentence ends the paragraph while summarily relating to the TS.

DIRECTIONS: Go ahead and write three body paragraphs about your 'Most Memorable Vacation' and remember the GREAT Burger format! When you return to next class the teacher will allow you to peer checklist these body paragraphs. Then, your job is to actually use your peer's suggestions to fix all mistakes in each of these paragraphs.

Bottom Buns are Toasted, & Top Buns Aren't!

For better scoring essays, you should avoid simply 'regurgitating' the same exact 'three reasons' in your Conclusion paragraphs!!!

Explanation: Notice how the top bun is much fluffier than the bottom one; it even has sesame seeds. In like fashion, an Introduction paragraph contains 'unprocessed data' that we must analyze during the three Body Paragraphs. Bottom paragraphs are flatter, shorter, and have no sesame seeds because data has been processed! Meaning, the writer has properly analyzed the prompt during the body of the essay.

Now, drafters should specifically present results, new observations based on results, and/or fresh ways to correct or fix the problem. Therefore, all writers should use the following four advanced Conclusion techniques:

a.) A Call to Action: Tell people with the power, to USE the Power! Ex. (I wholeheartedly insist that the principal of Anthony Arnold Middle should amend this dress code!) Senators could change laws, CEOs/Administrators could rescind policies, Teachers could instruct students, if properly persuaded.)

b.) <u>Look Into the Future:</u> Suggest exactly what might happen in 1, 3, 5, or 10 years into the future if a proper solution is not implemented. Ex. In ten years, Polar bears will become extinct if we do not stop polluting the ozone layer.

c.) <u>New Solution to the Problem:</u> Analyze the situation and specifically prove your newer idea is better. Ex. Instead of erasing our rights, Principal Johnson should allow casual Fridays; loose jeans and tee shirts.

d.) <u>New Moral Lesson:</u> Share the new insight or lesson you have learned from this experience. Or tell how your original opinion has shifted. Ex. Principal Johnson should immediately stop judging our 'outsides' and focus on our inner well-being!

Note: Every conclusion should include at least two or three of these advanced Conclusion techniques. Your Essay exam table readers will definitely be impressed because these techniques simply delve deeper. Imagine being a table reader who reads hundreds of very mechanical or robotic three reasons essays. Then, they pick yours up, and it is totally different; mouth-watering Intro and Conclusion. Don't you believe that these assessors would tend to grade upwardly? You need to leave them licking their 'mental fingers'; Umm, this is too delicious!

DIRECTIONS: Go ahead and complete the Conclusion paragraph using the GREAT Burger essay guidelines. When you bring it back to class, your peers will review it, and you'll revise a final copy at home.

Conclusion Paragraph Template

TS (Transition, Restate stance) Therefore, the magical city of Orlando will always be one of my fondest memories! SD 1 (Restate three activities in one sentence) The thrill-rides, spectacular attractions, and white sandy beaches totally rocked! EXP 1 (Transition, Conclusion Technique c) So, my sister and I have mutually agreed to save our allowances. EXP 2 (Conclusion Technique b) We will make next year's trip even better, and plan it earlier too. EXP 3 (Transition, Conclusion Technique d) Also, we learned that taking regular breaks keeps us de-stressed and 'out of each other's hair'. CS (Closing Sentence=Conclusion Technique a) You definitely need to see the hundreds of attractions in Florida to appreciate them.

Note: As you can see, it is quite easy to include the advanced strategies. (See the green, highlighted sentences above, and refer to the previous page's definitions). You should use no less that 2-3 advanced Conclusion techniques as demonstrated above).

Let's See Just How Overloaded with Flavor (or Style) this GREAT Burger Expository essay sample actually is!

As you peruse the upcoming sample:

Can you visualize the details in the stories? Does this essay offer twice the proof in each body paragraph—two stories? Does each paragraph have at least three complex adjectives, adverbs and transitions?

Do the sentence types vary?

Did the Introduction avoid three bland reasons, and provide a vivid story?

What grade would a Writing Exam Table reader give this essay?

MY MOST MEMORABLE VACATION
(GREAT BURGER EXPOSITORY SAMPLE)

There were merely two days until my family and I would be free for our Summer vacation of 2006! Stumbling into the darkened den, I gladly overheard my mother Sara confirming our reservations. We were going to stay at the luxurious Wyndham Resort in Orlando. Then, she exhaled a brief sigh and loudly proclaimed that it was packing time. My sister, dad, and I eagerly snatched our wrinkled clothes from overstuffed drawers. We randomly shoved them into our suitcases which my mom eventually repacked without criticizing us. Obviously, she felt as we did; this was truly going to be our greatest vacation ever!

Orlando was the place where I experienced an undeniably amazing movie! Yes, the Terminator 4-D show at Universal studios was unpredictable. There were about three hundred patrons who slowly crammed into the semi-lit auditorium. After putting on 3-D glasses, my eyes were truly shocked by the gunfire and explosions. Larger fragments of glass and concrete seemed to be coming right at me! Afterwards, two characters on motorcycles added an interactive element to the performance. They actually rode over several ramps through flaming hoops held by beautiful female stage-hands. For their finale, these two 'motor-heads' appeared to ride right into the immense movie screen behind them. These were the most realistic and fantastic special effects I'd ever seen.

I had never experienced a roller coaster ride quite like the one in Orlando either. Surely, 'The Kraken' at Sea World took my whole family by surprise. My sister sharply remarked that I thought I was so tough because of my bragging. Foolishly, I claimed that "no ride in this amusement park was too much for me!" I saw future riders rapidly shimmying out of their shoes towards the line's end. After asking why, Sharon leveled that they did not want their shoes to fly off. This was when the thought of an inverted coaster chopped ego down to size. Unexpectedly, my legs dangled in the air two-hundred feet over the ground. My reactions were a mixture of horror and absolute delight!

The golden sun seemed so close to the shore I could nearly touch it! My family and I got the chance to pull off our shoes to beach-comb. While there, my playful father dragged me into the warmer ocean while my sister splashed him. I tried to retaliate but he was just too fast for me; I fell down. As I looked up, my eyes caught a glimpse of a mesmerizing girl around my age. Her deep tan and shapely curves fascinated me, and so I introduced myself. Paoula--a tourist from Brazil--made my day when she told me I was cute. Ultimately, she gave me her telephone number, and we call each other every two weeks.

Therefore, the magical city of Orlando will always be one of my fondest memories! The thrill-rides, spectacular attractions, and the white sandy beaches totally rocked! So, my sister and I have mutually agreed to save our allowances. We will make next year's trip even better, and plan it earlier too. Also, we learned that taking regular breaks keeps us de-stressed and 'out of each other's hair'. You definitely need to see the hundreds of attractions in Florida to appreciate them.

(© 2011, GREAT Burger Essay Workshop, Stephen C. Simms Sr.)

For argument's sake, let's use the Florida Writes Rubric to assess the quality of the previous essay.

Florida Writing Assessment Program (FLORIDA WRITES!)
Assessment Home | Florida Writes Home

Score Points in Rubric

The rubric further interprets the four major areas of consideration into levels of achievement. **This rubric was used in the Spring of 2011**

6 Points The writing is focused, purposeful, and reflects insight into the writing situation. The paper conveys a sense of completeness and wholeness with adherence to the main idea, and its organizational pattern provides for a logical progression of ideas. The support is substantial, specific, relevant, concrete, and/or illustrative. The paper demonstrates a commitment to and an involvement with the subject, clarity in presentation of ideas, and may use creative writing strategies appropriate to the purpose of the paper. The writing demonstrates a mature command of language (word choice) with freshness of expression. Sentence structure is varied, and sentences are complete except when fragments are used purposefully. Few, if any, convention errors occur in mechanics, usage, and punctuation.

5 Points The writing focuses on the topic, and its organizational pattern provides for a progression of ideas, although some lapses may occur. The paper conveys a sense of completeness or wholeness. The support is ample. The writing demonstrates a mature command of language, including precision in word choice. There is variation in sentence structure, and, with rare exceptions, sentences are complete except when fragments are used purposefully. The paper generally follows the conventions of mechanics, usage, and spelling.

4 Points The writing is generally focused on the topic but may include extraneous or loosely related material. An organizational pattern is apparent, although some lapses may occur. The paper exhibits some sense of completeness or wholeness. The support, including word choice, is adequate, although development may be uneven. There is little variation in sentence structure, and most sentences are complete. The paper generally follows the conventions of mechanics, usage, and spelling.

3 Points   The writing is generally focused on the topic but may include extraneous or loosely related material. An organizational pattern has been attempted, but the paper may lack a sense of completeness or wholeness. Some support is included, but development is erratic. Word choice is adequate but may be limited, predictable, or occasionally vague. There is little, if any, variation in sentence structure. Knowledge of the conventions of mechanics and usage is usually demonstrated, and commonly used words are usually spelled correctly.

2 Points   The writing is related to the topic but include extraneous or loosely related material. Little evidence of an organizational pattern may be demonstrated, and the paper may lack a sense of completeness or wholeness. Development of support is inadequate or illogical. Word choice is limited, inappropriate or vague. There is little, if any, variation in sentence structure, and gross errors in sentence structure may occur. Errors in basic conventions of mechanics and usage may occur, and commonly used words may be misspelled.

1 Point   The writing may only minimally address the topic. The paper is a fragmentary or incoherent listing of related ideas or sentences or both. Little, if any, development of support or an organizational pattern or both is apparent. Limited or inappropriate word choice may obscure meaning. Gross errors in sentence structure and usage may impede communication. Frequent and blatant errors may occur in the basic conventions of mechanics and usage, and commonly used words may be misspelled.

Unscorable

The paper is unscorable because

- the response is not related to what the prompt requested the student to do.
- the response is simply a rewording of the prompt.
- the response is a copy of a published work.
- the student refused to write.
- the response is illegible.
- the response is incomprehensible (words are arranged in such a way that no meaning is conveyed).
- the response contains an insufficient amount of writing to determine if the student was attempting to address the prompt. the writing folder is blank.

March 31, 2011, Florida Writing Assessment Program (FLORIDA WRITES!), http://fldoe.org/asp/fw/fwaprubr.asp

Understand that this Florida Writes Rubric works from the bottom up as it is normally used. So let's look back at the previous essay and assess it together:

a.) The writing surpasses the Unscorable test. It has a definite subject matter, contains enough writing, and it is on-topic.

b.) The writing surpasses a score of '1': It does not minimally address the Memorable Vacation Prompt. Neither does the writing resort to simplistic listing of ideas, limited word choice, or erratic grammar. The sentence structures are varied. They are not filled with common misspellings, frequent errors, or disorganized ideas.

c.) The writing surpasses a score of '2': The writing is more than related to the prompt, and avoids extraneous or unrelated details. The entire essay is presented in an organized pattern, and has a great sense of completeness or wholeness. Development of support is twice as much as a normal essay instead of inadequate or illogical. The essay contains a lot of sentence variation, and word choice is precisely picked. Lots of support is included and no common misspellings or lapses in conventions are noticed. Mechanics and usage are well done.

d.) The writing surpasses a score of '3': This writing exceeds the level of generally focused. It doesn't include extraneous or loosely related material. Its organizational pattern is well established and Support is plenteous. Refreshing, specific word choice demonstrates a breadth of vocabulary knowledge. Ample variation of sentence structures and knowledge of the conventions of mechanics and usage are fully evident. No misspellings are presented.

e.) The writing surpasses a score of '4': The writing has a high level of focus and excludes extraneous or loosely related material. It only uses pertinent examples to answer the essay prompt. No lapses in the organizational pattern and the piece exhibits an overwhelming wholeness or completeness. The support, including word choice, is more than ample; six justifications instead of three reasons. Plenty of sentence variation is seen throughout the essay. Development of support is quite evenly distributed between body paragraphs and all sentences are complete. The paper follows the conventions of spelling, grammar, and usage very well.

f.) The writing surpasses a score of '5': The writing has focused on the topic well; and rare/or no lapses occur. The piece has provided a progression of ideas. The paper conveys a sense of completeness or wholeness. The support is at least ample. The essay includes 6 major 'mental snapshots' instead of three justifications for the stance. There precision in word choice and consistent sentence variation in the essay. There are no fragments and/or if there are, they are intentional and for a desired effect. The paper overwhelmingly

Note: The three major differences between a 4 or 5 Writing score are:

1. 'Support is ample' in a 5-score,   Yes, support more than ample.
   instead of 'support is adequate' in a 4-score?
2. 'Mature command of language' for a 5-score,   Yes, mature command of language.
   instead of a 4 score?
3. 'Much sentence variation' in 5-score instead of   Yes, varied sentence structures.
   'little variation in sentence structure'

g.) The writing meets the level a score of '6': The writing is focused, purposeful, and very insightful about the writing situation. The paper conveys a sense of completeness and wholeness with adherence to the main idea, and its organizational pattern provides for a logical progression of ideas. The overwhelming support is substantial, specific, relevant, concrete, and/or illustrative. The paper demonstrates a commitment to and an involvement with the subject by using six mini-stories. It also shows clarity in presentation of ideas, and uses creative writing strategies throughout the entire essay; they are appropriate to the prompt's purpose. The writing demonstrates a mature command of language (word choice) with 'personalized' freshness of expression. Sentence structure is varied, and sentences are complete. There are no stand-alone fragments. Few, if any, convention errors occur in mechanics, usage, and punctuation.

Notwithstanding, we have just proved that the GREAT Burger Method Persuasive Sample does meet the strictest guideline of the Florida Writes Rubric. This is not surprising to me since I created GREAT taking this very rubric into consideration nearly seven years ago.

Now, I am going to provide Adjective, Adverb, and Transition Sheets that your students should regularly use. When they write each paragraph, these sheets should be out on top of their desktops! Students must learn 10 newer adjectives, 10 complex –ly adverbs, and 10 newer transitions that they hardly used before.

In fact, the Appendices should become a required and permanent part of each student's portfolio. Literally, badger them if you have to ensure that they don't return to vocabulary as usual.

*Also, you should take time to review them and have learners circle your preferable, complex terms. That way, they will know that you insist upon more refined sentences rather than overly simple ones.

(Appendix A, Appendix B, and Appendix C begin on the next page.) They contain commonly used 144 adverbs, over 100 adjectives, and nearly 100 transitions.

(Appendix A) Topic: 144 Commonly Used Adverbs

Hint: *They describe how, when, where, and to what extent?*

1. accidentally	37. eventually	73. nearly	109. shrilly
2. afterwards	38. exactly	74. neatly	110. shyly
3. almost	39. faithfully	75. nervously	111. silently
4. always	40. far	76. never	112. sleepily
5. angrily	41. fast	77. noisily	113. slowly
6. annually	42. fatally	78. not	114. smoothly
7. anxiously	43. fiercely	79. obediently	115. softly
8. awkwardly	44. fondly	80. obnoxiously	116. solemnly
9. badly	45. foolishly	81. often	117. sometimes
10. blindly	46. fortunately	82. only	118. soon
11. boastfully	47. frantically	83. painfully	119. speedily
12. boldly	48. gently	84. perfectly	120. stealthily
13. bravely	49. gladly	85. politely	121. sternly
14. briefly	50. gracefully	86. poorly	122. successfully
15. brightly	51. greedily	87. powerfully	123. suddenly
16. busily	52. happily	88. promptly	124. suspiciously
17. calmly	53. hastily	89. punctually	125. swiftly
18. carefully	54. honestly	90. quickly	126. tenderly
19. carelessly	55. hourly	91. quietly	127. tensely
20. cautiously	56. hungrily	92. rapidly	128. thoughtfully
21. cheerfully	57. innocently	93. rarely	129. tightly
22. clearly	58. inquisitively	94. really	130. tomorrow
23. correctly	59. irritably	95. recklessly	131. too
24. courageously	60. joyously	96. regularly	132. truthfully
25. crossly	61. justly	97. reluctantly	133. unexpectedly
26. cruelly	62. kindly	98. repeatedly	134. very
27. daily	63. lazily	99. rightfully	135. victoriously
28. defiantly	64. less	100. roughly	136. violently
29. deliberately	65. loosely	101. rudely	137. vivaciously
30. doubtfully	66. loudly	102. sadly	138. warmly

31. easily	67. madly	103. safely	139. weakly
32. elegantly	68. merrily	104. seldom	140. wearily
33. enormously	69. monthly	105. selfishly	141. well
34. enthusiastically	70. more	106. seriously	142. wildly
35. equally	71. mortally	107. shakily	143. yearly
36. Even	72. mysteriously	108. sharply	144. yesterday

(March 31, 2011, 144 Commonly Used Adverbs, http://www.facebook.com/topic.php?uid=2212484282&topic=1470)

(Appendix B) Adjective List

An **adjective** modifies a <u>noun</u> or a <u>pronoun</u> by describing, identifying, or quantifying words. An adjective often precedes the noun or the pronoun which it modifies. In the following examples, the **highlighted** words are adjectives:

The **car-shaped** balloon floated over the treetops.
Mrs. Smith papered her **living room** walls with **hideous** wall paper.
The **large** boat foundered on the **wine dark** sea.
The **coal** mines are **dark** and **dank**.
Many stores have already begun to play **irritating Christmas** music.
A **battered music** box sat on the **mahogany** sideboard.
The back room was filled with **large, green** rain boots.

APPEARANCE	APPEARANCE CONTD.	CONDITION	CONDITION CONTD.	FEELINGS (BAD)	FEELINGS (BAD) CONTD.
adorable	glamorous	alive	impossible	angry	grumpy
adventurous	gleaming	annoying	inexpensive	annoyed	helpless
aggressive	gorgeous	bad	innocent	anxious	homeless
alert	graceful	better	inquisitive	arrogant	hungry
attractive	grotesque	beautiful	modern	ashamed	hurt
average	handsome	brainy	mushy	awful	ill
beautiful	homely	breakable	odd	bad	itchy
blue-eyed	light	busy	open	bewildered	jealous
bloody	long	careful	outstanding	black	jittery
blushing	magnificent	cautious	poor	blue	lazy
bright	misty	clever	powerful	bored	lonely
clean	motionless	clumsy	prickly	clumsy	mysterious
clear	muddy	concerned	puzzled	combative	nasty
cloudy	old-fashioned	crazy	real	condemned	naughty
colorful	plain	curious	rich	confused	nervous
crowded	poised	dead	shy	crazy, flipped-out	nutty
cute	precious	different	sleepy	creepy	obnoxious
dark	quaint	difficult	stupid	cruel	outrageous
drab	shiny	doubtful	super	dangerous	panicky
distinct	smoggy	easy	talented	defeated	repulsive
dull	sparkling	expensive	tame	defiant	scary

elegant	spotless	famous	tender	depressed	selfish
excited	stormy	fragile	tough	disgusted	sore
fancy	strange	frail	uninterested	disturbed	tense
filthy	ugly	gifted	vast	dizzy	terrible
	ugliest	helpful	wandering	dull	testy
	unsightly	helpless	wild	embarrassed	thoughtless
	unusual	horrible	wrong	envious	tired
	wide-eyed	important		evil	troubled
				fierce	upset
				foolish	uptight
				frantic	weary
				frightened	wicked
				grieving	worried

FEELINGS (GOOD)	FEELINGS (GOOD) CONTD.	SHAPE	SIZE	SOUND	TIME
agreeable	happy	broad	big	cooing	ancient
amused	healthy	chubby	colossal	deafening	brief
brave	helpful	crooked	fat	faint	Early
calm	hilarious	curved	gigantic	harsh	fast
charming	jolly	deep	great	high-pitched	late
cheerful	joyous	flat	huge	hissing	long
comfortable	kind	high	immense	hushed	modern
cooperative	lively	hollow	large	husky	old
courageous	lovely	low	little	loud	old-fashioned
delightful	lucky	narrow	mammoth	melodic	quick
determined	nice	round	massive	moaning	rapid
eager	obedient	shallow	miniature	mute	short
elated	perfect	skinny	petite	noisy	slow
enchanting	pleasant	square	puny	purring	swift
encouraging	proud	steep	scrawny	quiet	young
energetic	relieved	straight	short	raspy	
enthusiastic	silly	wide	small	resonant	
excited	smiling	difficult	tall	screeching	
exuberant	splendid	doubtful	teeny	shrill	
fair	successful	easy	teeny-tiny	silent	
faithful	thankful	expensive	tiny	soft	
fantastic	thoughtful	famous		squealing	
fine	victorious	fragile		thundering	
friendly	vivacious	frail		voiceless	
funny	witty	gifted		whispering	
gentle	wonderful	helpful			
glorious	zealous	helpless			
good	zany	horrible			
		important			

TASTE/TOUCH	TASTE/TOUCH CONTD.	TOUCH	QUANTITY		
bitter	melted	boiling	abundant		
delicious	nutritious	breezy	empty		
fresh	plastic	broken	few		
juicy	prickly	bumpy	heavy		
ripe	rainy	chilly	light		
rotten	rough	cold	many		
salty	scattered	cool	numerous		
sour	shaggy	creepy	substantial		
spicy	shaky	crooked			
stale	sharp	cuddly			
sticky	shivering	curly			
strong	silky	damaged			
sweet	slimy	damp			
tart	slippery	dirty			
tasteless	smooth	dry			
tasty	soft	dusty			
thirsty	solid	filthy			
fluttering	steady	flaky			
fuzzy	sticky	fluffy			
greasy	tender	freezing			
grubby	tight	hot			
hard	uneven	warm			
hot	weak	wet			
icy	wet				
loose	wooden				
	yummy				

(March 31, 2011, Adjective List, http://www.keepandshare.com/doc/12894/adjective-list)

(Appendix C) Transitional Words

Using transitional words and phrases:

a.) help papers read more smoothly.
b.) provide logical organization and understandability
c.) improve the connections and transitions between thoughts

A coherent paper allows the reader

to flow from the first supporting point to the last.

Transitions indicate relations,

whether within a sentence, paragraph, or paper.
This list illustrates "relationships" between ideas,
followed by words and phrases that can connect them.

Addition:

also, again, as well as, besides, coupled with, furthermore, in addition, likewise, moreover, similarly

Consequence:

accordingly, as a result, consequently, for this reason, for this purpose, hence, otherwise, so then, subsequently, therefore, thus, thereupon, wherefore

Generalizing:

as a rule, as usual, for the most part, generally, generally speaking, ordinarily, usually

Exemplifying:

chiefly, especially, for instance, in particular, markedly, namely, particularly, including, specifically, such as

Illustration:

for example, for instance, for one thing, as an illustration, illustrated with, as an example, in this case

Emphasis

above all, chiefly, with attention to, especially, particularly, singularly

Similarity:

comparatively, coupled with, correspondingly, identically, likewise, similar, moreover, together with

Exception:

aside from, barring, besides, except, excepting, excluding, exclusive of, other than, outside of, save

Restatement:

in essence, in other words, namely, that is, that is to say, in short, in brief, to put it differently

Contrast and Comparison:

contrast, by the same token, conversely, instead, likewise, on one hand, on the other hand, on the contrary, rather, similarly, yet, but, however, still, nevertheless, in contrast

Sequence:

at first, first of all, to begin with, in the first place, at the same time, for now, for the time being, the next step, in time, in turn, later on, meanwhile, next, then, soon, the meantime, later, while, earlier, simultaneously, afterward, in conclusion, with this in mind,

Summarizing:

after all, all in all, all things considered, briefly, by and large, in any case, in any event, in brief, in conclusion, on the whole, in short, in summary, in the final analysis, in the long run, on balance, to sum up, to summarize, finally

Diversion:

by the way, incidentally

Direction:

here, there, over there, beyond, nearly, opposite, under, above, to the left, to the right, in the distance

----

(March 31, 2011, Transitional Words for Essay Writing, http://www.studygs.net/wrstr6.htm)

| # Persuasive Essay Example

(Florida Comprehensive Assessment Test Persuasive Released Prompt 2008-2009)

The <u>purpose of a persuasive essay</u> is to convince a reader, using detailed justifications, to choose the stance that you personally believe is correct or true.

Read: The Florida Legislature is discussing the possibility of adding an hour to the school day to improve students' learning.

Think: Before you begin writing, think about the effects of adding an hour to the school day.

Explain: Now write to convince the adult reader of your paper on whether to add an hour to the school day.

Quick Persuasive Essay Planner

	Topic: Against Extra Hour School day	
Justification # 1 Students 'tune out'	**Justification # 2** Harder on teachers	**Justification # 3** Takes away social time
EXP 1a: After lunch, drowsy	**EXP 2a:** Overstresses teachers	**EXP 3a:** Can't date as long (**X**)
EXP 1b: Constant clock watching (**X**)	**EXP 2b:** Teachers mean to students	**EXP 3b:** Less time to relax
EXP 1c: Higher test failures	**EXP 2c:** Resistant teacher, busy work (**X**)	**EXP 3c:** No family time

Notice that all entries are written in caveman, fragments with recognizable details, not whole sentences. There isn't enough time to write complete sentences in a GREAT Quick Essay Planner!

Basically, the Persuasive layout or planner is completed in the very same way as an Expository essay.

However, the EXPs of Expository essays are normally denoted: Activity #1, Activity #2, & Activity #3

Contrariwise, EXPs of Persuasive essays are normally denoted: Justification # 1, Justification # 2, & Justification #3

Let's begin our two Introduction paragraphs, just like we would in the GREAT Burger workshop. I have chosen the Other Factors Introduction and Personal Testimony Introductions.

Other Factors Introduction: (Made-up Newspaper Article)

TS Extra, extra, read all about it! "Longer schooldays Lowering Student Scores" was the dismal daily headline of my Middle school's newspaper. EXP 1 Apparently, Math and Science grades--earned after lunch--were markedly declining. SD 1 I mentally attempted to process other ways our new nine hour days had affected me. EXP 2 This article discussed how the learning environment was changing before our eyes. SD 2 Notably, seasoned instructors actually seemed to hold a grudge about lengthier workdays as well. SD 3 They were more irritable than before; snapping at trivial occurrences. CS Teachers and students overwhelmingly disagree with this time-consuming measure.

Personal Testimony Introduction:

TS At first, I held unwavering support for longer schooldays, believing it would improve pupil performance. SD 1 Then, our practice assessment scores of the state test came out; quite disappointing! EXP 1 Adding an hour to the school-day had not staved off declining scores as administration had promised! SD 2 Instead, Reading scores remained flat, and overall Math marks drastically plummeted seven percent. EXP 2 Greater frequency of both student and teacher absences coupled with classroom time-wasting were to blame. SD 3 This could have easily been foreseen had the leadership of our school examined our over-tested, over-stressed atmosphere. CS: Therefore, I am ardently opposed to lengthening days at any Middle school in America!

Note: Hyphenated words generally count as one word in a sentence. Also, the writer only used the word 'I' twice in keeping with repetition free. One was in the first sentence and one in the last, spreading them far apart.

Likewise, 'administration' in (EXP 1) is replaced with the words 'leadership of our school' (SD 3).

Schooldays, school-day, and days are all different words even though they have similar meanings; these meet Repetition free as well.

Lastly, I tried my best to remain within 15 words or less; if you rarely have 16 words it is okay. But make it a habit to edit the sentence down to the established limit.

The Closing sentence provides a definite stance or position for the reader.

Both of these introductions meet the requirements of the GREAT Burger checklist.

Now we can begin on our Body Paragraphs. Make certain that you have your adjective, adverb, and transition sheets out to choose non-predictable terms. Let's use our planner to compose BP1, BP2, & BP3.

BP1:   TS Teenagers already have a lot to deal with, and they simply tune out! EXP 1a Specifically, we go to lunch remarkably late and that definitely does not help us focus. SD 1 Instead, we re-enter our later classes and display exhausted behaviors. SD 2 A visitor would mainly notice more frequent yawns and stretches during this extended hour period. SD 3 Furthermore, other classmates intentionally sassed teachers, and laid their heads on their desks. EXP 1c As a result, a larger portion of my peers cannot apply concepts on tests that the teacher just reviewed. SD 4 My friends get to about the fourth test item, and tragically they just go blank. CS Perhaps, this vividly explains why remaining in school longer than a workday is unwise.

BP2:   TS In addition, this cost-cutting measure unexpectedly made it harder on teachers to do their jobs. EXP 2a Already overstressed educators have been given a greater challenge in planning and implementing instruction. SD 1 Thus, they become resistant and apathetically passed out more worksheets; we weren't learning that way! SD 2 Both instructors and pupils emotionally decided to disobey this burdensome regulation. EXP 2b Moreover, teachers can sometimes cope with this hardship in harsher ways. SD 3 Picture an environment where the slightest giggling, off-task horseplay or confusion is answered with bitterness. SD 4 Personally, I recall one day when my snickering at a joke got me a detention. SD 5 This happened without a warning, reprimand or anything; it was right off the bat. CS The removal of empathy or compassion from my teachers is just too much to pay!

BP3:   TS Huge portions of our student body concur that this rule robs them of social time. EXP 3b Many relish the days when we could go home and watch our favorite cartoons. SD 1 After relaxing our bodies, we would be in a much better position to face challenging homework. SD 2 So we would typically perform better on these assignments. SD 3 With our extra-curricular activities, we constantly go straight to drudgery, and have no lives afterwards. EXP 3c Also, it is important that every teenager spend time with his or her family members. SD 4 How can we improve our coping skills if we are constantly busy, living like hermits? CS: We need to take family communication seriously and not undercut it with anything else!

Terrific Body Paragraphs 1, 2, & 3 came directly from our planner. 2 EXPs were used for each Body paragraph to present 'twice the proof' to our audience. The supporting details (SDs) were made up from my mind to bolster the effectiveness of each EXP.

Now let's use our Four Innovative Conclusion Techniques to draft two captivating Conclusion paragraph.

Conclusion # 1:   TS Therefore, it was a total mistake for our administration to have implemented the extra hour policy. SD 1 Students really can't focus, teachers truly can't take it, and it robs us of social time! EXP 1 Home economics and another elective could be shortened by fifteen minutes each. SD 2 In this scenario, everyone wins since it offers a half-hour of extra instruction while not actually lengthening each day. EXP 2 Perhaps, a teacher/administrator conference could positively assist instructors on better time management. SD 3 By removing prolonged, ineffective methods our school may be able to excel without schedule changes! CS Also, our principal should remove his misguided focus from length of instruction to its quality.
(New Solution To Problem, New Moral Lesson)

Note: EXP 1 offers a great solution, EXP 2 offers another cogent solution; and CS offers a new moral lesson. All of these make it effective, and not dwell on three reasons; summed up in SD 1.

Conclusion # 2:   TS Why should teachers and students endure the extra hour when our grades have declined? SD 1 Students can't actually focus, instructors can't stand it, and we lack family interaction. EXP 1 Twenty-five percent of students will leave in three years! SD 2 That is if we blindly allow this failed policy to continue. EXP 2 Also, teachers may begin 'teaching to the test' instead of offering pupils breadth of material. SD 3 This would be more injurious than the longer day itself. CS Every parent at Anthony Arnold Middle School should register a complaint with the principal's office.

(Look into the Future, Call to Action)

> Note: EXP 1 provides us with a three-year look into the future, EXP 2 is a secondary look into the future about teaching techniques, and finally CS is a universal call-to-action aimed at parents.

You can see for yourselves just how well this paragraph meets the GREAT Burger checklist.

'Extra Hour' School-day Sample
(GREAT Burger Persuasive Essay)

At first, I held unwavering support for longer schooldays, believing it would improve pupil performance. Then, our practice assessment scores of the state test came out; quite disappointing! Adding an hour to the school-day had not staved off declining scores as administration had promised! Instead, Reading scores remained flat, and overall Math marks drastically plummeted seven percent. Greater frequency of both student and teacher absences coupled with classroom time-wasting were to blame. This could have easily been foreseen had the leadership of our school examined our over-tested, over-stressed atmosphere. Therefore, I am ardently opposed to lengthening days at any Middle school in America!

Teenagers already have a lot to deal with, and they simply tune out! Specifically, we go to lunch remarkably late and that definitely does not help us focus. Instead, we re-enter our later classes and display exhausted behaviors. A visitor would mainly notice more frequent yawns and stretches during this extended hour period. Furthermore, other classmates intentionally sassed teachers, and laid their heads on their desks. As a result, a larger portion of my peers cannot apply concepts on tests that the teacher just reviewed. My friends get to about the fourth test item, and tragically they just go blank. Perhaps, this vividly explains why remaining in school longer than a workday is unwise.

In addition, this cost-cutting measure unexpectedly made it harder on teachers to do their jobs. Already overstressed educators have been given a greater challenge in planning and implementing instruction. Thus, they become resistant and apathetically passed out more worksheets; we weren't learning that way! Both instructors and pupils emotionally decided to disobey this burdensome regulation. Moreover, teachers can sometimes cope with this hardship in harsher ways. Picture an environment where the slightest giggling, off-task horseplay or confusion is answered with bitterness. Personally, I recall one day when my snickering at a joke got me a detention. This happened without a warning, reprimand or anything; it was right off the bat. The removal of empathy or compassion from my teachers is just too much to pay!

Huge portions of our student body concur that this rule robs them of social time. Many relish the days when we could go home and watch our favorite cartoons. After relaxing our bodies, we would be in a much better position to face challenging homework. So, we would typically perform better on these assignments. With our extra-curricular activities, we constantly go straight to drudgery, and have no lives afterwards. Also, it is important that every teenager spend time with his or her family members. How can we improve our coping skills if we are constantly busy, living like hermits? We need to take family communication seriously and not undercut it with anything else!

Therefore, it was a total mistake for our administration to have implemented the extra hour policy. Students really can't focus, teachers truly can't take it, and it robs us of social time! Home economics and another elective could be shortened by fifteen minutes each. In this scenario, everyone wins since it offers a half-hour of extra instruction while not actually lengthening each day. Perhaps, a teacher/administrator conference could positively assist instructors on better time management. By removing prolonged, ineffective methods our school may be able to excel without schedule changes! Also, our principal should remove his misguided focus from length of instruction to its quality.

(© 2010, Persuasive Essay Sample, GREAT Burger Essay Workshop)

For argument's sake, let's use the Florida Writes Rubric to assess the quality of the previous essay.

Florida Writing Assessment Program (FLORIDA WRITES!)
Assessment Home | Florida Writes Home

Score Points in Rubric

The rubric further interprets the four major areas of consideration into levels of achievement. This rubric was used to score papers in Spring 2010.

6 Points   The writing is focused, purposeful, and reflects insight into the writing situation. The paper conveys a sense of completeness and wholeness with adherence to the main idea, and its organizational pattern provides for a logical progression of ideas. The support is substantial, specific, relevant, concrete, and/or illustrative. The paper demonstrates a commitment to and an involvement with the subject, clarity in presentation of ideas, and may use creative writing strategies appropriate to the purpose of the paper. The writing demonstrates a mature command of language (word choice) with freshness of expression. Sentence structure is varied, and sentences are complete except when fragments are used purposefully. Few, if any, convention errors occur in mechanics, usage, and punctuation.

5 Points   The writing focuses on the topic, and its organizational pattern provides for a progression of ideas, although some lapses may occur. The paper conveys a sense of completeness or wholeness. The support is ample. The writing demonstrates a mature command of language, including precision in word choice. There is variation in sentence structure, and, with rare exceptions, sentences are complete except when fragments are used purposefully. The paper generally follows the conventions of mechanics, usage, and spelling.

4 Points   The writing is generally focused on the topic but may include extraneous or loosely related material. An organizational pattern is apparent, although some lapses may occur. The paper exhibits some sense of completeness or wholeness. The support, including word choice, is adequate, although development may be uneven. There is little variation in sentence structure, and most sentences are complete. The paper generally follows the conventions of mechanics, usage, and spelling.

3 Points   The writing is generally focused on the topic but may include extraneous or loosely related material. An organizational pattern has been attempted, but the paper may lack a sense of completeness or wholeness. Some support is included, but development is erratic. Word choice is adequate but may be limited, predictable, or occasionally vague. There is little, if any, variation in sentence structure. Knowledge of the conventions of mechanics and usage is usually demonstrated, and commonly used words are usually spelled correctly.

2 Points   The writing is related to the topic but include extraneous or loosely related material. Little evidence of an organizational pattern may be demonstrated, and the paper may lack a sense of completeness or wholeness. Development of support is inadequate or illogical. Word choice is limited, inappropriate or vague. There is little, if any, variation in sentence structure, and gross errors in sentence structure may occur. Errors in basic conventions of mechanics and usage may occur, and commonly used words may be misspelled.

1 Point   The writing may only minimally address the topic. The paper is a fragmentary or incoherent listing of related ideas or sentences or both. Little, if any, development of support or an organizational pattern or both is apparent. Limited or inappropriate word choice may obscure meaning. Gross errors in sentence structure and usage may impede communication. Frequent and blatant errors may occur in the basic conventions of mechanics and usage, and commonly used words may be misspelled.

Unscorable

The paper is unscorable because

- the response is not related to what the prompt requested the student to do.
- the response is simply a rewording of the prompt.
- the response is a copy of a published work.
- the student refused to write.
- the response is illegible.
- the response is incomprehensible (words are arranged in such a way that no meaning is conveyed).
- the response contains an insufficient amount of writing to determine if the student was attempting to address the prompt.
- the writing folder is blank.

March 31, 2011, Florida Writing Assessment Program (FLORIDA WRITES!),
http://fldoe.org/asp/fw/fwaprubr.asp

Understand that this Florida Writes Rubric works from the bottom up as it is normally used. So let's look back at the previous essay and assess it together:

a.) The writing surpasses the Unscorable test. It has a definite subject matter, contains enough writing, and it is on-topic.

b.) The writing surpasses a score of '1': It does not minimally address the Memorable Vacation Prompt. Neither does the writing resort to simplistic listing of ideas, limited word choice, or erratic grammar. The sentence structures are varied. They are not filled with common misspellings, frequent errors, or disorganized ideas.

c.) The writing surpasses a score of '2': The writing is more than related to the prompt, and avoids extraneous or unrelated details. The entire essay is presented in an organized pattern, and has a great sense of completeness or wholeness. Development of support is twice as much as a normal essay instead of inadequate or illogical. The essay contains a lot of sentence variation, and word choice is precisely picked. Lots of support is included and no common misspellings or lapses in conventions are noticed. Mechanics and usage are well done.

d.) The writing surpasses a score of '3': This writing exceeds the level of generally focused. It doesn't include extraneous or loosely related material. Its organizational pattern is well established and Support is plenteous. Refreshing, specific word choice demonstrates a breadth of vocabulary knowledge. Ample variation of sentence structures and knowledge of the conventions of mechanics and usage are fully evident. No misspellings are presented.

e.) The writing surpasses a score of '4': The writing has a high level of focus and excludes extraneous or loosely related material. It only uses pertinent examples to answer the essay prompt. No lapses in the organizational pattern and the piece exhibits an overwhelming wholeness or completeness. The support, including word choice, is more than ample; six justifications instead of three reasons. Plenty of sentence variation is seen throughout the essay. Development of support is quite evenly distributed between body paragraphs and all sentences are complete. The paper follows the conventions of spelling, grammar, and usage very well.

f.) The writing surpasses a score of '5': The writing has focused on the topic well; and rare/or no lapses occur. The piece has provided a progression of ideas. The paper conveys a sense of completeness or wholeness. The support is at least ample. The essay includes 6 major 'mental snapshots instead of three justifications for the stance. There precision in word choice and consistent sentence variation in the essay. There are no fragments and/or if there are, they are intentional and for a desired effect. The paper overwhelmingly

---

Note: The three major differences between a 4 or 5 Writing score are:

1. 'Support is ample' in a 5-score, instead of 'support is adequate' in a 4-score?   Yes, support more than ample.

2. 'Mature command of language' for a 5-score, instead of a 4 score?   Yes, mature command of language.

3. 'Much sentence variation' in 5-score instead of 'little variation in sentence structure'   Yes, varied sentence structures.

---

g.) The writing meets the level a score of '6': The writing is focused, purposeful, and very insightful about the writing situation. The paper conveys a sense of completeness and wholeness with adherence to the main idea, and its organizational pattern provides for a logical progression of ideas. The overwhelming support is substantial, specific, relevant, concrete, and/or illustrative. The paper demonstrates a commitment to and an involvement with the subject by using six mini-stories. It also shows clarity in presentation of ideas, and uses creative writing strategies throughout the entire essay; they are appropriate to the prompt's purpose. The writing demonstrates a mature command of language (word choice) with 'personalized' freshness of expression. Sentence structure is varied, and sentences are complete. There are no stand-alone fragments. Few, if any, convention errors occur in mechanics, usage, and punctuation.

Notwithstanding, we have just proved that the GREAT Burger Method Expository Sample does meet the strictest guideline of the Florida Writes Rubric. This is not surprising to me since I created it taking this very rubric into consideration nearly seven years ago.

| # GREAT Burger Workshop Results

(Two Classwide samples from my five 2008-2009 English classes)

Thus far, you have done an exemplary job of presenting and refining the twelve weeks of bell ringers with your classes. By now, you've witnessed how easily implemented and entertaining some of these activities could be. Then, you went through the admittedly intense two to three week essay workshop to tighten their writing skills. I already know how tired you must be, but the feeling of accomplishment at this point must be awe-inspiring.

You are about to witness the writings culminating from a three week period of instruction. These were carefully composed during a preplanned portion of the 2008-2009 school year. I am still proud of those 8th graders. These are some examples of the caliber of work each of your classes should yield as well. I wanted you to see for yourselves how the same exact prompt could yield diverse, imaginative responses. This was even when some of the EXPs were similar.

In retrospect, the writing workshop was one of the toughest challenges I had to face. It called for me to amiably prepare students, and constantly re-examine their checklists. Ultimately, it was my duty to control or at least calibrate how successfully my students were. My mission was to maintain a delicate balance between asserting my authority and being the cheerful facilitator. Plainly, I had to stay on their backs to drive them into success without turning them off.

If the students found it tough, this workshop would be quite tedious for teachers. Some reasons why were because I had to rewrite on the same prompt three times a day. Repeating the same two introductions over and over was typically exhausting. This was so because I had to appear as if each Introduction was a fresh product when some of it invariably was redone. It basically felt that same for the body paragraphs, and the two conclusions.

Then, there is the fact that eight graders are largely impatient and seek immediate gratification. So, professionals have to constrain themselves to use their 'friendly power' in keeping them on track. Take a peek at the culmination of my arduous work with my students. All the while, ask yourselves if these paragraphs are creative, focused, convincing, and grammatically sound.

The format you will see five times is exactly the way I did it. It will demonstrate how I utilized the smart board to present the GREAT Burger essay workshop. Of course, there was a lot of editing, rewording, sentence shortening, probing for better adjectives, adverbs, and transitions along the way. That is exactly what I want you to do. Allow your students to slowly improve the sentences and paragraphs so they grasp the concepts firmly. Also, pay close attention to how the two EXPs from each column of the planner allowed us to construct very juicy body paragraphs.

"MY PERFECT EXPOSITORY ESSAY" BY PERIOD 1 (2008-2009 SCHOOL YEAR)

The purpose of expository writing is to explain, define, or tell how to do something by giving information.

(2007-2008 Florida Comprehensive Assessment Test Released Writing Prompt)

Read: Most teenagers have chores.
Think: Think about why it is important for teenagers to have chores.
Explain: Now write to explain why it is important for teenagers to have chores.

	Subj: Teens should have chores.	
Justification #1: Builds character/discipline.	**Justification #2:** Prepares young for adult responsibilities	**Justification #3:** Relieves parents of workload.
EXP 1: Washing clothes builds patience	**EXP 1:** Cooking, for when mom not home.	**EXP 1:** Vacuuming floor, helps dad de-stress (X)
EXP 2: Caring for a dog, follows routine	**EXP 2:** babysitting, caring for innocents	**EXP 2:** Washing the car saves parents saves money
EXP 3: Mowing the lawn, exercise (X)	**EXP 3:** allowance, manage money (X)	**EXP 3:** Cleaning bathrooms, relax in a bubble bath

Intros: *Always insightful, creative, and unpredictable with a Clincher at the end!*

Five Types of Introductions: Three Expansions, Personal Testimony, Historical Review, Anecdote, and Other Factors (newspaper/news item/Television Shows, etc.).

Other Factors Introduction: 1/29/09

From the show 'George Lopez', I was absolutely disturbed when Angie completed all the chores. It seemed as if she were a lowly maid trapped in a miserable household. This was the incident that actually switched my entire perspective. Many of the leading characters' explosive quarrels might have been prevented if Max helped out. Perhaps, Carmen, the ungrateful teenager, could have used the dishwasher now and then. Even the grandmother only sat around their home drinking, smoking, and insulting her son. Likewise, millions of families would positively benefit from everyone getting involved with the chores.

Historical Review Introduction:

On Christmas Eve, my overworked and highly stressed mother plopped down on our leather futon. She had finally finished cooking for twenty-five relatives, and wrapped all the presents. Meanwhile, I could see the sheer desperation in her eyes as she glared into an absolute disaster zone. I resisted the temptation to be selfish, and instead washed every dish and wiped the countertops. Then, my nearly tearful mother released a heartfelt sigh of relief. She showed me how much my efforts made her Christmas that much better. So, I gained a new empathy for those unfortunate folks who always do chores alone.

*Body Paragraph Goal: 2 vivid EXPANSIONS that provide complete mental pictures for the reader.

Period 1: Body Paragraphs 1, 2, & 3.

BP1:   Initially, adolescents should definitely work around the traditional household to build character and discipline. For instance, the process of washing clothes develops a greater level of patience. Sorting, bleaching, tumbling, drying, and folding may seem never-ending, but it is an orderly cycle. By doing so, one absolutely learns to value the time parents spend finishing it. Another way to cultivate patience is caring for the family's Cocker Spaniel. By walking, then feeding, and even bathing Sparky, it teaches control of a teenager's temper. This is a valuable coping skill for childhood and adulthood.

BP 2:   Everyone should actually chip in with housework to prepare for adult responsibilities. To illustrate, mom would find it a tremendous and welcome surprise to eat a home-cooked meal. Imagine preparing a savory Arroz con Pollo; my mom's favorite dish. She'd be pleased, and making this meal would have been practice for my college years. Likewise, attentively caring for my smaller sibling would save lots of teaching time. Feeding Luna, burping her, and entertaining her would be an invaluable experience. Furthermore, it would definitely ready me for my own children someday.

BP 3:   In addition, being helpful in everyday chores provides an immense relief from parents' workloads. For example, if my brother Jerry washed our Lexus 300XL every weekend, he'd save dad hours. My father Jonathan could spend more time on Saturdays completing projects in his garage instead. In fact, my sibling Jerry would have saved my dad sixty dollars in a single month! My eldest sister Karmen could ensure that my mother's evening went more smoothly. After an exhausting workday she could have already tidied up the bathrooms. Compassionately, Karmen could run my mom's steaming hot bathwater and add her favorite bubble bath. No doubt, this would put my mother at ease; less complaining, less disciplining that night.

Conclusion Paragraphs: should not simply repeat the three reasons; sum those up in a single sentence; then complete two of the four following conclusion techniques:

1. Look into the future
2. Call to Action,
3. New Moral Lesson
4. New Solution to the Problem

Conc 1: In summary, teenagers should involve themselves in chores since they build character, responsibility, and lightens burdens. In 2011, many parents will be much more tranquil and will improve their job performances. Their worksite efficiency might increase significantly by twenty-three percent. Perhaps, young adults should not be so focused on their own desires. Because the more you help your parents, the greater your privileges will become. Hence, this modern world would flourish into a more civil place.

(Combined Look into future & New Moral Lesson)

Conc 2: Ultimately, housework is not to be avoided since it fosters discipline, maturity, and de-stresses. Every single adolescent should lend a hand to make everyone's lives easier. Meaning, filling the dishwasher or picking up after themselves does not inconvenience them at all. They spend much more time talking on the telephone or texting their friends. Instead of waking up at 11:30 AM or watching Cartoon Network, many chores could be completed. Another solution could be to have three different hampers for their clothes. If they filled them correctly, then they would already be sorting their laundry. There are many short-cuts for cleaning that could be implemented to reduce cleaning time and effort.

(Combined Call to Action & New Solutions to the Problem)

Period 1 has interactively written to at least two types of imaginative Introductions, three body, paragraphs, and at least two Conclusion techniques over a two week period. Now we can review the entire essay they drafted in its entirety. They chose their best Intro, their body paragraphs, & one conclusion:

Historical Review Introduction:

On Christmas Eve, my overworked and highly stressed mother plopped down onto our leather futon. She had finally finished cooking for twenty-five relatives, and wrapped all the presents. Meanwhile, I could see the sheer desperation in her eyes as she glared into an absolute disaster zone. I resisted the temptation to be selfish, and instead washed every dish and wiped the countertops. Then, my nearly tearful mother released a heartfelt sigh of relief. She showed me how much my efforts made her Christmas that much better. So, I gained a new empathy for those unfortunate folks who always do chores alone.

Initially, adolescents should definitely work around the traditional household to build character and discipline. For instance, the process of washing clothes develops a greater level of patience. Sorting, bleaching, tumbling, drying, and folding may seem never-ending, but it is an orderly cycle. By doing so, one absolutely learns to value the time parents spend finishing it. Another way to cultivate patience is caring for the family's Cocker Spaniel. By walking, then feeding, and even bathing Sparky, it teaches control of a teenager's temperament. This is a valuable coping skill for childhood and adulthood.

Everyone should actually chip in with housework to prepare for adult responsibilities. To illustrate, mom would find it a tremendous and welcome surprise to eat a home-cooked meal. Imagine preparing a savory Arroz con Pollo; my mom's favorite dish. She'd be pleased, and making this meal would have been practice for my college years. Likewise, attentively caring for my smaller sibling would save lots of teaching time. Feeding Luna, burping her, and entertaining her would be an invaluable experience. Furthermore, it would definitely ready me for my own children someday.

In addition, being helpful in everyday chores provides an immense relief from parents' workloads. For example, if my brother Jerry washed our Lexus 300XL every weekend, he'd conserve dad's hours. My father Jonathan could spend more time on Saturdays completing projects in his garage instead. In fact, my sibling would save him sixty dollars in a single month! My eldest sister Karmen could ensure that my mother's evening went more smoothly. After an exhausting workday she could have already tidied up the bathrooms. Compassionately, Karmen could run my mom's steaming hot bathwater and add her favorite bubble bath. No doubt, this would put my mother at ease; less complaining, less disciplining that night.

In summary, teenagers should involve themselves in chores since they build character, responsibility, and lightens burdens. In 2011, many parents will be much more tranquil and will improve their job performances. Their worksite efficiency might increase significantly by twenty-three percent. Perhaps, young adults should not be so focused on their own desires. Because the more you help your parents, the greater your privileges will become. Hence, this modern world would flourish into a more civil place.

(Combined Look into future & New Moral Lesson Conclusion)

"MY PERFECT EXPOSITORY ESSAY" BY PERIOD 5 (2008-2009 SCHOOL YEAR)

(2007-2008 Florida Comprehensive Assessment Test: Released Writing Prompt)

Read: Most teenagers have chores.

Think: Think about why it is important for teenagers to have chores.

Explain: Now write to explain why it is important for teenagers to have chores.

	Topic: Why Teenagers have chores.	
Justification #1: Teaches youngsters responsibility & useful habits	**Justification #2:** Helps parents from being overwhelmed	**Justification #3:** Stay out of trouble.
EXP 1: Washing dishes builds patience.	**EXP 1:** Clean own bedroom without being asked **(X)**	**EXP 1:** Washing your clothes keeps you busy **(X)**
EXP 2: Taking out trash, scheduling **(X)**	**EXP 2:** Vacuuming/dusting the living room to assist	**EXP 2:** Babysitting uses time wisely
EXP 3: Ironing clothes, personal hygiene.	**EXP 3:** Cooking a meal for tired mother	**EXP 3:** Caring for a pet occupies time

Intros: Always insightful, creative, and unpredictable with a Clincher at the end!

Five Types of Introductions: Three Expansions, Personal Testimony, Historical Review, Anecdote, and Other Factors (newspaper/news item/Television Shows, etc.).

Other Factors Introduction: 1/29/09

During my earliest years, the Flintstones was a cartoon in which Wilma worked extremely hard. I have vivid memories of her tirelessly washing dishes, babysitting, and sweeping out her rock-home. Moreover, it is quite disappointing to notice that many families are still run similarly today. For example, most women are definitely considered homemakers and they feel trapped by their responsibilities. Therefore, it would be much more advantageous for modern teenagers to share the workload.

Historical Review Introduction:

On Thanksgiving, many delicious aromas were airborne as I watched mom plummet onto the couch. She was apparently exhausted from preparing our wonderful feast all night long. Then, my compassionate thoughts led me to wash the dishes, wipe the countertops, and mop. Mom gratefully hugged me, and kissed my cheeks with tears in her eyes. From then on, I truly recognized the value of chipping in with our daily chores.

*Body Paragraph Goal: 6 vivid EXPANSIONS that provide complete mental pictures for the reader.

Body Paragraphs 1, 2, & 3:

BP 1: Primarily, teenagers should share the chores because it certainly teaches them responsibility and useful habits. The entire process of hand-washing dishes builds a greater level of patience. For instance, scrubbing greasy pans, rinsing soap suds, and then drying the silverware seem never-ending. This would assist me in understanding how much effort my parents normally put into it. Similarly, it would be shockingly preposterous to drag into a job interview with a wrinkled suit! Teenagers could gradually learn to present themselves by ironing their own slacks and shirts right now. Obviously, this would improve personal hygiene and help their social lives.

BP2: Also, lending a hand with the daily chores prevents my parents from being overwhelmed. One moment to remember would be when my overstressed guardian does not have to vacuum. Instead, she could finally relax in a warm bubble bath and forget her worries. Her tense muscles could be reinvigorated and rejuvenated so that she could manage another day. Meanwhile, I could ponder the positive reaction I would get after making zesty Fettuccini Alfredo. My mom Sonja would quickly bite into the crispy Texas toast and then gracefully complement me. This is another way to remove a part of the burden from my caretaker's shoulders.

BP3:   In addition, staying out of trouble is absolutely essential for teenagers. A responsibility like babysitting lends itself to keeping young adults inside of the house. This is especially true when caring for an infant who needs constant feeding, burping, and cleaning. Essentially, this chore would also prevent teens from being persuaded by 'peer pressure'. In like fashion, grooming and maintaining a Pomeranian named Foxy would be extremely constructive. Remembering her leash, walking her regularly, and brushing her thick fur are time consuming. Yet, these menial tasks are necessary, and would also occupy my idle hands; preventing distractions.

Conclusion Paragraphs: should not simply repeat the three reasons; sum those up in a single sentence; then complete at least two of the four following conclusion techniques:

1. Look into the future
2. Call to Action,
3. New Moral Lesson
4. New Solution to the Problem

Conc 1: Therefore, completing chores actually teaches responsibility, relieves parent's burdens, and keeps teenagers from peer pressure. By 2012, millions of guardians will dramatically increase their job performances. Larger drops in stress levels will then produce pretty fulfilled caretakers and more peaceful home-lives. Moreover, President Obama's message of hope will resonate that much clearer in citizens' minds. Perhaps, American adolescents should finally understand that doing their 'fair share' is essential. Another important moral is that clearing the table or taking out trash is no inconvenience. If they are assisting their parents, surely they are actually helping themselves.

(Look into the Future and New Moral Lessons)

Conc. 2: Teen diligence regarding housework is necessary to engender responsibility, relaxation, and independence. Thus, the time has come for tens of millions of my peers to acknowledge their duties! They should sincerely remove the focus from their own desires, to aiding their households. By doing this, these youths can convince their younger relatives to also chip in. Maybe, bigger brothers can patiently show their smaller sisters how to fold clothes. This would also conserve precious time at home. In addition, including more siblings definitely decreases the overall amount of effort each child would expend.

(Call to action and New Solution to the problem)

Period 5 has interactively written their two Introduction types, three Body Paragraphs, and two Conclusions with me over a two-week period. Later on, I taught two more Conclusions techniques, and two more Introduction types. Now, view their entire essay and assess it!

Other Factors Introduction:

During my earliest years, the Flintstones was a cartoon in which Wilma worked extremely hard. I have vivid memories of her tirelessly washing dishes, babysitting, and sweeping out her rock-home. Moreover, it is quite disappointing to notice that many families are still run similarly today. For example, most women are stereotypically considered homemakers and they feel trapped by their responsibilities. Therefore, it would be much more advantageous for modern teenagers to share the workload.

Primarily, teenagers should share the chores because it certainly teaches them responsibility and useful habits. The entire process of hand-washing dishes builds a greater level of patience. For instance, scrubbing greasy pans, rinsing soap suds, and then drying the silverware seem never-ending. This would assist me in understanding how much effort my parents normally put into it. Similarly, it would be shockingly preposterous to drag into a job interview with a wrinkled suit! Teenagers could gradually learn to present themselves by ironing their own slacks and shirts right now. Obviously, this would improve personal hygiene and help their social lives.

Also, lending a hand with the daily chores prevents my parents from being overwhelmed. One moment to remember would be when my overstressed guardian does not have to vacuum. Instead, she could finally relax in a warm bubble bath and forget her worries. Her tense muscles could be reinvigorated and rejuvenated so that she could manage another day. Meanwhile, I could ponder the positive reaction I would get after making zesty Fettuccini Alfredo. My mom Sonja would quickly bite into the crispy Texas toast and then gracefully complement me. This is another way to remove a part of the burden from my caretaker's shoulders.

In addition, staying out of trouble is absolutely essential for teenagers. A responsibility like babysitting lends itself to keeping young adults inside of the house. This is especially true when caring for an infant who needs constant feeding, burping, and cleaning. Essentially, this chore would also prevent teens from being persuaded by 'peer pressure'. In like fashion, grooming and maintaining a Pomeranian named Foxy would be extremely constructive. Remembering her leash, walking her regularly, and brushing her thick fur are time consuming. Yet, these menial tasks are necessary, and would also occupy my idle hands; preventing distractions.

Teen diligence regarding housework is vital in producing responsibility, relaxation, and independence. Thus, the time has come for tens of millions of my peers to acknowledge their duties! They should sincerely remove the focus from their own desires, to aiding their households. By doing this, these youths can convince their younger relatives to also chip in. Maybe, bigger brothers can patiently show their smaller sisters how to fold clothes. This would also conserve precious time at home. In addition, including more siblings definitely decreases the overall amount of effort each child would expend.

(Call to Action and New Solution to the problem)

| # Comparison/Contrast Essays

10th Grade Smartboard & Student Samples
(2010-2011 School year)

The major objective of this essay type is to thoroughly evaluate why one particular stance is more beneficial or appreciable than the other.

When one is completing a Comparison, he or she is typically looking for the similarities in two objects, events, concepts, or ideas.

However, when one is drafting a Contrasting essay then he or she is normally finding both sides of the differences between two objects, events, concepts, or idea.

Consider the following writing prompt:

Read: A teacher named Mr. Simms recently moved to North Carolina and he always enjoyed Miami-style barbeque.

Think: critically recall how North Carolina barbeque differs from Miami ribs.

Explain: Persuade essay readers why Miami-styled ribs are better than N.C. ribs using at least three convincing reasons.

Obviously, the first step we must take is to complete a Comparison/Contrast Quick Essay Planner. It should take no longer than 12-15 minutes to complete.

Ground rules for planner:

1. Use creative Intro
2. Label the parts
3. Write in caveman—no time for complete sentences

N.C. barbeque versus Miami-style barbeque
(Contrasting Essay Quick Planner)

> **A. New intro type:**
>
> **Historical review Intro. (Neg.)**
>
> *Smithfield's for first time*

> **B. Preference** *(recall brief pos. experience)*
>
> *Contrast Mom's home cooking during Memorial Day (in a single sentence)*

> **C. Thesis Statement:** *clear statement of position/ stance.*
>
> Obviously, I prefer the tender, juicy Miami-style spareribs to North Carolina's pulled pork.

Activity/Justification #1: Easier to prepare	Activity/Justification #2: Less resources & time	Activity/Justification# 3: Better tasting
Exp. A1: Miami bbq-shorter process	**Exp. A2:** Invite football fans over noon, eat Miami ribs by 2 pm.	**Exp. A3:** MIA bbq uses fruit juice, brown sugar, & citrus fruits.
Exp. B1: N.C. shoulder- 8-12 hours to prepare	**Exp. B2:** Invite friends at noon, run out of gas, friends eat snacks, leave at 3	**Exp. B3:** N.C. bbq uses some sweet spices but too much vinegar

As = (A1, A2, & A3) = Your favorite stance: (Supporting EXPs why you prefer Miami BBQ)
Bs = (B1, B2, & B3) = Opposing your stance: (Opposing EXPs why N.C. pulled pork is not better)

Now let's write together 10th graders: Example of BPs 1, 2, & 3

Goal: Clearing up the Expansion process using the Quick Essay Planner

Miami bbq vs. N.C. bbq

TS My famished wife and I eagerly pulled into the half-filled parking lot of Smithfield's BBQ and Chicken. SD 1 After quickly ordering, our entrees did not actually appear to be what we expected. SD 2 The chicken seemed to be drenched in hot sauce, and the pork was served to us 'off the bone'. SD 3 Obviously, these were not the sweet, delectable ribs from family reunions and special holidays in Miami, Florida! TS Our sparsely eaten entrees; proof positive that we preferred Florida spareribs to North Carolina's pulled pork.

BP 1:   TS Of course, I absolutely crave Miami-styled ribs because they are easily prepared. (EXP A1) Imagine only having to thaw your pork spareribs for one and a half hours. SD 1 Then, one could casually soak the raw meat in a tasty marinade of brown sugar and citrus fruit. SD 2 My slab could then be cautiously placed on the blazing rack of a George Foreman grill. SD 3 Tasty, tender pork in only three hours seems like a God-send! (EXP B1) On the other hand, North Carolina pulled pork always takes much longer to prepare. SD 4 Defrosting a larger pork shoulder would likely take at least four hours to accomplish. SD 5 Next, the juices and tart vinegar take around three more hours to marinade themselves into the meat. CS: The smoker takes even more time; twelve hours ultimately elapses for pulled pork.

BP2:   TS Another aspect that makes Miami ribs more convenient is that they take less resources. (EXP A2) For instance, I could probably invite my fantasy football team over for a draft party at 11 AM. SD 2 While they were watching pre-Game Shows, I could quickly prepare my Miami-styled ribs. SD 3 After a shorter cooking time and less charcoal the Florida ribs would be ready for everyone to devour by kickoff. (EXP B2)-Besides that, North Carolina pork would definitely consume more charcoal to cook than Miami ribs. SD 4 The griller could use a gas grill; cooking would certainly 'hog up' this flammable liquid. SD 5-In either case, it means that more gas must be purchased to complete the pulled pork. CS Clearly, the Florida ribs leave more money in the cook's pocket.

BP3:   TS In addition, Miami ribs are preferable because they are clearly better tasting. (EXP A3) SD 1 These tender spareribs can be easily drenched in a coating of fruit juices. SD 2 This will gradually tenderize the meat. SD 2 Then, the experienced chef could ready his charcoal briquettes and hickory chips to perfection. SD 3 We gently slide the ribs onto the open-flame and until they are medium done. EXP B3-On the other hand, N.C. barbeque is literally soaked in a similar solution of spices, herbs, and brown sugar. SD 4 The entire pork shoulder is saturated in vinegar which makes the meat taste too bitter. SD 5 Therefore, the tenderness of the pork becomes overpowered by the tartness of it! CS It is hard to stomach strong, sour foods like that!

Conclusion: **TS** Thus, it truly seems that the contest between Florida and N.C.'s pork is no contest at all. **SD 1** (Look into the Future) If our Fayetteville, Raleigh, and Charlotte cooks don't vary their recipes, Miami rib restaurants will begin popping up. **SD 2** Then, the N.C. barbeque will soon become a less popular Southern dish. **SD 3** (New Solution) I immediately urge more N.C. restaurant owners to begin offering Miami style ribs on their menus to accommodate more customers. **SD 4** By doing so, they will not lose out financially when this radical change occurs. **SD 5** (Call to Action) The USDA could actively impose rules to ensure fairness at barbeque competitions nationwide. Everyone should have the right to choose!

*Now that all five of my 10th grade classes were responsible for one paragraph, we can put them together. Let's assess this Contrasting essay in its complete state.

COMPARISON/CONTRAST ESSAY ON SMARTBOARD MIAMI-STYLED BBQ VS. NORTH CAROLINA PULLED PORK

My famished wife and I eagerly pulled into the half-filled parking lot of Smithfield's BBQ and Chicken. After quickly ordering, our entrees did not actually appear to be what we expected. The chicken seemed to be drenched in hot sauce, and the pork was served to us 'off the bone'. Obviously, these were not the sweet, delectable ribs from family reunions and special holidays in Miami, Florida! Our sparsely eaten entrees: proof positive that we preferred Florida spareribs over North Carolina's pulled pork.

Of course, I absolutely crave Miami-styled ribs because they are easily prepared. Imagine only having to thaw your pork spareribs for one and a half hours. Then, one could casually soak the raw meat in a tasty marinade of brown sugar and citrus fruit. My slab could then be cautiously placed on the blazing rack of a George Foreman grill. Tasty, tender pork in only three hours seems like a God-send! On the other hand, North Carolina pulled pork always takes much longer to prepare. Defrosting a larger pork shoulder would likely take at least four hours to accomplish. Next, the juices and tart vinegar take around three more hours to marinade themselves into the meat. The smoker takes even more time; twelve hours ultimately elapses for pulled pork.

Another aspect that makes Miami ribs more convenient is that they utilize less resources. For instance, I could probably invite my fantasy football team over for a draft party at 11 AM. While they were watching pre-Game Shows, I could quickly prepare my Miami-styled ribs. After a shorter cooking time and less charcoal the Florida ribs would be ready for everyone to devour by kickoff. Besides that, North Carolina pork would definitely consume more charcoal to cook than Miami ribs. More hours slow cooking requires plenty of briquettes! Even if the griller used a gas grill; the NC brand would certainly 'hog up' propane. Clearly, the Florida ribs leave more money in the cook's pocket.

In addition, Miami ribs are preferable because they are clearly better-tasting. These tender spareribs can be easily drenched in a coating of fruit juices. This will gradually tenderize the meat. Then, the experienced chef could ready his charcoal briquettes and hickory chips to perfection. We gently slide the ribs onto the open-flame and until they are medium done. On the other hand, N.C. barbeque is literally soaked in a similar solution of spices, herbs, and brown sugar. The entire pork shoulder is saturated in vinegar which makes the meat taste too bitter. Therefore, the tenderness of the pork becomes overpowered by the tartness of it! It is hard to stomach strong, sour foods like that!

Thus, it truly seems that the contest between Florida and N.C.'s pork is no contest at all. If our Fayetteville, Raleigh, and Charlotte cooks don't vary their recipes, Miami rib restaurants will begin popping up. Then, the N.C. barbeque will soon become a less popular Southern dish. I immediately urge more N.C. restaurant owners to begin offering Miami style ribs on their menus to accommodate more customers. By doing so, they will not lose out financially when this radical change occurs. The USDA could actively impose rules to ensure fairness at barbeque competitions nationwide. Everyone should have the right to choose.

Note: My students were so hungry and often complained about the way the vivid imagery was making their stomachs growl. Yet, it was one method to make certain I maintained their attention as we worked on the Smartboard. I had my 10th graders work on another Comparison/Contrast Essay as soon as possible.

As we were reading Elie Wiesel's Night, there was a teachable moment. Previously, I had already passed out a handout that expected the students to list 5 major differences and 5 major similarities. The completion of that activity uniquely prepared them to contrast the living conditions of the Concentration camps.

Comparison/Contrast Prompt:

The holocaust presented terribly difficult living conditions for millions of Jews across Europe. Ponder the advantages and disadvantages of both the Birkenau and Buna Concentration camps. Then, contrast three major differences between these 'labor houses' using vivid examples from the novel Night by Elie Wiesel. (Be sure to conform to GREAT Burger checklist).

Next, I will share an exemplary student sample based upon Elie Wiesel's Nobel Prize winning work:

You'll notice how the writer interweaves themselves into the historical review as if she were there. This is a powerful allusion technique that helps support her stance in this Comparison/Contrast essay.

Secondly, examine the breadth and depth of her responses. She does not sound like she is listing details as she tells the story. Instead, she provides a sequential set of details for the first side of the comparison, and then the same for the second. The effect is even-handed support for her preferred concentration camp, (if there could be such a thing). Then, she explains why she opposes a similar trait of the feared concentration camp.

Check out her careful choices of adjectives which are usually complex. Also, this formal writing mainly adheres to the three –ly adverb in the paragraphs. The essay contains vivid adjectives throughout, and each body paragraph does create 'mental snapshots' that the readers can envision. This is opposed to just being chatty with no real depth.

Admittedly, some of her sentences are over 15 words but they are not run-ons. (Avoiding run-ons is the primary purpose of imposing a word limit on sentences). Another positive was her choice to incorporate varying sentence structures-semi-colons, commas, etc.

Her stance is crystal clear and she masterfully thrusts the reader towards her contentions. One cannot help but notice the freshness of expression that the paper presents. Her unencumbered style truly shines a light on the atrocities at both camps.

In the Conclusion, the author uses a flashback to bring herself back to the present. Then, she shares at least two moral lessons she gained from the haunting experience. These are advanced techniques that she uses instead of boring the reader with an entire paragraph of the three reasons.

You could have groups in your class score this paper using the GREAT Burger checklist. Then, they can examine, firsthand, the level of writing that is expected of them.

GREAT BURGER INDEED! (REVISION) 10TH GRADE

It's been 67 years, but I still have the memories of my first hours at Birkenau. We spent days on those horridly cramped trains only to arrive at the gates of the hell. The smell of burning flesh met us as we escaped the clutches of the metal cans. As we separated from the men, ahead we saw the fiery pits of death. Later, we would soon realize that life in on camp would not be as brutal and terrifying. Therefore, my better memories of that awful time in the camps truly came from Buna.

To begin with, life was never suitable in the camps, but Buna was more humane. The barracks of Buna weren't beautiful but they had the necessary floors, walls, and roof. The bitter nights were astonishingly frigid and unkind, though not as tough with our precious blankets. At the age of thirteen I was set in my high stands; meaning I was exceedingly thankful for the washbowl and bar of soap the camp granted. Unfortunately, such treasures were not found at Birkenau. The conditions were harsh and unfair, with muddy, floorless barracks, but what's to be expected? With two people in one bunk, no blankets, absolutely no heat was produced. We were granted nothing, but a ration of bread, and some meals even soup.

In another ay it was more soothing to work and live in Buna than Birkenau. With fewer inmates, there were fewer fights and more bonds. Everyone stuck together, prayed, and never gave up faith. Me and the rest of my family never separated and did the best we could to go unnoticed. Death lurked in every corner of Birkenau. The smoke that arose form the furnace was a constant reminder; we no longer were people, only prisoners. Just one too many steps to the right could cause a fiery death in a hell hole, literally. It was everyone for his/her self. In that reliable situation, loneliness just put a cherry on top. One of the many blessings we received at Buna was working outside of the camp. For our family, physical labor was not our finest talent, so working at the warehouse was a heaven set. As we sat together, we counted bolts, bulbs, and electrical fittings. We worked with most polish and French civilians. We never talked much though, considering the language barrier. Back in Birkenau the labor was tremendously and ridiculously brutal. Lifting heavy rocks from one end of a field to another and digging meaningless holes in the intense heat.

Looking back on my life now, I realize that my family and I were the lucky ones. Through the pain and suffering we were dealt a good set of cards. I have used my experiences to help me better myself and my life. Birkenau will always haunt our dreams, but we will remember Buna as our savior. It restored our hope and our faith, in ourselves, in God, and the world. Everything happens for a reason.

You'll see that a few sentences exceeded 15 words but more than 90% of this essay conformed to the GREAT Burger Essay Method. Therefore, this student earned an A on this writing.

(Student Sample # 1)

Let's assess this paper according to the North Carolina Writing Rubric to be certain of its quality.

10TH GRADE WRITING ASSESSMENT RUBRIC (NORTH CAROLINA)

CONTENT RUBRIC

Points	Description
4	• Topic/subject is clear, though it may or may not be explicitly stated • Maintains focus on topic/subject throughout the response • Organizational structure establishes relationships between and among ideas and/or events • Consists of a logical progression of ideas and/or events and is unified and complete • Support and elaboration are related to and supportive of the topic/subject • Consists of specific, developed details • Exhibits skillful use of vocabulary that is precise and purposeful • Demonstrates skillful use of sentence fluency
3	• Topic/subject is generally clear, though it may or may not be explicitly stated • May exhibit minor lapses in focus on topic/subject • Organizational structure establishes relationships between and among ideas and/or events, although minor lapses may be present • Consists of a logical progression of ideas and/or events and is reasonably complete, although minor lapses may be present • Support and elaboration may have minor weaknesses in relatedness to and support of the topic/subject • Consists of some specific details • Exhibits reasonable use of vocabulary that is precise and purposeful • Demonstrates reasonable use of sentence fluency

2	• Topic/subject may be vague • May lose or may exhibit major lapses in focus on topic/subject • Organizational structure may establish little relationship between and among ideas and/or events • May have major lapses in the logical progression of ideas and/or events and is minimally complete • Support and elaboration may have major weaknesses in relatedness to and support of the topic/subject • Consists of general and/or undeveloped details, which may be presented in a list-like fashion • Exhibits minimal use of vocabulary that is precise and purposeful • Demonstrates minimal use of sentence fluency
1	• Topic/subject is unclear or confusing • May fail to establish focus on topic/subject • Organizational structure may not establish connection between and among ideas and/or events • May consist of ideas and/or events that are presented in a random fashion and is incomplete or confusing • Support and elaboration attempts to support the topic/subject but may be unrelated or confusing • Consists of sparse details • Lacks use of vocabulary that is precise and purposeful • May not demonstrate sentence fluency
NS	• This code may be used for compositions that are entirely illegible or otherwise unscorable: blank responses, responses written in a foreign language, restatements of the prompt, and responses that are off-topic or incoherent.

CONVENTIONS RUBRIC

Points	Description
2	• Exhibits reasonable control of grammatical conventions appropriate to the writing task • Exhibits reasonable control of sentence formation • Exhibits reasonable control of standard usage including agreement, tense, and case • Exhibits reasonable control of mechanics including use of capitalization, punctuation, and spelling

1	• Exhibits minimal control of grammatical conventions appropriate to the writing task • Exhibits minimal control of sentence formation • Exhibits minimal control of standard usage including agreement, tense, and case • Exhibits minimal control of mechanics including use of capitalization, punctuation, and spelling
0	• Lacks control of grammatical conventions appropriate to the writing task • Lacks control of sentence formation • Lacks control of standard usage including agreement, tense, and case • Lacks control of mechanics including use of capitalization, punctuation, and spelling

Let's begin with the appraisal of the Auschwitz Compare/Contrast essay's Content:

a.) **Bypass the score of 0:** This writing has control of grammatical conventions appropriate to the writing task. Also, it has quite a bit of control of sentence formations. It contains standard grammatical usage including agreement, tense, and case. It displays suitable control of mechanics including use of capitalization, punctuation, and spelling.

b.) **Bypass the score of 1:** Exhibits excellent control of grammatical conventions appropriate to the writing task. It contains control of sentence formation and standard usage; including agreement, tense, and case. The essay displays better control of mechanics including use of capitalization, punctuation, and spelling.

c.) **Bypass the score of 2:** Topic/subject is not vague neither does it exhibit major lapses in focus. It contains a well planned organizational structure that establishes a firm relationship between and among ideas and/or events. Also, there are no major lapses in the logical progression of ideas. The piece exhibits a overall sense of wholeness in the explanations of ideas and/or events. Ample support and elaboration lacks weaknesses in relatedness to and support of the topic/subject. Consists of vivid, specific, & quite developed detailed mini-stories. These are not presented in a list-like fashion but using creating writing strategies. The essay exhibits expressive use of vocabulary that is precise and purposeful. It contains varying sentence structures and demonstrates expert use of sentence fluency.

d.) **Bypass the score of 3:** Topic/subject is quite clear, and it is explicitly stated. May exhibit minor lapses in focus on topic/subject. Organizational structure establishes stronger relationships between and among ideas and/or events, although minor lapses may be present. Consists of a logical progression of ideas and/or events and is thoroughly complete, without minor lapses being present. Ample support and elaboration are strong in relatedness to and support of the topic/subject. The piece consists of some specific details. It exhibits expert use of vocabulary that is precise and purposeful. Likewise, it demonstrates large amount of sentence fluency.

e.) **This piece scores a 4:** Topic/subject is quite clear, and it is explicitly stated. Furthermore, it maintains focus on topic/subject well throughout the response. The well-planned organizational structure establishes relationships between and among ideas and/or events. The piece consists of a logical progression of ideas and/or events and is unified and complete. It displays twice the support and elaboration related to and support of the topic. Also, this elaboration specifically illustrates 'mental pictures' supportive of the topic/subject. These specific, developed details clearly agree with the writing's stance. It exhibits skillful use of vocabulary that is precise and purposeful. Most times, it demonstrates skillful use of sentence fluency.

CONVENTIONS RUBRIC

f.) **Bypass the score of 0:** Has control of grammatical conventions appropriate to the writing task. Contains control of sentence formation, and exhibits control of standard usage including agreement, tense, and case. Shows control of mechanics including use of capitalization, punctuation, and spelling.

g.) **Bypass the score of 1:** Exhibits better control of grammatical conventions appropriate to the writing task. Exhibits confident variation of sentences and good control of standard usage including agreement, tense, and case. Displays major control of mechanics including use of capitalization, punctuation, and spelling.

h.) **Earns the score of 2:** Exhibits skillful control of grammatical conventions appropriate to the writing task. Displays reasonable control of sentence formation, there are a few run-ons. Exhibits impressive control of standard usage including agreement, tense, and case. Shows commendable control of mechanics including use of capitalization, punctuation, and spelling.

Therefore, the Conventions earn a score of 2, and the Content earn a score of 4 from the first assessor (me). For the sake of argument, let's presume the second table reader decided it should only earn a 3 for Content.

Now, let's use the North Carolina Writing formula to calculate the student's Ausch sample's essay score:

(See following page for the computation).

Reader 1	Content	4	Reader 2	Content	3	Total Content Score	7
	Conventions	2		Conventions	2	Total Conventions Score	4
(Total Content Score x 2) + Total Conventions Score = Total Writing Score							
(4+3) x 2) + (2 + 2) = (7 × 2) + 4 = 18 (Achievement Level IV)-from below							

Achievement Level	Total Writing Score
Level I	4-7
Level II	8-11
Level III	12-16
Level IV	17-20

(April 4, 2011, North Carolina Writing Rubric, cectheforum.wikispaces.com/file/.../ Writing+Assessment+Rubric.doc)

As you can see, this young lady's impressive writing stands up to the rigorous standards of the North Carolina Writing Rubric. Thus, she receives the highest score possible for sticking with the GREAT Burger Essay Method most of the time! **(Teenager below was not my student).**

Just imagine the watermelon smile on the face of the young lady openly commended for her essay. Students like her do not have to be a fluke in your class. You could have many success stories just like this if you and they properly apply GREAT!

CHAPTER 8

Cause and Effect Essay

(10th Grade Essays: 2010-2011)
Powerpoint/Class Sample

The next page is a condensed version of the GREAT Burger Essay Workshop specifically for Cause and Effect. I have found this to be one of the most straightforward types of essay.

Of course, the writer should use the GREAT Burger Quick Cause and Effect Essay Planner found in this chapter's PowerPoint. Then, this author artfully crafts an enticing Historical Review or Personal Testimony introduction. These are the most effective for Cause and Effect Essays.

This introduction must have a clear Thesis statement at the end. That will make the reader desire to continue through the composition. He or she should hash out clear mental snapshots of either the effects or the causes of a topic. They should resist including the opposites though; all body paragraph discussion should be either effects. Or, the writer should be detailing all causes.

Conclusions are created using the Four Conclusion techniques described earlier. These are: a future look, a call to action, a new solution to the problem, or a new moral lesson. The writer will utilize at least two of them in each end paragraphs. They are to briefly detail their effects or causes in the second sentence only! (You succinctly overview the 3 effects/causes because nobody wants to reread the same drawn-out details).

SCHOOL YEAR 2010-2011
10TH GRADE
POWERPOINT PRESENTATION

CAUSE & EFFECT ESSAY & QUICK PLANNER

Objectives

- Choosing the stance you can support best!
- Harnessing data from the given information.
- Saving your time by writing plan in 'caveman'.
- 'Going for the gusto' in the Conclusion paragraph.

You may have a million ideas just floating around in your heads when given a Cause & Effect prompt.

Yet, there are some things you should know:

1. Cause and Effect Essays never ask for both causes and effects. Causal chains or Effects Chains

2. Graders of these essays expect very specific examples that may be real or made-up.

3. A Historical review Introduction or Anecdote Introduction would be the most ideal beginners.

4. When provided with research information, you must use one or two pieces of it in your paper.

Here is a released 10th Grade North Carolina Writing Assessment used by my students in preparation for their 2010-2011 Writing Exam.

Write an article for your school newspaper explaining the effects of working a part-time job while in school. You may use the following information, your own experiences, observation, and/or readings.

Research shows that school absences rise and scores on standardized tests fall as teens' work hours increase. Working students takes fewer classes, get fewer school honors, hold fewer leadership positions in school are less involved in extracurricular activities.

Source: Wall Street Journal Classroom Edition, "Benefits of a Part-Time Job, "March 2008

"The activities and courses students choose vary considerably, so it's important for young people to keep their individual situations clearly in mind," says Brad MacGowan, director of the Career Center at Newton North High School in Massachusetts. He continues, "For example, student actors should allow for the fact that they won't have as much time during performance seasons. Student Athletes need to remember the times of the year that they'll be tied up with games and practices. Other students who are in classes that make considerable demands outside of the classroom must keep that reality in mind."

Source: College Board, "Balancing High School and Part-Time Work"

Jobs that offer the opportunity to acquire skills and take on responsibility lay the ground work for mobbing up in the work world. These jobs can also be more interesting and rewarding, even if they pay less. Flipping burgers leaves you with short term money in your pocket but not much else A job that gives you the chance to learn a skill, oversee other people or take significant responsibility allows you to add accomplishments to your resume or your college application.

Source: SF Gate, "Best Part-Time Jobs for High Schools and College Students," December 18, 2005

As you write your article for your school newsletter explaining the effects of working a part while in school, remember to:

- Focus on the effects of working a part-time job while in school
- Consider the purpose, audience, and context of your article.
- Organize your article so that your ideas and details progress logically.
- Include specific details that clearly develop your article.
- Edit your article for standard grammar and language usage.

Use the blank sheet of paper given to you by your teacher to plan your article. Anythiyou write on the blank sheet will not be scored. You must write the final copy of your article on the next page.

GRADE 10 PROMPT: Write an article for your school newspaper explaining the effects of working a part-time job while in school.

<u>Simple planner</u>: stopping here will only produce vague, general examples; not upper score worthy!

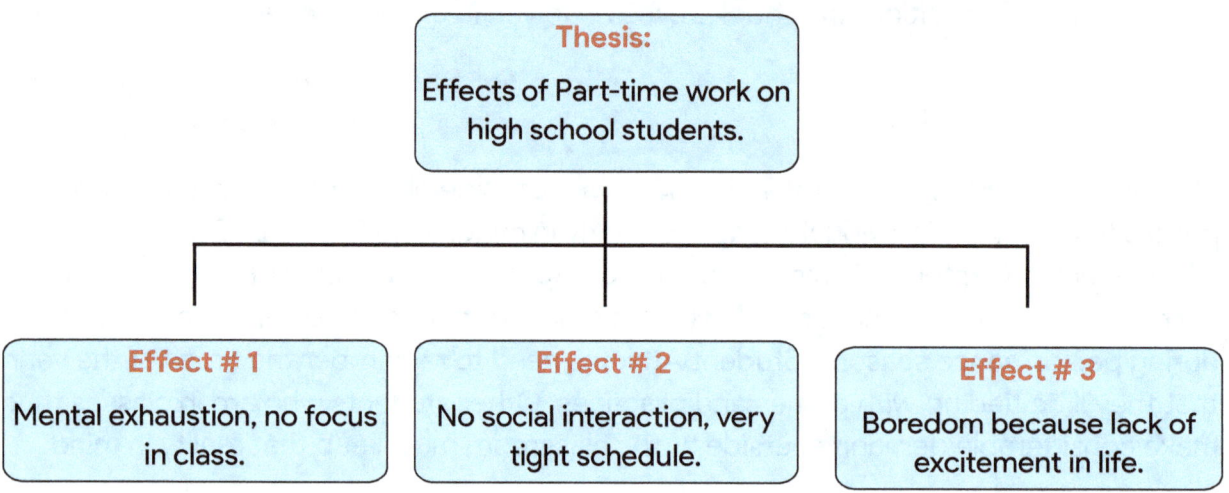

Thesis:
Effects of Part-time work on high school students.

Effect # 1
Mental exhaustion, no focus in class.

Effect # 2
No social interaction, very tight schedule.

Effect # 3
Boredom because lack of excitement in life.

Of course, you can't stop here...

You must create your <u>Expansions!</u>

Expansions: Facts, Reasons, Incidents, Examples, & Statistics that <u>specifically</u> make your points more clearly!!!

(Expansions in **green writing**; eliminate or **X** weakest one per column.)

GREAT QUICK ESSAY PLANNER

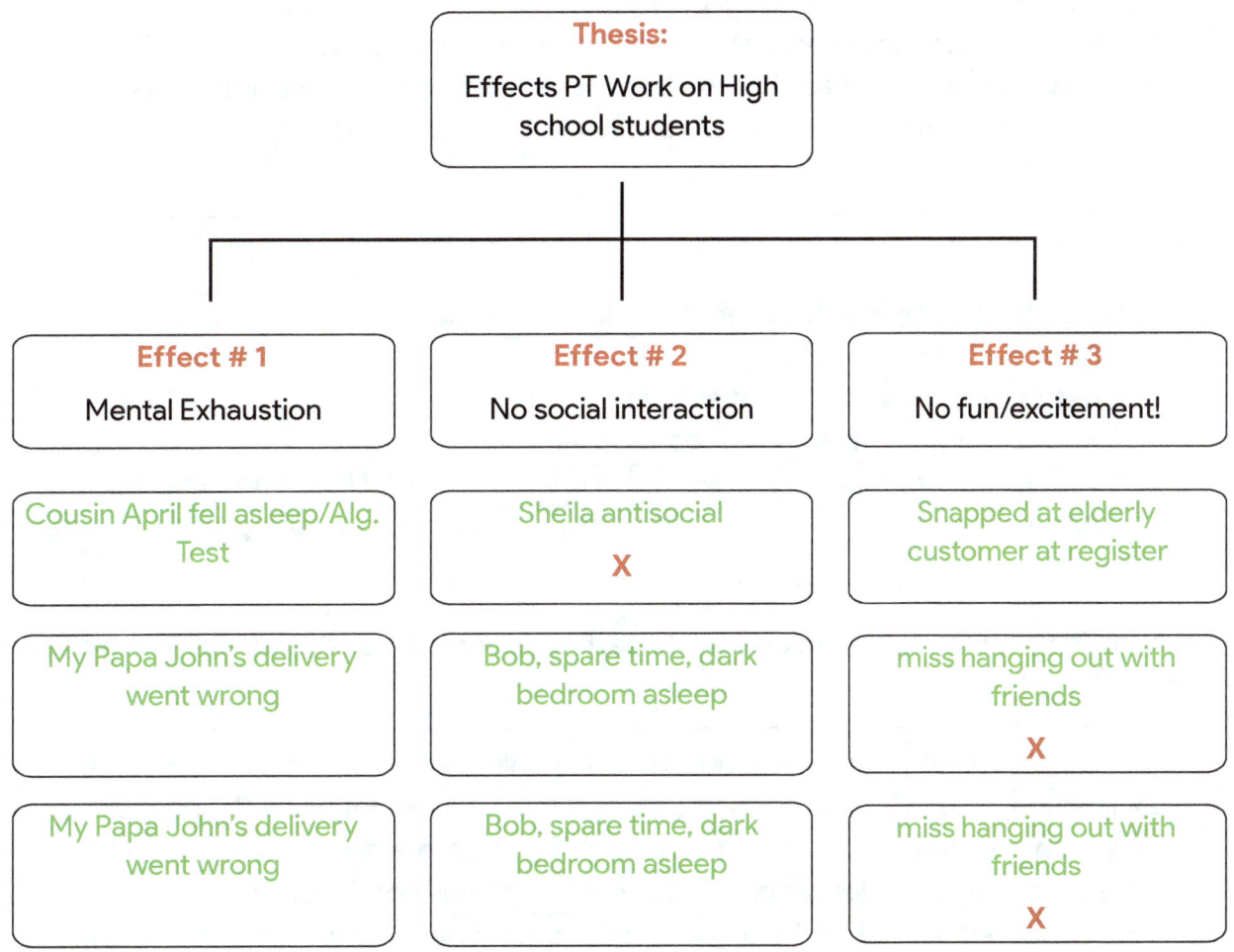

Thesis:

Effects PT Work on High school students

Effect # 1

Mental Exhaustion

Effect # 2

No social interaction

Effect # 3

No fun/excitement!

Cousin April fell asleep/Alg. Test

Sheila antisocial

X

Snapped at elderly customer at register

My Papa John's delivery went wrong

Bob, spare time, dark bedroom asleep

miss hanging out with friends

X

My Papa John's delivery went wrong

Bob, spare time, dark bedroom asleep

miss hanging out with friends

X

Our Effects Essay Introduction used provided Information from the testing prompt. (October 2010, Grade 10)

> *__Anecdote Intro:__* The oddest moment actually occurred on my way to Geometry class yesterday! Apparently, I picked up our school newspaper called the Falcon News, and was immediately engrossed. Bold, type-faced words of an article's title seemed quite relevant to my own situation. Then, it briefly mentioned that high schooler's stress levels were at all-time, elevated levels. Moreover, "research shows that school absences rise and scores on standardized tests fall as work hours increase." Therefore, several effects of part-time work on struggling students include mental exhaustion, social avoidance, and constant dullness.

Effects Essay Introduction is GREAT Burger because:

- It has three complex –ly adverbs. (underlined in black)
- It has four transitional words. (highlighted in red)
- It has quite a few complex adjectives (highlighted in green)
- Sentence length is less than or equal to 15 words.
- Sentence four paraphrases & sent. five quotes provided info from prompt.
- It has a clear thesis statement (Clinchers no longer used in 10th grade.)

Body Paragraph # 1 must remain GREAT!!

Grammatically Correct, **R**epetition Free, **E**xpertly Supported, **A**dverb & Adjective Packed, & **T**ransition Filled.

> Initially, one effect of part-time work is absolutely feeling a sense of mental exhaustion. After a long work-night, my cousin April was definitely drained. She only managed to get five and a half hours of rest before school. Tragically, she entered her Algebra class unprepared, and completely bombed her polynomials test. It did not seem like it was her fault, as much as she was overwhelmed. Personally, I have managed to mess up in my work duties as well. Two days ago, I accidentally fell asleep near the stoplight; then calamity struck! My car quickly jolted backwards, and the Papa John's extra large pizza was tossed onto the floor. So much for our thirty minutes or less guarantee!

Effects Essay Body Paragraph # 1 complies with GREAT Burger:

- It has five complex ' –ly' adverbs; (underlined in black)
- It has five transitions; (highlighted in red)
- It has quite a few complex adjectives (highlighted in green)
- 'Twice the proof'; two complete stories proving Topic Sent.
- Sentences 15 words or less; 7-8 sentences in a paragraph

Body Paragraph # 2 comes right out of the Planner as well.

Grammatically Correct, **R**epetition Free, **E**xpertly Supported, **A**dverb & Adjective Packed, & **T**ransition Filled.

> In addition, an effect of part-time work is the lack of social interaction. Two days ago, I coincidentally bumped into a middle school buddy of mine named Bob. I decided to spontaneously interview him on this topic. Surprisingly, he mentioned that all his spare time was spent in his darkened bedroom sleeping. I pitied his lonely existence while most of his friends were at the mall, movies, or bookstores. Later, I seriously considered my classmate Angela's turbulent relationship. She'd been dating a muscular football jock named Gregory for the past four months. All of a sudden, he rashly decided to get a part-time job against Angela's wishes. She foresaw that Greg would push her aside; they hadn't dated in a month! Soon, Angela dropped that zero, for a hero--a guy who'd spend time with her.

Effects Essay Body Paragraph # 2 meets GREAT burger standards:

- It has four complex ' –ly' adverbs; (underlined in black)
- It has five transitions; (highlighted in red)
- It has quite a few complex adjectives (highlighted in green)
- 'Twice the proof'; two complete stories proving Topic Sent.
- Sentences 15 words or less; at least 7-8 sentences.

Effects Essay Body Paragraph #3: Don't get weary, continue writing skillfully.

Grammatically Correct, **R**epetition Free, **E**xpertly Supported, **A**dverb & Adjective Packed, & **T**ransition Filled.

> Another instance of part-time work affecting a student negatively impacted my work performance. It was fifteen minutes until my cashier shift was over; 10:45 to be exact. Then, an older lady walked into Papa John's at a snail's pace and methodically searched the entire menu. She finally decided to order at 10:58 PM, but I was already grouchy from my previously sleepless night. I rudely interrupted, "listening to you is like watching paint dry!" In the end, I was nearly fired because my tight schedule had me so uptight. The next day was supposed to be a trip to remember! My friends and I quietly boarded our packed bus and arrived two hours later. As we disembarked, I felt a bit sluggish and unwisely decided to slouch on a nearby bench. Finally, I awakened to the sound of a loudly slamming door three hours later. There was no sign of my peers; I'd slept through the entire North Carolina Aquarium field trip!

Effects Essay Body Paragraph # 3 meets GREAT burger standards:

- It has seven complex '–ly' adverbs; (underlined in black)
- It has six transitions; (highlighted in red)
- It has quite a few complex adjectives (highlighted in green)
- 'Twice the proof'; two complete stories proving the Topic Sent.
- Sentences 15 words or less; at least 7-8 sentences.

Conclusion Paragraphs should use at least two or three of the techniques we discussed in the packet.

Grammatically Correct, **R**epetition Free, **E**xpertly Supported, **A**dverb & Adjective Packed, & **T**ransition Filled.

> Although there are many effects of part-time work, the negative outcomes definitely outweigh the positives. Essentially, mental exhaustion, no social interaction, and intense boredom should steer students away from it. Three years from now, this hardworking senior may have wisely saved $1,500 for college, but lack enough credits to graduate! Instead, conscientious individuals should either work less hours or wait to get part-time jobs. These solutions are quite relevant unless the youngster is genuinely well-balanced. It is up to every learner to make this controversial choice for him or herself.

Conclusion Paragraph also meets the GREAT burger standard:

- It has seven complex '–ly' adverbs; (underlined in black)
- It has six transitions; (highlighted in red)
- It has quite a few complex adjectives (highlighted in green)
- Uses three advanced conclusion techniques; does not repeat three reasons for the entire paragraph!
    - a.) Sentence #2: Repeats three main reasons in a single sentence; good.
    - b.) Sentence #3: A look into the future (what happens in three years?)
    - c.) Sentence #4: A new solution to the problem (less hours or wait for job)
    - d.) Sentence #6: A Call to Action (calls upon every student to decide)
    - e.) Sentences 15 words or less; at least 7-8 sentences.

As always, you should read this *10th Grade Class Sample Effects Essay* in its uninterrupted entirety.

The oddest moment actually occurred on my way to Geometry class yesterday! Apparently, I picked up our school newspaper called the Falcon News, and was immediately engrossed. Bold, type-faced words of an article's title seemed quite relevant to my own situation. Then, it briefly mentioned that high schooler's stress levels were at all-time, elevated levels. Moreover, "research shows that school absences rise and scores on standardized tests fall as work hours increase." Therefore, several effects of part-time work on struggling students include mental exhaustion, social avoidance, and constant dullness.

Initially, one effect of part-time work is absolutely feeling a sense of mental exhaustion. After a long work-night, my cousin April was definitely drained. She only managed to get five and a half hours of rest before school. Tragically, she entered her Algebra class unprepared, and completely bombed her polynomials test. It did not seem like it was her fault, as much as she was overwhelmed. Personally, I have managed to mess up in my work duties as well. Two days ago, I accidentally fell asleep near the stoplight; then calamity struck! My car quickly jolted backwards, and the Papa John's extra large pizza was tossed onto the floor. So much for our thirty minutes or less guarantee!

In addition, a downside of part-time jobs is the lack of social interaction. Two days ago, I coincidentally bumped into a middle school buddy of mine named Bob. I decided to spontaneously interview him on this topic. Surprisingly, he mentioned that all his spare time was spent in his darkened bedroom sleeping. I pitied his lonely existence while most of his friends were at the mall, movies, or bookstores. Later, I seriously considered my classmate Angela's turbulent relationship. She'd been dating a muscular football jock named Gregory for the past four months. All of a sudden, he rashly decided to get a part-time job against Angela's wishes. She foresaw that Greg would push her aside; they hadn't dated in a month! Soon, Angela dropped that zero, for a hero—a guy who'd spend time with her.

Another instance of part-time work affecting a student negatively impacted my work performance. It was fifteen minutes until my cashier shift was over; 10:45 to be exact. Then, an older lady walked into Papa John's at a snail's pace and methodically searched the entire menu. She finally decided to order at 10:58 PM, but I was already grouchy from my previously sleepless night. I rudely interrupted, "listening to you is like watching paint dry!" In the end, I was nearly fired because my tight schedule had me so uptight. The next day was supposed to be a trip to remember! My friends and I quietly boarded our packed bus and arrived two hours later. As we disembarked, I felt a bit sluggish and unwisely decided to slouch on a nearby bench. Finally, I awakened to the sound of a loudly slamming door three hours later. There was no sign of my peers; I'd slept through the entire North Carolina Aquarium field trip!

Although there are many effects of part-time work, the negative outcomes definitely outweigh the positives. Essentially, mental exhaustion, no social interaction, and intense boredom should steer students away from working. Three years from now, this hardworking senior may have wisely saved $1,500 for college, but lack enough credits to graduate! Instead, conscientious individuals should either work less hours or wait to get part-time jobs. These solutions are quite relevant unless the youngster is genuinely well-balanced. It is up to every learner to make this controversial choice for him or herself!

Did the Previous Essay Meet the GREAT Burger Criteria?

f.) Did the author include complex adjectives, adverbs, and transitions?

g.) Did the Introduction begin with a story that grabbed your attention?

h.) Does this writing flow very well?

i.) Does the writer make valid and effective double arguments in each body paragraph?

j.) Were Facts, Reasons, Incidents, Examples, and/or Statistics included?

k.) Can you actually picture each example in your mind?

l.) Did the author skillfully conclude this essay?

m.) Are you convinced that these negative effects outweigh the positive effects?

A resounding yes on all counts! This essay could stand up to any rigorous state or national standardized Writing exam standards. That is so because it surpasses the GREAT criteria.

For the sake of argument, let's assess this Cause and Effect essay using the North Carolina Writing Rubric. Then, we can determine how well GREAT Burger actually prepares a student for these rigorous writing exams.

10TH GRADE WRITING ASSESSMENT RUBRIC (NORTH CAROLINA)

CONTENT RUBRIC

Points	Description
4	<ul><li>Topic/subject is clear, though it may or may not be explicitly stated</li><li>Maintains focus on topic/subject throughout the response</li><li>Organizational structure establishes relationships between and among ideas and/or events</li><li>Consists of a logical progression of ideas and/or events and is unified and complete</li><li>Support and elaboration are related to and supportive of the topic/subject</li><li>Consists of specific, developed details</li><li>Exhibits skillful use of vocabulary that is precise and purposeful</li><li>Demonstrates skillful use of sentence fluency</li></ul>
3	<ul><li>Topic/subject is generally clear, though it may or may not be explicitly stated</li><li>May exhibit minor lapses in focus on topic/subject</li><li>Organizational structure establishes relationships between and among ideas and/or events, although minor lapses may be present</li><li>Consists of a logical progression of ideas and/or events and is reasonably complete, although minor lapses may be present</li><li>Support and elaboration may have minor weaknesses in relatedness to and support of the topic/subject</li><li>Consists of some specific details</li><li>Exhibits reasonable use of vocabulary that is precise and purposeful</li><li>Demonstrates reasonable use of sentence fluency</li></ul>

2	• Topic/subject may be vague
	• May lose or may exhibit major lapses in focus on topic/subject
	• Organizational structure may establish little relationship between and among ideas and/or events
	• May have major lapses in the logical progression of ideas and/or events and is minimally complete
	• Support and elaboration may have major weaknesses in relatedness to and support of the topic/subject
	• Consists of general and/or undeveloped details, which may be presented in a list-like fashion
	• Exhibits minimal use of vocabulary that is precise and purposeful
	• Demonstrates minimal use of sentence fluency
1	• Topic/subject is unclear or confusing
	• May fail to establish focus on topic/subject
	• Organizational structure may not establish connection between and among ideas and/or events
	• May consist of ideas and/or events that are presented in a random fashion and is incomplete or confusing
	• Support and elaboration attempts to support the topic/subject but may be unrelated or confusing
	• Consists of sparse details
	• Lacks use of vocabulary that is precise and purposeful
	• May not demonstrate sentence fluency
NS	• This code may be used for compositions that are entirely illegible or otherwise unscorable: blank responses, responses written in a foreign language, restatements of the prompt, and responses that are off-topic or incoherent.

CONVENTIONS RUBRIC

Points	Description
2	• Exhibits reasonable control of grammatical conventions appropriate to the writing task • Exhibits reasonable control of sentence formation • Exhibits reasonable control of standard usage including agreement, tense, and case • Exhibits reasonable control of mechanics including use of capitalization, punctuation, and spelling
1	• Exhibits minimal control of grammatical conventions appropriate to the writing task • Exhibits minimal control of sentence formation • Exhibits minimal control of standard usage including agreement, tense, and case • Exhibits minimal control of mechanics including use of capitalization, punctuation, and spelling
0	• Lacks control of grammatical conventions appropriate to the writing task • Lacks control of sentence formation • Lacks control of standard usage including agreement, tense, and case • Lacks control of mechanics including use of capitalization, punctuation, and spelling

Let's begin with the appraisal of the essay's Content:

a.) **Bypass the score of 0:** This writing has control of grammatical conventions appropriate to the writing task. Also, it has quite a bit of control of sentence formations. It contains standard grammatical usage including agreement, tense, and case. It displays suitable control of mechanics including use of capitalization, punctuation, and spelling.

b.) **Bypass the score of 1:** Exhibits excellent control of grammatical conventions appropriate to the writing task. It contains control of sentence formation and standard usage; including agreement, tense, and case. The essay displays better control of mechanics including use of capitalization, punctuation, and spelling.

c.) **Bypass the score of 2:** Topic/subject is not vague neither does it exhibit major lapses in focus. It contains a well planned organizational structure that establishes a firm relationship between and among ideas and/or events. Also, there are no major lapses in the logical progression of ideas.

The piece exhibits a overall sense of wholeness in the explanations of ideas and/or events. Ample support and elaboration lacks weaknesses in relatedness to and support of the topic/subject. Consists of vivid, specific, & quite developed detailed mini-stories. These are not presented in a list-like fashion but using creating writing strategies. The essay exhibits expressive use of vocabulary that is precise and purposeful. It contains varying sentence structures and demonstrates expert use of sentence fluency.

d.) **Bypass the score of 3:** Topic/subject is quite clear, and it is explicitly stated. May exhibit minor lapses in focus on topic/subject. Organizational structure establishes stronger relationships between and among ideas and/or events, although minor lapses may be present. Consists of a logical progression of ideas and/or events and is thoroughly complete, without minor lapses being present. Ample support and elaboration are strong in relatedness to and support of the topic/subject. The piece consists of some specific details. It exhibits expert use of vocabulary that is precise and purposeful. Likewise, it demonstrates large amount of sentence fluency.

e.) **This piece scores a 4:** Topic/subject is quite clear, and it is explicitly stated. Furthermore, it maintains focus on topic/subject well throughout the response. The well-planned organizational structure establishes relationships between and among ideas and/or events. The piece consists of a logical progression of ideas and/or events and is unified and complete. It displays twice the support and elaboration related to and support of the topic. Also, this elaboration specifically illustrates 'mental pictures' supportive of the topic/subject. These specific, developed details clearly agree with the writing's stance. It exhibits skillful use of vocabulary that is precise and purposeful. Most times, it demonstrates skillful use of sentence fluency.

CONVENTIONS RUBRIC

f.) **Bypass the score of 0:** Has control of grammatical conventions appropriate to the writing task

Contains control of sentence formation, and exhibits control of standard usage including agreement, tense, and case. Shows control of mechanics including use of capitalization, punctuation, and spelling.

g.) **Bypass the score of 1:** Exhibits better control of grammatical conventions appropriate to the writing task. Exhibits confident variation of sentences and good control of standard usage including agreement, tense, and case. Displays major control of mechanics including use of capitalization, punctuation, and spelling.

h.) **Earns the score of 2:** Exhibits skillful control of grammatical conventions appropriate to the writing task. Displays reasonable control of sentence formation, there are a few run-ons. Exhibits impressive control of standard usage including agreement, tense, and case. Shows commendable control of mechanics including use of capitalization, punctuation, and spelling.

Therefore, the Conventions earn a score of 2, and the Content earns a score of 4 from the first assessor (me). This time, let's presume the second table reader also decided it deserved a 4 for Content. Let's apply the North Carolina formula for calculating the Student sample's essay score:

Reader 1	Content	4	Reader 2	Content	4	**Total Content Score**	8
	Conventions	2		Conventions	2	Total Conventions Score	4
(Total Content Score x 2) + Total Conventions Score = Total Writing Score							
(4+3) x 2) + (2 + 2) = (7 × 2) + 4 = 18 (Achievement Level IV)-from below							

Achievement Level	Total Writing Score
Level I	4-7
Level II	8-11
Level III	12-16
Level IV	17-20

(April 4, 2011, North Carolina Writing Rubric, cectheforum.wikispaces.com/file/.../ Writing+Assessment+Rubric.doc)

| # Cause and Effect Anchor Essays

I want to share some individual samples of Cause and Effect Essays with you. This is after we previously completed a classwide sample of the writing type. This time the prompt will specifically ask for the effects rather than the causes. You may see that some aren't exactly perfect but they appear to have higher scores. Yet, most are noteworthy considering where these students began in my classroom. So prepare yourselves for the good, the bad, and the ugly, so to speak.

You'll notice that names have been intentionally wited-out to protect students' privacy. Needless to say, paperwork would be absolutely endless if I were to gather signatures for each sample I have in my possession. Feel free to share these samples with you students. Label them **Sample A, Sample B, Sample C, and Sample D,** and then have them compare these good to excellent anchor papers. Allow them to use the GREAT Burger essay checklist or your state writing standards to properly assess each essay. (You will notice how well it still works on Cause and Effect, and Comparison/Contrast essays.) This is even though it was designed specifically for Persuasive and Expository essays. I have included the one-page assessment instrument at the end of this chapter. Then, have them assign each paper with a percentage and/or grade.

For this prompt, I provided all of these students with the Historical Review Introduction during class. They planned the rest on the Quick Burger Essay planner, and then wrote it quickly. Then, we collected them in haste. Of course, we wrote Final Revisions that served as their Mid-Term Essays two days later. So, I added 8 points to each score as incentive for completion. Sometimes offering extra points for great effort also helps them improve effort levels.

See if your groups of students could properly critique each essay, paying no mind to the scores on top of the pages. (My mistake was not alloting several days for them to prepare; you should never curve using GREAT Burger as a general rule). Students must see their real writing level at the beginning of the year!

Here are their actual scores (without the curve):

Sample A: Content = 4, Conventions = 2   (His actual score was a 98-8 = 90 B+)

Sample B: Content = 4, Conventions = 2   (Her actual score was a 98-8 = 90 B+)

Sample C: Content = 2.5 or 3, Conventions = 1   (His actual score was a 91-8 = 83 C)

Sample D: Content = 4, Conventions = 1   (She actually scored a 95-8 = 87 B)

Prompt: Write an article for your school newspaper explaining the effects of working a part-time job while in school.

THE CAUSE AND EFFECT QUICK PLANNER

10/14

Bonus

You may have a million ideas just floating around in your heads when given a cause and effect prompt.

Yet there are some things you should know:

1. Cause and effect essays never ask for bathe effects and causes.
2. These essays expect very specific examples that maybe fake or real to prove your stance. {Causal chain and effect or Effect Chain
3. When provided with research information, you must use one or two pieces of it to focus your intro.

Grade 10 Prompt. Write an article for your school newspaper explaining the effects of working a part-time job while in school.

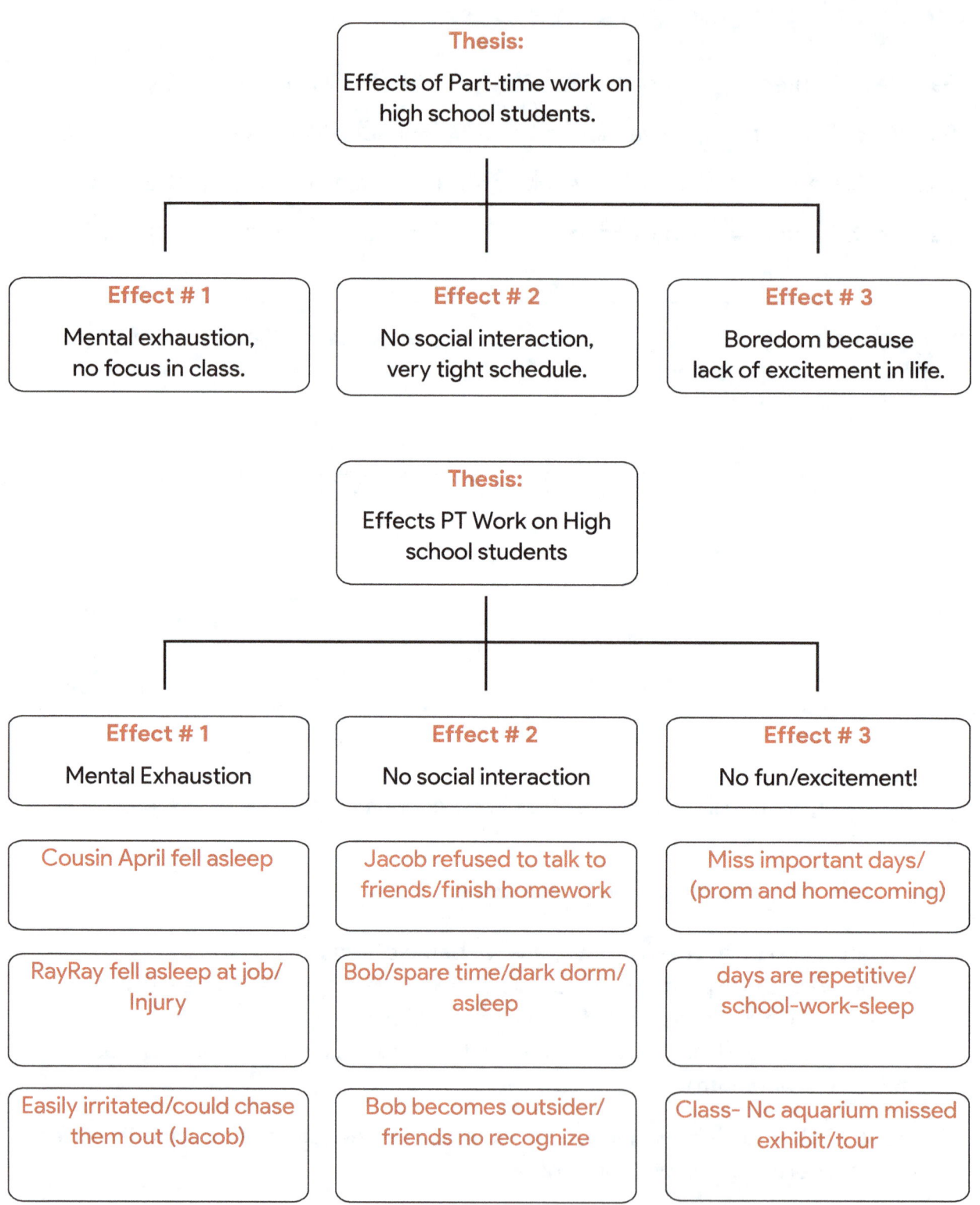

Essay- Midterm

④ Nc Writing Rub.

-excellent intro
-realistic bp1, bp2, bp3
-analtyical conclusion

98

The oddest moment actually occured on my way to Geometry class yesterday. Apparently, I picked up our school newspaper called the Falcon News, and was immediately engrossed. The bold, type-faced words of all article's title seemed quite relevant to my own situation. Then, it briefly mentioned that high schoolers' stress levels were at all time, elevated levels. Moreover research shows that "school abscenses rise and standardized test scores fail as work hours increase." These examples are proof-positive that working a part-time job extensively ultimately leads to mental exhaustion, no social interaction and a lack of fun or excitement.

Being employed while attending school can result in outrageous result of side-effects and included in that is mental exhaustion. I remember the account of my cousin April and has disaster on Algebra test. She shared with me that she had unexpectedly been asigned to mark a double shift. Relief reached her at 12:00 A.M. but by then she had to go to bed, leaving her zero time to study for her upcoming Algebra test. The next day, April entered the room drowsily and bombed on the test. My friend Franco has also been outwardly affected by having a part-time job. One day, at work, Franco was working the counter at McDonald's when an elderly lady came up to order. She was taking rather long to order and eventually Franco became and angrily said, "Hurry the HELL UP!"

Moreover, part-time jobs leave little to absolutely no time for social interactions and separates you from loved ones. Jacob, a classmate would always be doing homework during lunch hours and would refuse to talk to others that wanted to hold a conversation with him. I've come to notice that this occured after about two weeks Jacob started his job at the mall. Likewise, Bob has also became socially awkward due to his recent uptake on a part-time job. On any given day, when Bob has free time, he would spend it in his dimly lit room heavily dormant. These two have both been negatively affected from taking part-time job while still attending school.

Being deprived of having any fun or excitement is also a negative aspect of associating in part-time employment while still in school. I am reminded of the time that poor April missed her last prom of her high school years. She was completely ecstatic about it and told me she would remember the night always. Unfortunately, she didn't even get the shame to experience it due to the hours she was assigned to work. And now I am entitled to tell of the tragic story that occured to me on our field trip to the North Carolina State Aquarium. As excited as I was, that didn't excuse the fact that I worked long hours the other night and was practically hafl asleep. At the start of trip, I rested on a wooden bench and within a minute I was out.

✓+ There is no doubt that working a part-time job has great benefits and you should take the opportunity do so. However, take hold of the opportunity and get an occupation when it will not affect your school work, such as over the summer or Christmas. You could formally request to have your employer do lessen the hours that you must work os well. It is of greatest signifcance that you do not permit your occupation to subdue your existence. I maintain that having a part-time job causes negative effects that included mental exhaustion, deprivation of social interaction, and a loss at fun and excitement to your life.

THE CAUSE & EFFECT QUICK PLANNER
Objectives

You may have a million ideas just floating around in your heads when given a cause and effect prompt.

Yet there are some things you should know:

1. Cause and effect essays never ask for bathe effects and causes.
2. These essays expect very specific examples that maybe fake or real to prove your stance. {Causal chain and effect or Effect Chain
3. When provided with research information, you must use one or two pieces of it to focus your intro.

Grade 10 Prompt. Write an article for your school newspaper explaining the effects of working a part-time job while in school.

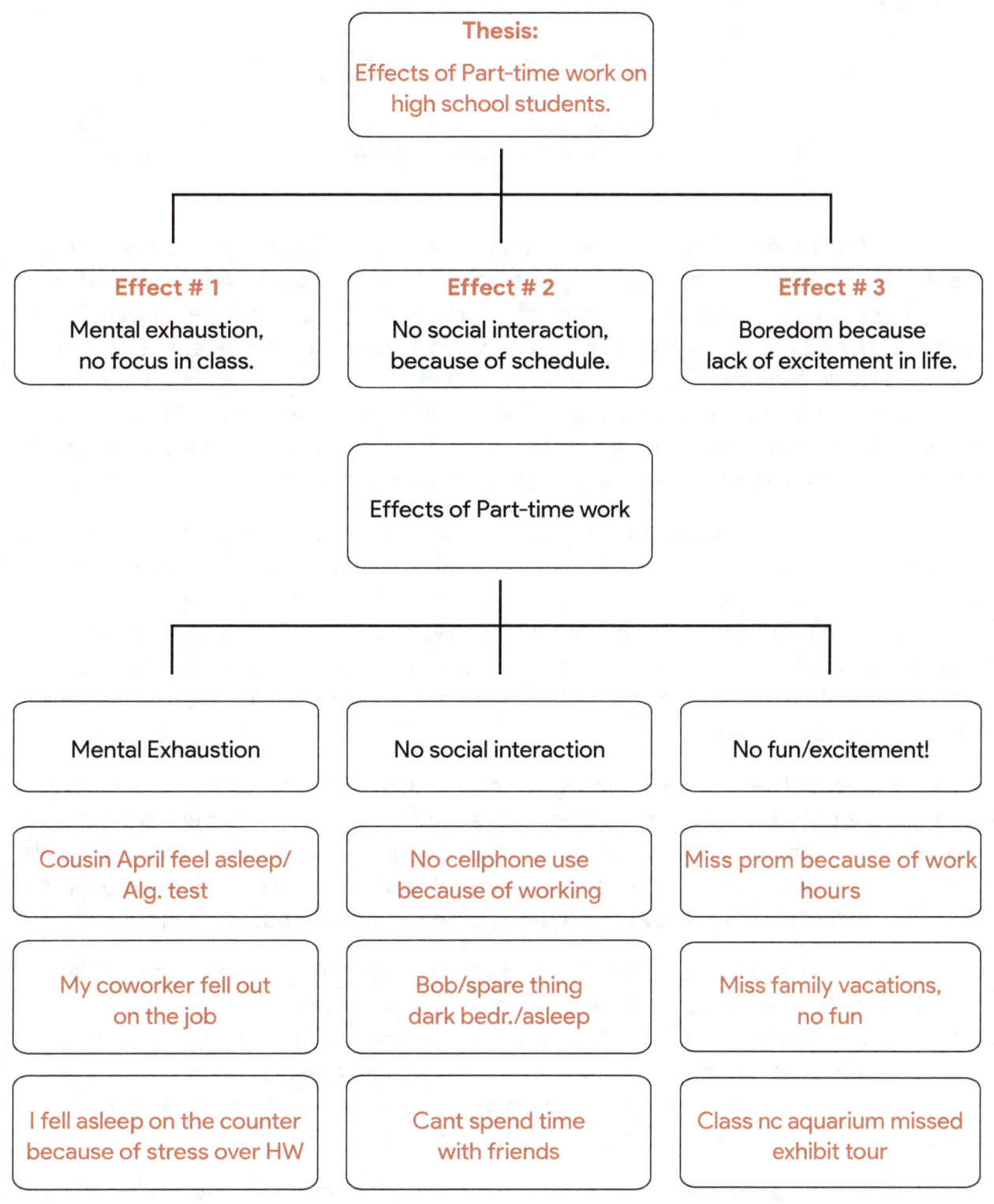

Essay

④ Nc Writing Rub.   **98%**   10/27.10   Bonus

-excellent intro
-realistic bp1, bp2, bp3
-analtyical conclusion   Beautiful!

The oddest moment actually occurred on my way to Geometry class yesterday. Apparently, I picked up our school newspaper called the Falcon News, and was immediately engrossed. The bold, type-faced words of all article's title seemed quite relevant to my own situation. Then, it briefly mentioned that high schoolers' stress levels were at all time, elevated levels. Moreover, research shows that "school absences rise and standardized test scores fall as work hours increase." Therefore, three negative effects of part-time work while in school absolutely are lack of social life, can cause absences, decrease in test scores on standardized test, and it harms student athletes.

First, working late hours at night and after school can cause students to miss out on school the next day. Research shows that school absences rise, as teen work hours increase. Outstandingly, this can affect all high school students. As soon as the school bell rings, a lot of us are rushing out to make it to work on time. More than likely, most of us work at least four hours, that only allows us to make it home at 8 or even after that. We are probably tired, just want to shower, then go to bed! We would not even want to think about homework or projects.

As the school year progressively goes on, I notice that teachers are beginning to prepare their students for standardized tests. Several of my peers frequently do not even come to school enough to take advantage of enough remediation. Without valuable tutoring there will most likely be a decrease in test scores for my friends. A tremendous decrease in test scores can give the country, even the state a negative reputation.

I myself am a student athlete I play softball, volleyball, basketball, and I dance. Maintaining these extra activities, and balancing school and excellent grades is already hard enough. When students athletes come home late from games and practice, it makes us feel drowsy and sluggish. We get so tired that we can barely keep our eyes open to write our names on our own papers. From experience one little slip up with one grade can cause you to be benched, or temporarily suspended from the team.

Although, there are many effects of part-time work, the negative outcomes definitely outweigh the positive ones. I myself am surprised that students can maintain everything all at once. From school, to projects, sports, homework, and even a part-time job, these can stress a person out. Basically, I have one simple solution to solve this problem. I say that school should come first, then worry about working later. I know most of you would rather study and participate in sports rather than stocking shelves, and flipping burgers anyways.

Bonus

A

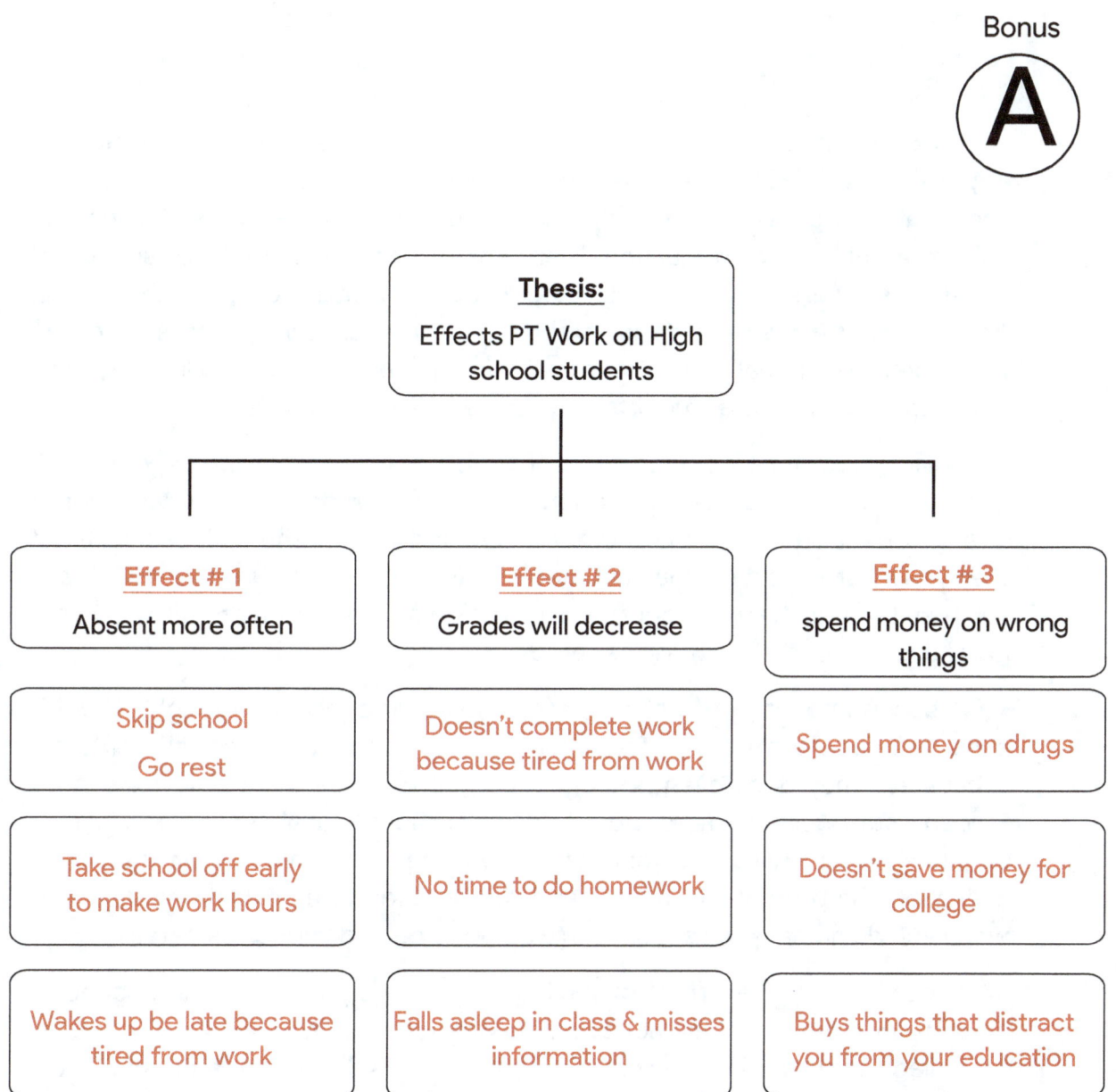

Thesis:

Effects PT Work on High school students

Effect # 1

Absent more often

Effect # 2

Grades will decrease

Effect # 3

spend money on wrong things

Skip school

Go rest

Doesn't complete work because tired from work

Spend money on drugs

Take school off early to make work hours

No time to do homework

Doesn't save money for college

Wakes up be late because tired from work

Falls asleep in class & misses information

Buys things that distract you from your education

Quite Enjoyable
Nc Writing Skillls
3.5/4

10/27.10

✓+ The oddest moment actually occurred on my way to Geometry class yesterday. Apparently, I picked up our school newspaper called the Falcon News, and was immediately engrossed. The bold, type-faced words of all article's title seemed quite relevant to my own situation. Then, it briefly mentioned that high schoolers' stress levels were at all time, elevated levels. Moreover, research shows that "school absences rise and standardized test scores fall as work hours increase." Therefore, three negative effects of part-time job are absences will rise, grades will decrease, and some students don't spend their money wisely."

Having a part time job during school can be very tough. Having to go through good eight hours of school and 4 hours of work everyday, can build up a lot of stress. You will be tired at the end of the day, and leave homework behind. If not then you'll just leave it for the next morning right before its due, which will make you rush through it, and do poorly on it. That's why most students with part time jobs have dropped at least a letter grade.

A second negative effect of having a part time job during high school is absences rise enormously. After a long day of school and work students are exhausted. They don't even bother waking up early the next day. For school, Students start worrying more about work than school. Your absences start gaining up and you could fail a class, and take it again next year. When your absent you mist a lot of important information and you have to make up a lot of work. Then when you do go back to school, you're going to behind your classmates.

The third negative effect of having a part time job during high school is students are spending their money on the wrong things. Instead of saving money for college some students buy drugs. That distracts them from their education. This is not all students. Some are very responsible with their purchases, once students get caught up with drugs, it could take over their lives, at such a young age. This is a reason, why dropouts are high in North Carolina.

This is why having a part time job during high school is a negative thing. Only responsible roll students should be given the privilege to have a part time job. The majority of high school students can not balance school and a part time job. It builds up too much stress.

Bonus

Expansions:

Effects Part Time Work

Mental Exhaustion

No social interaction

No fun or excitement

Cousin April fell asleep/ alg test

Jamie lost gf b/c barely sees her

Misses biggest party ever

John fell asleep while sweeping

Bob spare thin dark bdr/ asleep

Misses bday party

Jacob irritable/ no sleep/ curses on customer

Spends less time with family/ kid

Class NC aquarium missed exhibit tour

Excellent Work!

④ Nc Writing Rub.

excellent intro
-bp1, bp2, bp3 Ample support
-conclusion

The oddest moment actually occured on my way to Geometry class yesterday. Apparently, I picked up our school newspaper called the Falcon News, and was immediately engrossed. The bold, type-faced words of all article's title seemed quite relevant to my own situation. Then, it briefly mentioned that high schoolers' stress levels were at all time, elevated levels. Moreover, research shows that "school absences rise and standardized test scores fall as work hours increase." Therefore, it was my duty as a journalist to uncover more effects on part-time work and struggling students. Although there many positive effects of working a job during high school there are also many negative effects such as mental exhaustion, lack of social interaction and deprivation of fun and excitement.

✓+ As I briefly stated, mental exhaustion take a tremendous toil on ones life and attitude. My friend Jacob was faced with the dilemma once while working at our local Chuck-E-Cheese. He grumpily approached a customer's table dull look upon his face. Welcome to the Chuck, What the heck you want to eat" he blurted out arrogantly. "Excuse me young man?" the old woman asked with a startled look on her face. "Ummm,,,, I'd like a,,,, wait no,,," Come on!" Jacob exclaimed in an enraged tone. The infinitesimal amount of inappropriate language that escaped from his mouth not only stunned the woman but costed him job.

yes! Social interaction is a key part of life. However, relationships seem to come last and fixing things between you two can be had. Jamie, my friendly neighbor, Who I have been friends with since Elementary School had some issues with his girlfriend of 3 years. Since he always worked a late shift, there were no more movie nights or extravagant dinners. With all the work and no "quality time", his girlfriend broke up with him. He was shocked and even more stunned with the allegation of him not working but cheating with another girl.

✓+ From personal experience, I understand how awful it is to miss out on all the fun while working a part time job. Earlier this month, I was invited to the biggest party of the Senior year. The problem was that it was on the night I had to work a late Shift so there was no possible way I could attend without getting fired. The next day after the party everyone was overly enthusiastic and ecstatically overjoyed to tell me the memorable events at the superior Sorree. Apparently, my favorite rapper was in town and made a surprise appearance. Without my 9 to 5 I would have been able to dance the night away with my friends.

Although, working while Striving to earn an education may seem like a good idea there are many negative effects. Setting your priorities straight is of high importance. Maybe, its time to fully focus on your education and do away with your job. Working can wait, and you can always get another position.

Persuasive and Expository Essay Checklist

I. Intro Paragraph

_____ (Yes or No) Does it have a hook or attention grabbing Topic Sentence?

_____ (Yes or No) Includes THREE Reasons or Interesting Story relevant to TS

_____ (Yes or No) Does it clearly state a stance in the Clincher Sentence?

Gram. Corr.____   Repet. Free___   Exp. Supported___   3 Adj. & Adv.__   3 Trans_____

II. Body Paragraph I

_____ (Yes or No) Does Topic Sentence clearly state your 1st Reason w Trans.?

_____ (Yes or No) Did you use FRIES to 'fully support' your reason?

_____ (Yes or No) Does the Clincher sentence sum up/close out your paragraph?

Gram. Corr.____   Repet. Free___   Exp. Supported___   3 Adj. & Adv.__   3 Trans_____

III. Body Paragraphy II

_____ (Yes or No) Does Topic Sentence clearly state your 2nd Reason with

_____ (Yes or No) Did you use FRIES to 'fully support' your 2nd reason?

_____ (Yes or No) Does the Clincher sentence sum up/close out your paragraph?

Gram. Corr.____   Repet. Free___   Exp. Supported___   3 Adj. & Adv.__   3 Trans_____

IV. Body Paragraph III

_____ (Yes or No) Does Topic Sentence clearly state your 3rd Reason w Trans.

_____ (Yes or No) Did you use FRIES to 'fully support' your 3nd reason?

_____ (Yes or No) Does the Clincher sentence sum up/close out your paragraph?

Gram. Corr.____   Repet. Free___   Exp. Supported___   3 Adj. & Adv.__   3 Trans_____

V. Conclusion Paragraph

_____ (Yes or No) Does 1st two sentences briefly reword and restate 3 Reasons?

_____ (Yes or No) Does final 3-4 sentences include: a future looking statement? #

and/or

a call to action?# ____

and/or

a solution to the problem # ____

I carefully crafted this mini-checklist for Persuasive and Expository essays about four years ago.

Don't let the name at the top of it deceive you. This very elaborate checklist works for any type of essay. That is, it truly defines the typical errors found in Persuasive, Expository, Cause and Effect, Comparison/Contrast, Narrative, or Definition essays. Meanwhile, a savvy assessor can readily identify the strong-points in the writings as well. There is only one adjustment you would need to make to it.

Note: Three Reasons = Three Expansions (mental snapshots)

Remember:

Reason 1: We went to the beach at Orlando.

Expansion 1: Orlando's sunny rays heated my head and shoulders as we casually strolled through white sands.

Now ask yourself, which one of these sentences triggers you imagination and reads better? Obviously, Expansion 1 does while Reason 1 leaves you yearning for a little more.

Make sure you reiterate the difference between three reasons and three expansions. Perhaps you could have them cross out Three Reasons, and jot Three Expansions for memory's sake. So, they will remember doing away with Three Reasons.

CHAPTER 10 | 2008-2009 Student Testimonials

One of the major curricular benefits of the International Baccalaureate Programme is it's Reflective component. Learners are expected to consciously and continuously reflect upon an assignment, their reactions, and what else they need to accomplish. They are to re-evaluate at the beginning, towards the middle, near the end, and at the culmination of projects. By doing so, pupils tend to put much greater thought or focus into each separate step. In turn, such emphasis on reflection holistically strengthens the quality of long-term assignments.

I want you to realistically consider the GREAT Burger Workshop, its (writing portion) done over three weeks, a long-term assignment. Therefore, you should have your essayists write a journal entry about their predictions as you announce it a week ahead. Somewhere towards the middle, a one-page reflection of what the learners have understood thus far would suffice. In these three paragraphs they could mention the packet, the burger metaphor, and use of transition, adverb, and adjective lists. Also, their emotional reactions to the instruction so far would be appropriate, as it will be hard work. Finally, they should re-assess how well GREAT Burger worked based the essay that you do next: Rough draft, checklist, Revision, etc. In any case, reflections will cause them to take GREAT more seriously.

I have provided several student Reflections and demographics from 2008-2009 for your consideration. Unfortunately, my (2007-2008) reflections were somehow misplaced, but were just as wonderful! At any rate, you will see how many students' opinions on GREAT Burger Essay Method changed over time. Realize that cynical teenagers can definitely be resistant against such a huge change. I taught these teens for two years in a row: 7th & 8th grade. I had to employ 'friendly power', vigilant scrutiny, and interactive smart board exercises to win them over. In addition, take a look at the brief descriptions of each learner and the challenges that he/she overcame. These certainly serve as a reminder that GREAT Burger can work for any student, any writing level! I had the students compare 4th Grade score to their 8th Grade scores. Since this was the last time writing was emphasized for the FCAT Writes.

Just analyze the diversity of students, their differing Writing levels, and how GREAT addressed the variety of their needs.

DEMOGRAPHICS OF WRITING STUDENTS

Reflection A: Learner Profile

This multi-ethnic young lady was a shyer student who possessed plenty of potential. Her mother was Oriental and her father was of Black Caribbean heritage. She normally did enough to receive a B or B+ when it came to writings, even though she was an avid reader. However, she wondered why they were never A's in my class in the beginning. After using GREAT Burger workshop, she began to notice that she could be even more specific and creative. As a result, she shone when it counted most **impressively earning a 5.5 score** on her 8th grade Florida Comprehensive Assessment Test, as opposed to her 4th grade score of 4. This was a one and a half score jump!

Reflection B: Student Profile

This student was a playful African American male who was not a very descriptive writer. He was obviously resistant to frequent reading and this was illustrated by poor spelling above. Moreover, he wrote more like he spoke instead of skillfully drafting formal essay writings. After accepting GREAT Burger standards, he markedly improved his grasp of essays. We pulled out those adjective and adverb sheets and he purposefully began using them. These had long been missing from his plainer writings. Fortunately, his dedication paid off on his Florida Writes Essay score. He only earned a 3.0 which was the minimum passing score in 4th grade. As an 8th grader, he dramatically improved to a 4.5 score. (Meaning, one table reader gave him a 4 and another table reader gave him a 5. Therefore, their combined average scores was a 4.5, and he was so excited about it). He could hardly believe it himself but I knew he could do it!

Reflection C: Student Profile

Judging by her thick accent, this Cuban immigrant seemed to have recently entered the country. Yet, her mother's even thicker accent during a parent conference revealed that this was not the case. The young lady simply patterned her words after her mother's heavily accented ones. Despite this, she seemed to have a so-so grasp of English syntax and grammar as an ESOL level 5 student. It seemed that GREAT Burger provided that next level of writing foundation she desperately needed. It gradually removed the shackles of limitation from her vocabulary use and sentence structures. Eventually, she enhanced her simpler adjectives and adverbs by using more complex ones. Moreover, she learned how to use the pronoun antecedent rule which was quite important for her.

Reflection D: Student Profile

This Italian American male was always the ideal student. As a matter of fact, he earned a 5 on his 4th Grade FCAT Writes. At first, he was convinced that he could make it without GREAT burger. Then, he found that he could expand his already detailed writing to a higher level of elaboration. Eventually he sang the praises of this system after the initial hard work. He wound up being the Valedictorian of his middle school class.

Reflection E: Student Profile

This Mexican American teenager could dole out quite the yawner in the beginning. She would turn in non-descriptive, barebones words. Meaning, her paragraphs usually read like sterile lists more than well thought out words. These compositions would not really grab the reader's attention and would be in an informal voice. Nonetheless, she diligently worked on her dry sense of expression and lack of vivid adjectives and transitions. Sooner or later, she experienced how GREAT Burger's guidelines all cumulatively worked together. She confidently exhibited what she learned during our Florida Writes standardized test, and shocked us all! An incredible 2.5 change; from a 2 score in 4th grade to a 4.5 score in 8th grade! She is one of my fantastic success stories.

Reflection F: Student Profile

Here was an African American male who had one parent from a Caribbean island; another Muslim. He was a profoundly gifted artist, and this was displayed frequently in tagging, graffiti (on paper), etc. His drawings were so realistic and polished that he displayed them during his IB World Project. The youngster possessed better than normal writing skills but knew that he could do better. Yet, he had a very fast learning curve and that was to his own credit. It must be added that he was a frequent reader which made conforming to GREAT Burger methods simple. He admirably followed the writing program and emerged as one of my most prolific writers. His Florida Writes scores went from a 4.5 in fourth grade, to a superb 6 in eighth grade! His hard work earned him the highest score possible!

Reflection G: Student Profile

This chatty, somewhat mischievous, and jokey Latina absolutely enjoyed turning in work that was barely enough. Her goal was earning either a B- or C+ This would keep her grade point average around a 2.5. Her truly caring father—an overly fatigued business owner— would always find time to check up on her. It actually seemed that she was wrestling his attention away from his entrepreneurial pursuits. Oddly, this was even though he'd done five or six conferences to stay on top of her. (We struggled all year to make her remain a B- student despite her intentions to do otherwise). She wouldn't I had to convince her to accept GREAT as the next best thing, while she did not necessarily love it. Nevertheless, she wisely chose to adhere to GREAT, and started noticing a smoother, more convincing tone. Look at her results: a 3.5 in 4th grade, up to a marvelous 5 score in 8th grade.

Reflection H: Student Profile

(Not shown below). I literally saved the best for last here. This next pupil was a quieter Jewish American male who developed literary chutzpah. He was already a very good writer when he entered my classroom. Perhaps, he had the highest Emotional Quotient (EQ), more important than IQ, in that year's group of students. He understood responsibility, teamwork, and leadership. There was positively no wonder why he became President of the National Junior Honor Society. (School year 2008-2009 was my second year as Chapter Adviser of the NJHS). This mild-mannered, future journalist found several ways to ameliorate his above average writing. He worked on his sense of Voice and Style. Also, he made insertion of 3 –ly adverbs, and three transitions every other sentence paramount. These extras would prove to be 'the icing on the cake'. **You see, he earned an incredible 6 score in 8th grade** instead of the 4.5 in fourth grade. His mother came in and personally thanked me as did a dozen parents. Emotionally, she made his journalistic aspirations known to me and insisted GREAT brought him much closer! We hugged and I later bragged about the incident to my wife; another superb teacher.

These students demonstrated major upward shifts in their scores from 4th to 8th grades. Also, they showed dramatic improvement over their essay pretests earlier in the school year. So, I had the reflect upon how their writing had grown once they'd learned the GREAT burger essay workshop process.

(REFLECTION A)

Great Burger Writing Program

Throughout the last two years of learning language arts here at Frank C, I've learned more than I possibly ever could've imagined. I've been fortunate enough to be able to learn many new strategies of writing. At first, GREAT Burger, seemed like such a useless way to write an essay, I thought it took up too much time and my essays were fine the way I wrote them. However, I came to see that my assumptions was clearly wrong. As time progressed, I realized that my writing truly did improve. My writing sounded more intelligent, and at the same time, it wasn't boring.

For my FCAT Writes in fourth grade, I got a solid 4. And that was using the boring "Three Reasons". Yet, because I took the time to think about what I was really writing, the GREAT Burger method helped me achieve a 5.5 for my 8th grade Writes. Honestly, this method has shaped the way I write, as well as speak. It may seem like alot, but looking for repitions, and adding transitions, adverbs & adjectives isn't. It will pay off in the long run; I can tell you from experience.

FCAT WRITES 4th: 4   FCAT WRITES 8th: 5.5

(REFLECTION B)

Great Burger Writing Program

There are several quality strategies towards writing an overly achieved essay. However, the one that simply taught me to write with perfection is the Great Burger Method. Inquisitively, G represents grammarly correct and that everything makes sense. Also the R States one must be repetition free with it's writing. Basically, E renders as expertly supported examples, qoutation had much evidence. Additionally, A depicts adverbs, and adjectives, which add to a tasteful paragraph. And lastly, T enacts that you use three transition per paragraph. Henceforth, Using this method will lead you to an extraordinary essay.

There are several ways to improve an essay. However the Great Burger Method increased my writing the most. Without this method my skills would be worthless and only judge on improvasion instead of strategy. From 4th grade to 8th grade with this extravagant method made a big increase

4TH Grade: 3.0   8TH Grade: 4.5

(REFLECTION C)

GREAT Burger Writing Program

By learning the GREAT Burger I have been able to enhance my grammar. Simply by not using the same words over and over again. Such as, and, I, is, etc. Now using GREAT Burger I use Adverbs and much more adjectives. Also, I got to learn about transitions, which before learning GREAT Burger I didn't know what transitions were. But now in my writing I use adverbs, adjectives, and transitions.

GREAT stands for -G- Grammatically correct. Meaning theres no "I is" or "He are". Next, the R-stands for repitition free. This just checks to make sure you aren't using "I" or common words more than 3 times in one paragraph. The E stands for Expantions. This help you give "the proof or why this is five" to any answer or opinion you might be stating. A stands for adverbs and adjectives. In a good paragraph you should have at least 3 adverbs and 3 adjectives. Finally, the T, which stands for transitions. Transitions are words covered at the begining of a sentence. Then, by using this method of writing its sure to help you write any report.

4th Grade FCAT writes score- 3.5   2009 FCAT Writes Score 5.5

(REFLECTION D)

GREAT Burger Writing Program

This year, we were taught the 'GREAT Burger' method to writing an essay. GREAT stands for a series of word that you use to check your paragraphs to make sure they are good. 'G' stands for grammatically correct', which includes, spelling, syntax, punctuation, etc. 'R' and 'E' stand for 'repetition free' and 'expetly supported.' Those prompt you to check for overly used words or phrases and to make sure you support what you say. 'A' is the big one that stands for 'adjectives & adverbs', which says to check for at least 3 of each. 'T' stands for transitions and makes sure that you have 3. In addition, a person writing in GREAT makes positive that he or she had is or less words per sentence, and 6 to 7 sentences for paragraph.

The GREAT Burger writing method has definitely changed my style of writing. Now, my subconscient mind checks for adjectives, adverbs, and transitions while keeping my sentences short and expertly supported. I have seen an increase in how much better my writing sounds and how much more sense I make GREAT Burger really helped changed my style of writing for the better. I think it is a great program, and should be taught in more classrooms.

4th Grade Score: 5   8th Grade Score: 6

REFLECTION E PERIOD 4 5/4/09

GREAT Burger Writing Essay

The GREAT or Grammar Rpetition free, expertly supported, Adverbs/adjectives and transitions has been a great help these two years. I was and still am very amazed at the fact I got an 4.5 in 8th grade. Sure, it could have been a much higher point and I know I could have done better. But to see how much improvement, I've done since 4th grade (at the time, I was ESOL) and now (I'm still not a pro at the english language), I'm proud of getting my point.

Painfully, I've only gotten 2's & 3's in my FCAT scores, therefore, this makes me real proud to have gotten a 4.5.

What amazed me the most was that I did better than some kids that I know for a fact, are super brilliant, & their knowledge is way bigger than mine, but I did better. I feel strong because the Great Burger really helps & makes you get higher points. If I had know the Great Burger in 4th grade, I would have probably gotten a much better score. I want to thank Mr. Simms for teach us this GREAT method.

(REFLECTION F)

GREAT Burger Writing Program

GREAT Burger, in all its steps, has greatly enhanced my writing abilities, Grammar repetition, support, adverbs and adjectives plus transitions all affect the outcome and score. This method makes essays sound mature and sophisticated. With these skills I have improved greatly and obtained a six on the FCAT writing test. Before great Burger, my vocabulary was very limited, but the constant deed of having to look transitions, adverbs, and adjectives has doubled my knowledge and It has become increasingly easy to find -ly words and it taught me to use vibrant and descriptive writing. I used to count my sentences until I got to 5 for a paragraph, now the joy of expressing what needs to be addressed keeps me writing longer and more college level sentences. Repetition in writing make the illusion that the story is being stretched think but inventing new ways to explain the same subject proves to be a helpful way of prolonging paragraphs and expanding on the topic. Incorrect grammar also ruins a perfect essay and makes it appear childish and uneducated. Use of strong and correct words give the proper justification and shows what the writer learns what he is talking about. My essays and stories have became more creative and extravagant and I am thankful.

4th Grd Score: 4   8 grade score: 6

(REFLECTION G)

GREAT Burger Writing Program

Throughout, the last two years we have been taught a "skeleton" of writing. This marvelous skeleton is called "GREAT Burger Method". Of course, we have complained about the method 3 adverbs, 3 adjectives, 3 transitions but deep down we know it got us were we are today. Second in the count of Mam Dade in FCAT writing. Grammar, Repetition free, Expertly supported, Adverbs/Adjectives, Transitions.

The slogan is content and easy to remember. Think, food, think Great Burger and you've got a 5 or 6. Though, saying it and remembering it come cosin, it's just the structure of writing to avoid a "robotic" paragraph or essay. Mr. Simms has pounded us with the things proven to enhance our writing. Ultimately, it is in the writers hand, literally! Even though, it is tideous at times, just think GREAT automitcally transforms you're writing style.

I scored a 5.0 in 8th grade.   I scored a 3.5 in 4th grade.

CHAPTER 11

2009–2010 Student Testimonials

This was quite an unusual year in which it seems like we never had enough time. However, we made sure that we complied with GREAT Burger instructions. We set the goal in November 2009 that if 95 percent of the students passed the FCAT Writes they would be rewarded. I had been told 'unflattering news' about this so-called group of students. Much of the 'bad news' was substantiated by former teacher's grades, comments, and/ or assessments. Many in this 2009–2010 did not have the same fervor for reading novels as the previous learners. Nevertheless, I defiantly clung to my position that I could teach any set of students to write effectively. Thankfully, it paid off even better than before.

Unfortunately, my learner's scores came out too late for me to afford their GREAT Burgers or whoppers with cheese. However, I did what I could. Lack of money did not prevent me from bragging on them and personally congratulating each class period. I remember giving all of them a bonus A, and allowing their last GREAT Burger essay to count as their Final Essay Exam. I did so since we'd gone over it together and all they had to do was revise it using GREAT Burger essay guidelines. Nearly everyone did a tremendous job on it, and they were currently busy with their World Projects anyway. They only had to complete an Objective Final Exam and they were done!

Though it was hard-fought, I prudently managed to ignite the spark of confidence that led to fantastic results. Every single learner in my classes passed the FCAT Writes that year; 100% passing score. All of their scores came in later during this second year our 8th graders had taken the exam. Ultimately, this writing method is only as motivating as the teacher who is imparting it; so include compassion. Don't let them catch a glance of 'give-up' in your eyes, or they will fulfill it.

The next few pages are GREAT Burger Reflections drafted using the same method. However, students were asked how they believed they did with GREAT since scores were not available yet. They were graded according to my specified format of three paragraphs. (Essentially these 2010 essayists were to employ GREAT Burger writing about GREAT!)

Student Profile Hardworking African-American student
who greatly improved her scores

The great burger is a system to help me skillfully write an essay or perfect paragraph. With this system, I can make sure that my paragraphs are grammatically correct, repetition free, expertly supported, adjective & adverb filled, and has at least three transitions. This great burger system is essay for me to follow. When I finish with an essay. I always check and make sure my paragraphs deliberately are GREAT burger. Furthermore, GREAT burger has been tested and included into past essays. These essays have received high and overachieved scores.

Great burger has has changed my writing style tremendously. For instance, instead of listing three reason's why in my introduction, I use historical review or other factors. New and more mature transitions and topic sentences replace simple ones use as First, second, and third. In addition, adjectives and adverbs such as tiny, big, happily and playfully have been replaced with minature, enormous and giddily. Furthermore, GREAT burger increases the sense of organization and corrected grammar found in my paragraphs. This way, I can receive higher grades in my writing ability.

Fortunately, I was able to incorporate the GREAT burger system into my FCAT writes. With this advantage, I am sure I received a five to a six in my FCAT writes. The GREAT Burger was able to help me in knowing what the judges were looking for. Thanks to my teacher, Mr. Simms, I have developed a unique writing style. In which, I can express my feelings thoroughly & thoughtfully.

Haitian American girl who included many but not all elements of the writing program. (Reflecion B) 4/7/2010 P3 B+

Reflection: Great Burger

The "Great burger is an acronym that stands for; Grammatically Correct (G) Repetition Free (R), Expertedly Supported (E), Adverbs, Adjectives (A), Transitions (T). The name comes from the analogy that the more you fill the burger (Essay or Paragraph), the "greater" it tastes. This writing tool creates a balanced and knowledgeable essay/paragraph, or in this case, a mouth-watering burger.

Using "GREAT Burger" definitely helped improve my writing style. Consequently, my vocabulary has expanded and my use of adverbs has reached new heights. Gradually, my paragraphs grew from 5 sentences to 7 or 8. I now use a variety of adjectives that enhance my essays to high levels.

Naturally, I have kept my sense of creativity in my essays but now with more of a studios approach. In the future, I will continuously use GREAT Burger to create efficient, well rounded essays.

FCAT Writes: 4.5

The outcome of how I did on the writing test should, should be O.K. I predict I gota 4.5 or 5. Unfortunately, my use of all GREAT Burger tools was not present in the essay. Throughout the essay I slacked off and didn't add many transitions or adverbs etc. Periodically, I began to add more writing tools, or in this instance concliments to my burger. Hopefully, the outcome of this test will be GREAT!

Hispanic girl always in a rush
actually takes her time on FCAT Writes. 3/7/10 A

The GREAT Burger is a writing tool. You use it to help write and edit your paragraphs. Each paragraph must be GREAT. The G stands for Gramatically correct; each paragraph must use correct grammar and that it all sounds not. The R stands for repetition free. You use this to make sure that you don't use any words more than twice per paragraph. It sounds better when words aren't over used. The E stands for expertly supported. It must have detail and sound good together. A is for adjectives and adverbs. For a well written paragraph you need 3 of each. And last is transitions. Each paragraph should have 3 transitions and then you have your perfect paragraph.

This writing style has improved and changed my writing for the better. It has taught me to write better. Now, I make sure I have correct grammar, that its repetition free, expertly supported, and 3 transitions. I'm sure my writing has improved because of this, I probably did better in my FCAT and overall in general.

I feel that I got a 5 on the FCAT Writes. I used GREAT Burger, planned well and did my best. I am confident using this writing method helped my overall performance of this years FCAT.

I could genuinely identify with many of these 2009-2010 students who were prematurely counted out. Although enlightening, revisiting their overall academic and behavioral struggles was not fair to them. Most of our faculty and teachers were careful not to bring the matter up but somehow it got back to them. They were the problem kids, they would never score as well as the preceding class had. After all, a 98% passing rate was definitely hard to top! Two or three of my students even brought it up during my class. To which I responded, "you'll notice that I never agreed with that because everyone in this classroom has the ability to succeed!" I had a stiffneckedness about them succeeding no matter what discouraging limitation was spoken over them. Occasional chats between lessons reinforced my belief that each of them had the potential to excel.

Negative comments left a looming shadow of defeat and failure over their heads that they had to prove absolutely wrong. And so they did with every single student passing the FCAT Writes in 2010. It was a feat that nobody could believe happened but me. Suppose I had given up in the middle of the year based upon the so-called 'past evidence'? Or what if I conspired to count these learners out along with a few others? They would have never realized **the best 8th Grade FCAT Writing scores of any graduating class in that school thus far.** Who could top a 100% passing rate; 3.5 or higher on the FCAT writing test (Florida Writes)?

I began very much like these learners and recall the days when my own outlook was not so promising. My educational experience actually began as an energetic, lanky boy attending a Title I elementary school. Mainly, poorer students on free lunch went there because of their nearby address. There I was, a fairer skinned boy with reddish hair who could barely remain in my seat for fifteen minutes. This son of a working mom and dad sometimes acted out for positive or negative attention; it didn't matter to me. What I knew was that both my parents were always working. I assumed that I ranked lower on their priority list. I did not know or care that it took two people to earn a decent living in the 1980s.

By fifth grade, a stigmatizing label was placed on me prematurely! It was as if this school marm inscribed the letter 'D' for dummy directly onto my forehead with her words. "Oh he's just so hyperactive, he just won't sit still;" was this particular teacher's appraisal. It meant 'I would never learn anything.' That was before there was a specific and treatable disorder called Attention Deficit Hyperactivity Disorder (ADHD). Little did she know that I felt detached from the learning environment. Because it seemed like an endless stream of easy worksheets I was shutting down. Or, maybe she did not understand how to properly differentiate instruction for her differing levels of students. Many of my peers were slower readers and writers.

During those years, there would be occasions when I'd sit and read entire passages of the Bible non-stop. Or, I'd finish my work and actually grab a dictionary off the shelf to learn more 'e' or 'g' words. Then, state assessment test scores revealed that I wasn't slow at all. Upper 70th percentile in Reading, lower 90th percentile for Mathematics, was a far cry from learning disabled. In fact, the tests revealed that I was a bored and untapped scholar. You must understand that my major obstacle, then and sometimes now, is a wandering level of focus. It occurs unless I am fully engrossed with a topic. The findings of this data were doubly confirmed when I won the 5th Grade Spelling Bee. Then, I proudly represented A. L. Lewis Elementary in the Miami Herald Spelling Bee!

At any rate, my middle and High school marks were rather average until the end of my 10th grade year. I was hiding behind the mediocre marks to fit in because I was pretty popular. All I really embraced during these formative days was music. It could be Jazz, classical, or the newest pop hit. I loved to play the trumpet from 6th grade on, and was one of the first chair instrumentalists. By 9th grade, I began playing the french horn for concert band as well. My fingers seemed to naturally tickle the ivories too. I was already playing for my church services by then and doing so was quite fulfilling to me. I'd developed an acute ear and could play almost anything I heard instantly. Still, teachers did not necessarily notice my number and level of talents.

Mrs. Reid was my proverbial hero who stepped up instead of throwing another teenager under the bus. She skillfully unraveled the intricacies of "The Crucible" and "Of Mice and Men". Her use of interesting discussions, crossword puzzles, games, skits, and projects helped me accept these selections as works of art. Moreover, completing each of the novels with a complete understanding left me with a tremendous sense of accomplishment. I never got the chance to formally express my thanks to her but I'll treasure her influence forever. She gave just the push I needed to thrive in academia by simply performing her job well. Not only that, she cultivated what was there instead of just standing by, wishing! Hoping that learners had more of this or that was a waste of time. Instead, she nurtured me—the quieter one in the back--without being mushy-gushy. Perhaps her greatest accomplishment was using my own favorite learning styles to reach me.

Ever since then, I absolutely envied Mrs. Reid's talent for making text not only clearer but more relevant to my classmates' experience. I was seemingly re-programmed, and my attitude towards reading had drastically changed from avoidance to affinity. Deep within the recesses of my heart was the wish to follow in Mrs. Reid's shoes. First, I needed to start taking every mark seriously by extending my full efforts to each assignment. Next, my brain envisioned the day when I could help shape minds, inspire new goals, and enlighten those on the verge of giving up.

From 11th grade until the 12th, I devoted myself. I had to complete all of my work and balance that with extra-curricular activities like band. I'd managed to raise my GPA to a 3.4 by graduation, and won a High School Achievement Award. This was a full-tuition scholarship to Miami-Dade Community College including books. I wasn't quite ready to leave my parents so this was an attractive offer. I accepted, and completed my Associate of Arts with Honors; 3.63 GPA. I soon attempted my first novel named "Treachery" by Chris Stephens in 2002 but never adequately released it. But I did prove to myself that I had what it took to write a novel. Eventually, I finished my Bachelor of Science in English Education (grades 6-12) in 2004; with a 3.71 GPA.

I began teaching high school Language Arts for three years and then middle school for the same amount of years. I also became a National Junior Honor Society Chapter Adviser for three years, and pressed my students towards community service. Recently,

I even earned a Master's degree in Business Administration with a 3.58 GPA. Yeah, 'the limited one who couldn't learn anything' label was proven terribly wrong when I ended up with a 3.7 Ph. D of Business Administration. This goes to show that a little inspiration goes quite a long way, and the cruelest thing an educator can do is count out his or her students early. That is why I personally empathize with frustrated students because I once was one. This passion for enhancing learner's writing skills is one that was borne from my own experiences. No doubt it was an arduous journey but I did get there.

My parting advice is that every Language Arts instructor of Middle, High, and College students recall that we were not always scholars. Essentially, different teachers took turns molding us into better writers and gifted speakers. It will take an abundance of patience, empathy, and even tough love to shape your pupils' futures. Instead of being bogged down in the perception of failure insist that these learners save themselves. Undoubtedly, reading and writing are the tools to success; entreat them to love it for their own collective good. Turn away from condemning 'problem students' paradigm, and succor them where they hurt! In these days, marred with more dysfunctional families than ever, we must roll up our collective sleeves. There is an alarming percentage of college entrants who have to take preparatory classes to catch up (60% for math and reading/writing courses). This, in itself, undeniably proves that educators must improve instruction. Our strategies, delivery, and even our responses to controversial behavior in the classroom must evolve.

Language Arts teachers must toss 'limited resources' out by the ears, so to speak. Meaning, they need to clear out their handouts and collections of worksheets every one-to-two years. During the past seven years, I've started my handout files from scratch at least five times! If my delivery wasn't fresh then my students would only be receiving a lesser byproduct of the topic. This sharply contrasted with providing a deeper understanding of a subject matter. Another issue is that transmitting knowledge in stale, outdated manner causes more harm than good; students simply tune out. Embracing technology--especially Smart boards, iPads, laptops, MP3s, Wikispaces, WebCTs, Prezis, and other newer gadgets— is absolutely vital for reaching 21st century youth. It is all but impossible to reach today's generation with yesteryear's technology; we've got to keep up. This is assuredly correct since those devices are the way they mentally process information now.

Breadth of instructional domains should be evident in every Reading teacher's strategies. Constantly shifting your methods between Aural, Oral, Speaking, Kinesthetic-Tactual, Visual, and even technological will forge well rounded learners. Then, they will eventually make you, their parents, and the world proud. Please maintain an 'every learner can succeed' spirit during this workshop. Hopefully, you will experience the same caliber of results.

Good luck and God speed!

Dr. Stephen C. Simms